The Low Countries

Cover:

Tim, child refugee from Burundi, 2010.

Photo by Lieve Blancquaert.

2011

The Low Countries

ARTS AND SOCIETY IN FLANDERS AND THE NETHERLANDS

19

Published by
the Flemish-Netherlands
Association
Ons Erfdeel vzw

Contents

(Self-) Images of the Low Countries

Chronicle

Philosophy and Science

Politics

Society

Visual Arts

Next page:
Jan van Eyck, *The Arnolfini Portrait,* 1434. Detail.
Oil on oak, 82.2 x 60 cm.
The National Gallery, London.

Johannes de eyck fuit hic
1434

Mirrors, Windows, Reflections

In June 1667 the Dutch Admiral de Ruyter mounted a devastating raid on the English fleet moored at Chatham in the Thames estuary. At that time Holland was referred to in Britain as 'that indigested vomit of the sea' and an official propagandist wrote a pamphlet in which he derived *belgia* from *belregia, Beelzebub's realm.* By *Belgia* the author meant… the Dutch Republic. What's in a name? And what's in an image?

What do we see in the mirrors we look into and the mirrors others hold up to us? What do we see when we look at things through windows, and so through frames?

To form the theme of this edition we have put together a collection of images: images of Flanders and the Netherlands to be found in other countries and images that the Flemish and Dutch have of themselves. How does a Scotsman who fled Thatcher's England in 1979 and eventually landed up in Brussels regard the Low Countries? What does an American historian who teaches in Amsterdam think of a Dutch state that within the space of a single decade seems to have done a complete about-face? What do the antitheses 'Protestant-Catholic' and 'Calvinist-Burgundian' say about the Low Countries? What responses are evoked by Orange, the colour, the rallying-cry and the dynasty? And what do such emblematic books as *Turks fruit*, *La Légende d'Ulenspiegel* and *Het Verdriet van België* and *Max Havelaar* tell us about Flanders and the Netherlands?

LUC DEVOLDERE | *Chief Editor*

And then of course there are the actual images: photos which in one way or another put across the image and the self-image of Flanders and the Netherlands.

All these images ultimately produce some sense of identity. And in the end identity is the never-ending debate about identity.

In the general section of the yearbook you will encounter the usual mixture of articles. We explore the royal houses of the Netherlands and Belgium, writers such as the Fleming Maurice Maeterlinck who wrote in French and won the Nobel Prize for Literature in 1911 and Gerard Reve who once tried writing in English, painters like the sixteenth-century Lucas van Leyden and the contemporary Koen van den Broek. The belfries of the Southern Netherlands, proud guardians of civic independence, have been proclaimed Unesco World Heritage sites. Five hundred years ago Erasmus' *In Praise of Folly* was published: a divertimento that became a cult book. Graphic novels, music festivals and uninhabited islands in the Wadden Sea will parade before you.

Look in mirrors, through windows. Let everything be reflected back. There are more things in the heaven and earth of the Low Countries than are dreamt of in the vomit of a British pamphleteer.

(Self-) Images of Flanders

Renaat Veremans at the Yserbedevaart in Diksmuide, 1950.
Photo by Paul Van den Abeele.

The composer conducts Flemish part-song at the IJzerbedevaart in Diksmuide. This annual pilgrimage to the Yser, to the graves of the fallen in the First World War ("Here lie their bodies like seeds in the sand. Hope for a harvest O Flandersland"), has grown into a *lieu de mémoire* for the Flemish movement, which cannot shake off its Catholic origins: "All for Flanders, Flanders for Christ" (AVV-VVK).

Ernest Claes at Averbode Abbey, 1950.
Photo by Paul Van den Abeele.

The popular Flemish author, in 1950, flanked by two priests.
Literature in Flanders is still embedded.

Hugo Claus and Sylvia Kristel, Paris, 1976.
Photo by Paul Van den Abeele.

The Flemish writer has become a dandy, hooked on the soft porn star *Emmanuelle* (in reality a Dutch girl). In Paris, by the way, the writer is addressed as *Monsieur* Kristel.

Vic Anciaux, Komen / Comines 1979.
Photo by Paul Van den Abeele.

A Flemish Nationalist party president averts smouldering violence at a demonstration.
Flemings are opposed to the Belgian state but don't throw bombs.

Inner courtyard. Holy Sepulchre boarding school, Bilzen, 1992.
Photo by Annie van Gemert.

The photographer captures a disappearing world: girls in Catholic boarding schools in Flanders.

Snellegem (fair-time cycle race).
Photo by Stephan Vanfleteren.

Flanders and cycle racing: a mystical marriage. The photographer shows a fair-time cycle race going round and round a Flemish church tower. The spectator is the archetypal fan of the most popular sport in Flanders, silently saluting those toiling on the road, to whom he's invisible.

Zaventem. Between the Olmstraat and the Brussels Ring.
Gardening in the no-man's-land of the Vuurberg.
Photo by Michiel Hendrickx.

"What's nature now in this country?" sighs the poet. But all over Flanders there's resistance to ribbon development and asphalting. The vegetable garden survives in the desert.

Zellik, 2000.
Photo by Stephan Vanfleteren.

This photo was taken from the Brussels Ring. In the distance, the Koekelberg Basilica in Brussels. In a single picture the photographer captures the tension between rural and urban in Flanders.

Oast. Passendale, 1996.
Photo by Filip Claus.

Chicory is a substitute for coffee. The roots of the chicory plant used to be washed and dried and roasted on the heated floor of the oast house. Working in these closed, sweltering hot drying sheds was hard. The photographer captures this *huis clos*. What is almost unimaginable is the *gleichzeitige Ungleichzeitigkeit* with the picture you see opposite.

District patrol. Lanaken, 2003.
Photo by Filip Claus.

Immaculate villa with just the right four by four on the drive. Gated community.
As of the 60s of the last century Flanders quickly became rich.

The Guide Has Become Anxious

How the Netherlands Has Changed

As an American with Dutch roots I have always had an eye for the reputation of the Netherlands in the world. To be sure, one should not exaggerate the attention that the world gives the Netherlands most of the time. Nevertheless, the country has often generated strong images – often positive, as the land of unlimited freedom, but sometimes too as a country that had grown overly tolerant and permissive. The effective decriminalization of soft drug use, the legalization of euthanasia and, in a different vein, the legalization of same-sex marriage for the first time in history would seem, depending on the commentator, to prove either assertion.

The international reputation of the Dutch is currently under evaluation, as I shall analyse below, and for good reason. But I think there was good reason to think of the Netherlands, from the 1960s to the 1980s or perhaps the 1990s, as a place where various progressive projects combined to create a striking political habitus. It was a country that already in the 1950s demonstrated a noticeable interest in the Third World – a reflection, I think, of both postcolonial guilt and a strong religious and moral impulse to change the world. Secondly, in the 1960s and 1970s the Netherlands was a country where Roman Catholics – some 40% of the population – transformed themselves almost overnight from a reliably orthodox part of the church to some of the church's most progressive critics. At the same time, Amsterdam changed from a rather sleepy European capital into one of its leading countercultural scenes. Not only did the country as a whole become a centre of social experimentation that included drugs policy and euthanasia, but a wave of 'new social movements' committed to issues like peace and human rights put the Netherlands at the forefront of broader forms of international engagement; for a short time, no country showed a greater involvement in such groups as did the Dutch.

All of these progressive projects strengthened the image of the Netherlands as an uncommonly liberal country – both within the Netherlands and abroad. But it was not only progressive movements and legislation that informed the Dutch image of themselves. They also tended to think of themselves as a well-regulated country – certainly in contrast to others – and as a place relatively free from conflict. Although the metaphor of the polder – meant to illustrate the Dutch tendency to work together in order to keep their feet dry – became a recurring reference only in the 1990s, pride in their ostensibly consensual way of dealing with problems has older roots. But in a crucial way this self-image reinforced its other progressive image: the Netherlands was a country that disliked political extremism and confrontation (a 1994 survey showed the Dutch tolerance for such things as among the lowest in Europe) and thus was able to develop a sober and clearheaded approach to social issues that perplexed other societies. In this way the Netherlands was able to develop strong brand recognition. It was not only a charming country of dikes and tulips, but a country with a different moral ethos. For that reason the Netherlands could become a Mecca not only for the hordes of tourists who visited the country's coffee shops and Amsterdam's Red Light District, but also for the occasional sojourner who sought – unrealistically as it turned out – assistance from a Dutch physician in ending his or her life. Even Jack Kevorkian – the American physician convicted for his own role in ending the life of one his patients – thought erroneously that Dutch doctors routinely offered their services to those who expressed their desire to die.

But even for those many visitors who made no attempt to avail themselves of these temptations, the abiding perception was often that the Netherlands was a remarkably free society.

None of this meant, of course, that the Dutch reputation for being either progressive or free and easy earned plaudits from everyone. In the early 1980s, the American neo-conservative intellectual Walter Laqueur argued that the Netherlands suffered from *'Hollanditis,'* a historically recurrent tendency toward neutral and pacifistic policies – a tendency he regretted in the face of the Soviet threat. And in 1994 *Der Spiegel* portrayed *'Frau Antje'* – known in Germany as the costume-clad purveyor of Dutch cheese – as a cannabis addict. TIME Magazine asserted in 1987 that Dutch tolerance had surely reached its absolute limits: the enormous increase in criminality, including problems with drug addicts and violent squatters, were prompting the Dutch to retreat from their easygoing ways.

Frau Antje as cannabis addict. *Der Spiegel*, 1994.

The end of tolerance

To be sure, the proclamation of the end of tolerance did not put an end to Holland's reputation; in his documentary the British filmmaker Jonathan Blank praised Dutch libertinism in his 1994 *Sex, Drugs and Democracy*, which seemed to confirm the Netherlands as a commonsensical place that let people do whatever they wanted. And indeed until the very end of the last century, the Netherlands did seem to have almost reached the end of history. In the 1990s the faintly progressive ethos presided over a society that had grown wealthy through neoliberal policies. The public seemed content and politics were dull; there were few problems that technocratic solutions could not solve. But TIME Magazine was not entirely misplaced in its sense that the Dutch cultural landscape was heading in a more conservative direction, a trend also evidenced elsewhere. From the early to mid-1980s there were increasing doubts, expressed publicly within the Netherlands, about the decay of the public sphere and the decline of collective *'values.'* That had a lot to do with changes in the social structure of Dutch society. The very aspects that made much of Dutch society so notably progressive in the 1960s and 1970s were actually rooted in older patterns; the social engagement and the sense of solidarity of that era had a lot in common with the *'pillarized'* society of the 1950s, with its tight-knit communities. Now the processes of individualization – in whose name the cultural revolution of the 1960s had been unleashed – slowly undercut the progressive ethos of Dutch society. This did not bring an immediate end to Dutch progressive ideals, but from the 1980s on there was an increasingly decisive rejection of what was felt to be the exaggerated and militant leftism of the 1970s. By the 1990s, too, globalization in general and the expansion of the European Union in particular led to a gradual growth of interest in the Dutch nation and how its *'heritage'* might be preserved, a rather striking development in a country where most public voices had disdained such interest. And even though the Dutch found it hard, perhaps more than other publics in Europe, to give form to the very squishy debate surrounding national identity, a new discussion arose about the 'value' (*nut*) of the Netherlands. Who were the Dutch anyway, and who would see to it that the Netherlands would be around in the future?

Meanwhile, some – though by no means all – of the trademark features of progressive Holland ran into trouble. A few emblematic developments may illustrate this development. The Dutch were compelled by its neighbours in 1995 to curtail the amounts that its coffee shops could sell customers and the number of coffee shops themselves began to decline. It was one sign that Holland's social policies would have to fit within the patterns of a wider Europe. Much more important was the catastrophic failure of the Dutchbat contingent in Srebrenica in July of 1995, which at the end of a badly-conceived UN mandate handed 7,000 Muslim men over to the Bosnian Serbs, who promptly executed them. The early rejoicing that followed the return home of the Dutchbat troops had the effect of deepening the shame many Dutch soon felt about their indirect role in the massacre. 'We are cowardly,' the prominent Amsterdam sociologist Abram de Swaan told a military audience not long after the event. For years, Srebrenica would continue to haunt the Dutch, not only as the tragic outcome of government policy, but as a failure of national character. But Srebrenica was not the last event that would disquiet the Dutch. The 2000 discovery of structural and massive fraud in the construction sector prompted the Dutch to question whether they were really the upright and corruption-free society that they imagined themselves to be. Similarly, though with considerably more unease and pathos, the politically-motivated murders of the politician Pim Fortuyn in 2002 and the filmmaker Theo van Gogh in 2004 caused a new wave of soul-searching. The Netherlands was not as peaceable as the Dutch had thought. Others saw in the murder of Van Gogh by an Islamic radical primarily an external act of violence, but also a severe indictment of Holland's progressive Establishment, which refused to take the Islamic threat seriously.

Srebrenica.

So Dutch history seems to have taken a turn no one expected. It seems now not that the Dutch had reached the end of history, but that they had denied history. NRC-columnist Bas Heijne argued in his little book *Onredelijkheid* (Unreasonableness) that religion and nation were more resistant forces than many had thought. In contrast to an almost studied casualness about norms a couple of decades ago, the Dutch now often state an appreciation for explicit moral norms, even if they remain ambivalent about how rigorously they should be applied.

Pim Fortuyn.
© Photo by Onno de Wit, 2002.

A country in conflict with itself

Although I could not possibly have predicted the future, I did wonder back in the fall of 1999 if the Dutch progressiveness which had so much been the focus of my historical research was necessarily guaranteed a much longer life. In a small essay I wrote then for *The Low Countries* I wrote about the myth of Dutch progressiveness, pointing to some of the more conservative features of Dutch society and wondering if the Dutch might not at some point be all too confident about the progressive spirit they projected. In my first book *Nieuw Babylon in aanbouw* (New Babylon under construction, 1995), too, I asked if Dutch Establishment politics, with its moderately progressive but not always very critical stance, would be well prepared to deal with new challenges surrounding the retreat of the welfare state, immigration and social cohesion. Although Dutch political elites could have done much worse, their ability to identify, engage and channel disaffected segments of the population proved much less effective than they believed a decade ago.

Part of the reason is indeed that the Netherlands had for a long time been more conservative on issues such as crime and immigration than Establishment politics had admitted. In this respect, the vision of the Netherlands as a progressive country was only a part of a more complex reality, even in the relatively liberal 1960s and 1970s. That is why from the late 1990s on it was not such a very long way toward new demands that newcomers integrate quickly into Dutch society, that norms be reasserted in society, and that more attention be given to national identity. For a long time mainstream politicians had ignored this

A memorial in 2009 for Theo van Gogh, who was murdered on 2 November 2004, Linnaeusstraat, Amsterdam.

programme. But now the political climate demands a harder, more radically assertive approach to these problems, and once trusted institutions are held in suspicion by a large segment of the electorate.

These new developments have their advantages – the Dutch complacency about their own society is largely gone – but it is primarily the disadvantages that we feel. The Dutch live in a society full of disunity and uncertainty. In this respect, the Netherlands is hardly unique, though it is striking that some of the most vociferous international critics of Islam, Geert Wilders and Ayaan Hirsi Ali, have been parliamentarians from the Netherlands. In many parts of Europe populist movements have asserted themselves powerfully, and mainstream institutions are challenged by a deep divide over the place of Islam in Europe and more generally over angst about globalization. In this respect, one could say that the Netherlands has merely been compelled to give up the pretension that it was a moral beacon to other nations.

Therein lies the difference, and perhaps it helps explain the rather sharp political culture that has characterized Dutch public life since the murder of Pim Fortuyn in 2002. For a long time prior to that Dutch politics was characterized by an even keel. Since the early 1980s, when the previous period of political polarization came to an end, Dutch public life had allowed little room for rowdy politics, celebrating its '*poldermodel*' instead. The Dutch have been playing catch-up with, according to some reports, some of the raucous and no-holds-barred political cultures in Europe, deeply intensified of course by ready access to the Internet, which 93% of the Dutch, from all walks of life, enjoy. The result of this uncomfortable discussion is a country that is in conflict with itself, and in which there is a sense of alienation. That was one of the main messages of Paul Scheffer's *Land van aankomst* (Land of Arrival, 2007), in which the famous publicist viewed the process of migration as a process of alienation, including for the long-established inhabitants who have to watch their own country change before their eyes. That last sentiment is certainly expressed by many Dutch who, whether they live in immigrant-rich neighbourhoods or not, see demographic change as an uprooting experience. Progressive citizens have often claimed that they no longer recognize their now xenophobic country and that they long for the 1990s, when the public sphere was not dominated by anxiety. And anxiety it often certainly is: many Dutch with whom I have spoken – and I really do mean many – do fear that Muslims some day will seize power in the Netherlands and impose Islamic rule.

These anxieties have helped the Dutch to develop a new, more nostalgic view of the past. Paul Schnabel, the director of the government-run Netherlands Institute for Social Research (Sociaal en Cultureel Planbureau, SCP), rightly observed that in recent years the Dutch have tended to see the best period of the Netherlands as lying in the past. That is certainly true of more politically conservative citizens, who long for a time when the Netherlands was less in the grip of Europe, or of migration, than it is presently (though I find it interesting that Wilder himself, in contrast to many populists, does not offer a very articulate vision of a past he sees as exemplary). But, as noted above, progressive Dutch, typified perhaps by the popular Dutch writer Geert Mak, feel this way too. In Mak, who has attracted a large following with his sympathetic historical portraits of the Netherlands, one often sees a desire for a return to the 1970s, a period long before the triumph of neo-liberal principles and right-wing radicalism.

And these anxieties have led to a new insistence on national identity. Although such a project inevitably remains elusive, the tens of thousands of residents living in the Netherlands have learned as a result what it ostensibly means to be Dutch. Required films, courses and exams thus point to signature features of Dutch society, from the toleration of topless beaches to the intolerance for messy front yards. They are perhaps the clearest statements at present of what it means to be Dutch, destined ironically to be better known by newcomers than by the Dutch themselves. Such statements do not in any event give the Dutch a greater sense of security about who they are.

However one may judge recent developments, there is little left of the Netherlands as a *'guide land'* (*Gidsland*) in the first decade of the twenty-first century. That is not only because of Dutch uncertainty, or because of traumatic events like Srebrenica. It also has to do with the fact that gay marriage is more widely accepted in more places than ten years ago, and the same is true of euthanasia. Shooting rooms for addicts and the decriminalization of cannabis are hardly exclusively Dutch achievements any more. That the Dutch can take at least a small degree of credit for these changes they may choose to take as comfort. But for the time being the confusion and uncertainty over what the Netherlands is, and what its place in the world should be, will continue. Perhaps that should be recognized as the normal state of affairs in Europe at the moment. At least the Dutch still have their dikes and tulips. ■

Geert Wilders in Berlin, 2 October 2010.© Photo by Michael Zellman.

Crossing Over

Thirty Years on the Wrong Side of the English Channel

› **Play**
Groot Bijgaarden Station
2 January 2010

It was the coldest winter for thirty years. Eurostar trains were seizing up in the Channel Tunnel, brought to a standstill by the new Ice Age. I was standing on a station platform next to an industrial estate outside Brussels waiting for the 18.57 train from Aalst. What am I doing here? I asked myself. How did it come to this?

« **Rewind**
De Vingerhoed, Utrecht
18 September 1979

First impressions are lodged in the mind for evermore when you move to a new country. I remember the solid black bicycles, the yellow signs, the insistent tram bells. I remember the sky that seemed to go on forever.

I arrived, like James Boswell, in the Dutch city of Utrecht. Boswell left Britain in 1763 on a ship from Harwich to acquire a Dutch legal education in the Netherlands. I left on a Stena ferry from the same port to escape the right-wing politics of Margaret Thatcher, who had become Prime Minister on 4 May.

Utrecht in those days seemed like Utopia compared to the crumbling island monarchy I had left behind. The bright yellow trains with their cute yellow noses ran on time. The spacious libraries had more English books than the ones back home. The country seemed rationally organised compared to the mess I had left behind. And the language was full of amusing oddities, like the *vingerhoed* (finger hat) that was their word for a thimble and the *handschoen* (hand shoe) that translated quite logically into a glove.

Quite soon I had settled into a life that revolved around cycling, sitting in warm cafes and studying "Dutch for Beginners". Of course, it wasn't all rosy. I would soon be confronted with the difficulties of finding a place to live in the world's most overcrowded country. Not to mention the complexities of speaking a language in which the verb normally at the end of the sentence placed is.

Utrecht.

• **Pause**
Geneva
14 February 1980

What on earth brought me to Utrecht? I'd like to say it was the paintings of Vermeer, which I first discovered in a Phaidon art book in Edinburgh Public Library. But that would be a little too neat. I think the true explanation is that I moved to the Netherlands because it was on the other side of the English Channel. I had jumped ship and, though I didn't realise it then, would remain an exile for the next thirty years and more.

Yet Mrs Thatcher's booming voice carried across the North Sea. I still remember that speech she made in Dublin on November 29, 1979, while I was settling into an apartment in a Utrecht suburb. 'I want my money back,' she demanded, hitting the table with her handbag. 'I must be absolutely clear about this.' Oh, how I wished at that moment that I had been born Dutch.

Yet I was finding it hard to fit into this perfect society. During those early weeks, I wandered the streets like Boswell. 'My heart sank to think of living in such a place,' wrote my unhappy Scottish compatriot. I felt the same, much of the time. The Netherlands was such an open and yet such a closed society. It was like visiting an art gallery where you were allowed to look but not to touch.

Boswell finally found a woman to offer some consolation. 'I have met a Dutch woman,' he noted in his diary. I, too, fell for Belle de Zuylen. I read *De Noble* in Utrecht, and bought the first volume of her letters, in French, in a bookshop in

Geneva. It was also in Geneva where, wandering through the Musée des Beaux-Arts, I first saw Maurice Quentin de La Tour's Portrait of Belle de Zuylen, aged 25. For all of ten minutes, I couldn't take my eyes off her.

» Fast forward

Maastricht
30 April, 1982

I was living in Maastricht when Thatcher went to war with Argentina. From the peaceful Low Countries this looked like an act of imperial madness, a return to the Victorian age. I was shocked to see the people of Britain waving enthusiastically as Royal Navy warships sailed from Portsmouth, bound for the other side of the world. Each day, I walked to the newsagent in Grote Straat to pick up yesterday's copy of *The Guardian*. Each day, the news got worse. At home, people of my age, or a few years younger, were beginning to realise that they could be called up to fight. I had not imagined that we could do such a thing.

› Play

Baarnedesteeg 13, Amsterdam
10 July, 1983

Maastricht finally seemed a bit dull and provincial. So I moved to Amsterdam and settled into an old apartment on the edge of the red light district. A short walk in one direction led to the mediaeval Sint Antonis city gate where Rembrandt painted Dr Tulp's anatomy lesson. A few steps in the other direction brought me to a glowing neon-lit canal where sex was sold behind heavy curtains.

The Nieuwmarkt in those days was a dingy area with hungry cats and nervy junkies and rusted bicycle parts. Yet I liked it. I liked the bookshops that smelled of damp and old coffee, and the distant bells of the Oude Kerk where Rembrandt's Saskia was buried under a blank grey stone. I liked the shops selling useful gadgets for mariners and the smoky café De Engelbewaarder where the dim interior seemed to have been imported from a seventeenth-century painting.

I liked the way that the Dutch got the small things just right, like the Nationaal Strippenkaart, a bus ticket that could be used everywhere in the country, and the Museumjaarkaart, which gave access to virtually every museum collection in the country. Once you had bought a *strippenkaart* and a *jaarkaart*, you could travel almost everywhere and visit any museum you wanted from the erudite Pipe Museum to the vast Rijksmuseum.

I liked the slow pace of Amsterdam, the gentle humour and the bicycles that rattled along the canals. I liked the way everyone owned a car, because it was seen as essential, but no one ever drove anywhere, because you would never find a parking place again. So parked cars slowly rusted on the canals, gradually buried under the dead leaves.

The Amsterdammers I knew were laid-back, a little world-weary, somewhat wind-blown. Everyone had read Anja Meulenbelt and disliked Ronald Reagan and voted PvdA. I noticed odd little signs of idealism, like a squat on the Wa-

Maastricht.

terlooplein with wooden birds on the roof and strange rusted structures where white electric cars were parked, apparently abandoned. I did once see one puttering along a canal, but in 1986 this utopian system was finally abandoned.

I read a lot of books in Amsterdam and gradually found out about some of the people that had lived near the Nieuwmarkt. I was particularly fond of Jan Jacobsz Swammerdam, who ran a chemist's shop at 18 Oude Schans in the early seventeenth century. Here he dabbled in science and amassed a cabinet of curiosities that included a unicorn, three Hottentot catapults, a mermaid's hand and a mechanical mouse.

His son, also Jan, built up a more scientific collection that embraced such items as the ear-drum of a walrus, a silkworm's testicles and the nostrils of a horse. On a visit here in 1668, Cosimo de Medici was so impressed with what he saw that he offered Swammerdam a position in Florence and the sum of 12,000 guilders for the entire collection, but the Dutch collector declined the offer.

Swammerdam wrote books on unusual subjects. I particularly liked the sound of "A Treatise on the History of Bees", which contained 60 extremely detailed drawings as well as a calculation of the number of eggs in a queen bee's ovaries. Nor was he afraid of taking risks in the pursuit of knowledge and in one experiment he ate larvae to observe the taste. The raw larvae struck him as "very disagreeable" and tasting of "rusty bacon," whereas boiled larvae "have a more agreeable taste, but if one continues chewing them, the former taste prevails again."

Amsterdam.

While studying the mayfly, Swammerdam met the Flemish mystic Antoinette Bourgignon to discuss religion. She described the mayfly as a "little beast which lives only a single day, and throughout that time endures many miseries". The meeting profoundly influenced Swammerdam, and in 1675 he produced his classic work on the mayfly entitled *Ephemeri vita*, or "Life of the Ephemera", which became famous for its extremely detailed illustrations.
Swammerdam, like the mayfly, did not live long. He died of malaria in 1680, aged just 43, and his entire collection was sold off. He bequeathed his unpublished writings to a friend, who failed to publish them, and they lay forgotten for almost half a century. In 1727 Herman Boerhaave of Leiden University discovered Swammerdam's extraordinary collection of drawings and descriptions of animals and published them as *Bybel der Natuure*, or 'The Bible of Nature', in two handsome volumes.

This contains remarkable scientific descriptions, but also some odd ideas and digressions that reflect the seventeenth-century mind. Swammerdam told a story of a maidservant who tried to thread woodlice thinking they were pearls. He also offered a description of how to go fishing using cormorants, as well as instructions on the proper method of engraving pictures on sea shells.

• **Pause**

What is it about Amsterdam that makes people turn their attention to miniature things? Three centuries after Jan Swammerdam pored over the mayfly, the American artist Donald Evans lived in Amsterdam creating tiny paintings in the form of postage stamps issued by imaginary countries. He loved cooking and invented countries based on Italian recipes he read in Elisabeth David cookbooks. There was the country of "Mangiare" (Eat), Castello Pisello" (Pea Castle), "Lago Divinorosso" (Lake of Red Wine) and the church of "S. Fagiolo in Olio" (St Haricot Bean in Oil).

Bruce Chatwin wrote an essay on Evans for the New York Review of Books. "'I can't think of another artist who expressed more succinctly and beautifully the best aspirations of those years: the flight from war and the machine; the asceticism; the nomadic restlessness; the yearning for sensual cloud-cuckoo-lands; the retreat from public into private obsessions, from the big and noisy to the small and still."

Evans' reclusive life ended suddenly on April 29, 1977, when he was trapped in a fire in his Amsterdam apartment. He was just 31 years old, and left behind almost nothing apart from 4,000 tiny paintings of places that never existed.

• **Record**

The world changes. By the late 1980s, I was beginning to sense a transformation in the Netherlands. People were beginning to take Thatcher's brutal capitalism seriously. Her hard line message that there was no alternative was creeping across the Channel to the debating chamber in Den Haag. Maybe we need to introduce Thatcherism to the Dutch, they were saying. It felt like a good time to leave. I found a job in Brussels.

→ **Play**
Brussels, Central Station
November 11, 1989

Brussels looked grim on the day I arrived. I noticed the dark town houses with their net curtains permanently drawn, as if someone had recently died. I noticed the gloomy metro stations and the trams the colour of faded newspaper.

I didn't really like Belgium at first. It wasn't like the Netherlands. It wasn't love at first sight. It seemed a sullen country, silently resentful, nursing some grievance.

Slowly, I began to get accustomed to the place. I began to discover the noisy street markets, the blend of languages like Italian and Arabic and something that might have been Hungarian. I liked the quiet melancholy of the cafes, which reminded me of the paintings of Spilliaert. I liked the way Belgian literature was always gloomy and Belgian films almost always included one scene set in grim industrial wasteland.

I think you can understand a country by listening to train announcements. In Britain, they broadcast messages in a loud authoritarian tone that makes you think that the Battle of Britain is still raging. In the Flemish area of Belgium, they have someone speaking quite softly and with just a hint of seduction, as if your train journey to Leuven might possibly be the start of an affair.

Oh, I don't know what to think. Sometimes Belgium seems old-fashioned and a bit cynical. Other times, it is right up there with the world's most progressive countries. Sometimes it is a country of Catholic priests under investigation for sex scandals. Other times it is the first country in Europe to have a gay church.

I didn't realise it back in 1989, but a young politician called Guy Verhofstadt was beginning to have an impact in Belgium. Someone dubbed him "baby Thatcher" because he was young and apparently supported Mrs Thatcher's economic policies. It is probably just as well I wasn't reading the newspapers too closely at the time. He eventually became prime minister, but much later, after he had matured a bit and softened his liberalism.

• Delete

Brussels
2 November, 2004

On a sunny day in September, 2001, two planes brought down the Twin Towers in New York. The whole world shifted slightly in the aftershock. The Netherlands was deeply affected, more so perhaps than Belgium. Maybe the ancient ties with New Amsterdam made it more personal.

Strange things began to happen in the months that followed. I gradually became aware of Pim Fortuyn, a neatly-suited Rotterdam politician known for being both gay and anti-Muslim. I was only just beginning to understand his policies when I saw a news report showing his body lying in the street outside the Hilversum broadcasting centre, shot dead by an angry activist who afterwards explained that he was enraged at Fortuyn for 'using Muslims as scapegoats'.

I had come to see Belgium as surreal and the Netherlands as orderly. But nothing in Belgium could match what came next. On 2 November 2004, in the busy Linnaeusstraat in eastern Amsterdam, a 26-year-old Dutch Moroccan pulled out a gun and shot the Dutch filmmaker Theo van Gogh as he cycled to his office.

Van Gogh fell to the ground and staggered across the street to a nearby building. The attacker advanced towards him and raised his gun. Van Gogh cried out: "We can still talk about it! Don't do it! Don't do it!" The plea for understanding had no effect. The attacker fired another shot and then slit Van Gogh's throat. He then left a note pinned to his chest with the knife and fled to the nearby Oosterpark.

The Dutch like to be unshockable, but these two murders appeared to knock them sideways. The last political assassination in the Netherlands was the murder of William of Orange in 1561. This was a country where the strongest political statement I can remember is when a newspaper called Reagan a 'nitwit'. It was a country where political opponents would be 'polderised' into agreement through endless dull discussions. It wasn't a country where you fired a gun at your political enemies.

The weirdness only got worse. At the time he was murdered, Theo van Gogh had just finished a film about the killing of Pim Fortuyn titled 06-05. But his killer had been enraged by another film – "Submission" – that Van Gogh produced earlier in 2004 in collaboration with the Somali refugee Ayaan Hirsi Ali.

The film told the story of a Muslim woman forced into an arranged marriage, abused by her husband and then brutally punished for adultery. It included scenes in which verses of the Koran were painted on the woman's naked body. The aim, Van Gogh said in an interview, was "to provoke discussion on the posi-

Brussels.

tion of enslaved Muslim women." He could hardly have imagined that a film, any film, would cost his life.

Then there was his name. Van Gogh? What, like the artist? people asked, confused by the news story coming from peaceful Amsterdam. Theo was in fact related to Vincent's brother, another Theo, who had supported Vincent while he struggled to succeed as an artist. The brother had a son whom he named Vincent. Van Gogh was in an asylum near St Rémy in Provence when he heard the news of young Vincent's birth. He painted a work called "Branches with Almond Blossom" and sent it to Theo to hang above the couple's bed.

Vincent had a son, yet another Theo, who was executed as a resistance fighter during the German Occupation of The Netherlands. Another son, Johan, worked for the Dutch secret service and it was his son, Theo, who was shot dead in an Amsterdam street.

A monument to the murdered filmmaker titled 'The Scream' was unveiled in the Oosterpark in 2007. I knew this park because I had walked through it on 22 October 1987, a day of violent storms, a few hours after my first daughter was born. I remember the midwife saying that it was like the end of the world, but I hoped for Anna's sake it was the beginning.

More than any storm, the murder of Theo really seemed like the end of the world. How could something like that happen in a country I loved so much? How could everything change so totally? How could anyone ever again express an opinion, cycle through the streets, make a film?

That country of bright primary colours had suddenly turned dark. Where would it go from there?

Henry Le Boeuf Hall at the Centre for Fine Arts, Brussels.

» **Fast forward**
Amsterdam, Rokin
14 April, 2008

The last time I went back to Amsterdam, I found that much of the old city had gone. The Rijksmuseum was still closed and the centre had been ripped apart to lay down a new North-South metro line. The newspaper De Volkskrant had shrunk in size and the politician Geert Wilders had made a film attacking Muslims.

And then I read Ray Kluun's novel *Love Life*, which was the book everyone was talking about at the time. It is the story of a man who parties and sleeps with prostitutes while his girlfriend is dying of cancer. And it's largely a true story. It was a nasty book, I thought, the kind of novel that was being published in London and New York during the Thatcher-Reagan years.

I realised then that the Netherlands was no longer Utopia.

→ **Play**
Brussels, Central Station
1 September, 2010

I stepped off the train one evening at Luxembourg Station in Brussels. This is a busy station next to the European Parliament. Trains arrive and depart all the time. People pour into Brussels in the morning and leave the city again at 6 pm. The city ebbs and flows.

No one stays for long, I realised. No one belongs. Not really. Not the way a Parisian belongs. Or a New Yorker. Everyone is a migrant here, crossing Europe in search of somewhere they can call home. People pause in Brussels, eat a good meal, have an interesting conversation, stand in the middle of Grand'Place, and then move on somewhere more solid.

Yet I feel fond of Brussels. It seems a hopeful place, despite the chaos. It has an ability to adapt, to bend with the rules, to listen. It accepts different people, different ideas, and tries to make everything work in the end. There's no fixed plan, no big idea, just a willingness to listen.

It's now more than 30 years since I arrived in the Low Countries. I've spent more than half my life here, yet it still doesn't feel exactly like home. I admire the art, the hospitals, the food. But I still can't fit in, even though Brussels is, as capital of Europe, *my* capital.

My final question, as we approach the 500th anniversary of the publication of Thomas More's *Utopia*, is whether we are nearing the end of Utopia in the Low Countries. I sense that this region is in danger of losing those ideals like tolerance and optimism that first brought me here in 1979.

It feels like it might be time to move on again. And, if that is so, is there anywhere that is Utopia now? ■

^ **Eject**

Orange: a Colour that Unites and Divides

[MARNIX BEYEN]

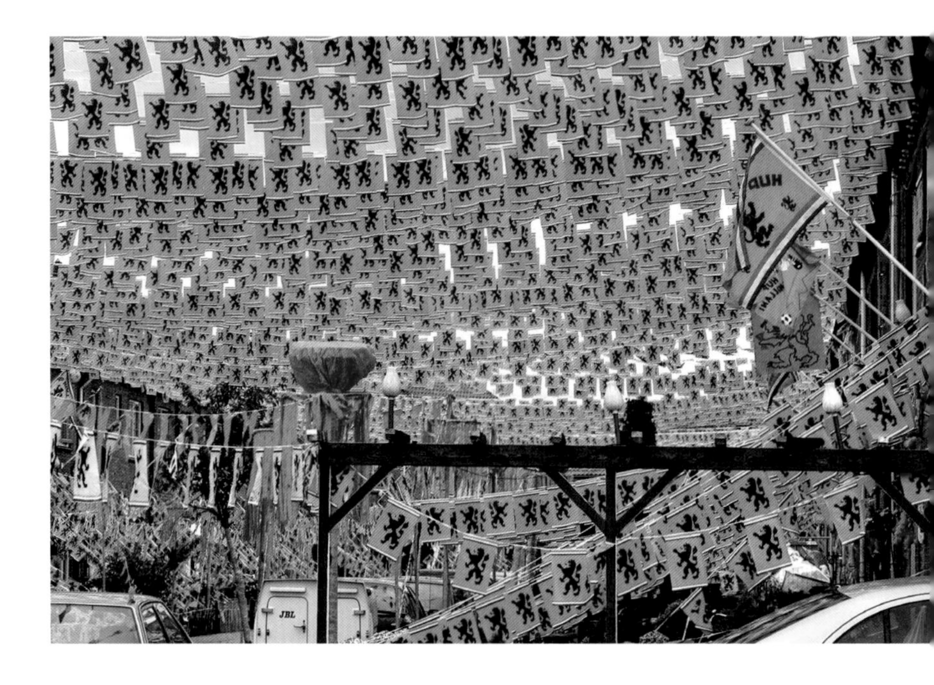

Doetinchem, Gelderland during the European Football Championship, 2004. Photo by Marcel van den Bergh.

'O, how quiet they are! How quiet the Belgians are!' This taunt, echoing across the sites of the 1988 Belgian pop festivals, was indeed met with a deafening silence. It was chanted by small groups of youths, dressed conspicuously in flags and strange headgear, many with painted faces. What reduced the Belgians to silence was not only the slogan but also the predominant colour in this masquerade: a garish orange that painfully underlined the significance of the words.

At first glance its significance was obvious to everyone: the Dutch football team had just become European Champions while the Belgian Red Devils had failed even to qualify. But although this particular interaction was tied to a specific set of events, for the participants it also formed part of an old, one might almost say timeless, ritual. Those particular young people may not have had much historical awareness, but they were playing a game that embraced four centuries of history. For most of them the exact references were undoubtedly buried in some historical subconscious, but perhaps that is why they could have so much impact; they summoned up responses which a judicious historical approach would have smothered. The colour Orange, which absorbed all these historical memories and bundled them together into a single icon, functioned as a powerful detonator for these reflex reactions.

The Father of the Nation divides and unites

It was a pure dynastic accident that added the French principality of Orange to the German and Netherlandish estates of the eleven-year-old German nobleman William of Nassau. But the consequences of that accident were far-reaching. When the higher nobility in the Netherlands started to grow restless under the Spanish King Philip II, it was Prince William who held the senior title. In spite of his intimacy with the Habsburg court, in which he had largely been brought up, and despite his reservations about any form of religious fanaticism,

Statue of Willem of Orange, Petit Sablon, Brussels. Photo by Jonas Lampens.

he gradually emerged as the 'natural' leader of the Dutch Revolt. In his search for something that would mobilise and unite together his heterogeneous troops, this dynastic accident again served him well. The name of his principality was also a colour that was heraldically unusual and therefore instantly recognisable. The armies with which he invaded the Netherlands in 1568 rallied behind the Prince's flag of orange, white and blue. Even the republic that emerged from the revolt presented itself to the outside world under the 'orange-white-blue'. After William's death, however, 'orange' was less and less able to hold the young republic together. As 'Stadholders', the House of Orange-Nassau exercised important executive and military functions in each of the provinces. Since they no longer represented the Habsburgs as viceroys or provincial governors, however, many people in the republic believed that ultimate sovereignty now rested with the provincial Estates.Consequently, they regarded the Stadholders with suspicion and at times with outright hostility. Moreover, as Stadholders William's immediate successors were drawn into the complex political and religious conflicts between the orthodox Calvinists who looked to Orange and the religious moderates who championed the Estates. In these circumstances it is not surprising that the orange stripe in the Republic's flag was soon replaced by red, definitively so after the first Stadholderless Period (1650-1672),. Although various reasons were given for the change, it was clear that orange had become the colour of the Stadholder's party rather than of the nation as a whole. This was even more the case in the eighteenth century when the restored Stadholders started to behave more and more like monarchs, and during the Batavian and French period when they disappeared from the political stage.

It was precisely during this period when the Stadholders were losing power to the enlightened bourgeoisie that they became the object of a movement of popular support which took light-hearted if at times also violent forms, the followers of which decked themselves in orange ribbons and bows. In an attempt to prevent a rebellion, in 1784 the Estates of Holland even banned the wearing of orange. Incidentally, the growth of Orange as an ideological force was not confined to the Netherlands but was international. After a bloody encounter with Catholic militia in the village of Loughgall in 1795 a group of Irish Protestants swore allegiance to the memory of William III, the Orange Stadholder who a century earlier had put an end to the Catholic rule of Britain's James II. This eventually became the Orange Order whose purpose was to testify to Protestant liberties anywhere on British soil. The annual Orange Marches that it has organised since then have been a smouldering fuse in the powder-keg of Northern Ireland, particularly in the last decades of the twentieth century. In former British colonies, too. this influential organisation proudly holds Orange aloft as a symbol of militant Protestantism.

In the Netherlands Orange gradually lost its ideological character. After the establishment of the Orange monarchy in 1813, the Orange movement ceased to be illegal and a much broader, emotional form of Orangism developed. However, it did not immediately become the main unifying element of the nation. Orange remained the colour of the common man, who viewed with mistrust the liberal elites who dominated the Dutch state. It was not until the last two decades of the nineteenth century that this began to change. During this period when democratisation, expansion and social pillarisation (*verzuiling*) threatened the unity of Dutch society, the political elites realised that they needed a unifying principle. Since the constitutional reforms of 1848 had left the Princes of Orange with very little political power, they seemed ideally suited to fulfil this symbolic role. Unfortunately, William II and William III had so little charisma that they achieved very little. It was only with the accession of Queen Wilhelmina in 1890 that an emotional bond between the monarchy and the people developed that would last for over a century. The renewed bond between the House of Orange and the Dutch people was ritually confirmed at Wilhelmina's inauguration in 1898 and during the celebrations of 1919, when the predominant colour was orange.

Against this background the historical perception of William the Silent also changed. While the 300th anniversary of his death in 1884 had been marked by fundamental ideological disagreements, the 400th anniversary of his birth in 1933 saw the various sections of the population uniting to commemorate the

'Father of the Nation'. The myth of Orange was not troubled by the historical uncertainties surrounding him. In particular, by emphasising his Erasmian attitude to religion, even the Dutch Catholics could incorporate William of Orange into their pantheon.

If the figure of William of Orange fostered Dutch unity, the colour orange continued to be divisive. A growing number of people thought that orange should be reintroduced into the Dutch flag, but since the most vociferous supporters of the change were the self-confessed fascists of the National Socialist Movement, nothing came of it. In February 1937 the red, white and blue was officially proclaimed to be the flag of the Netherlands, which was all the more painful for the orange supporters because the Union of South Africa had chosen Orange, White and Blue in 1928. But their revenge was sweet. Banned from the national flag, Orange made increasing headway on its own. The cult of Orange which underpinned Dutch nationalist activities during the Second World War was an example of this. After the war, when Fascism was no longer regarded as a threat, a blind eye was turned to the fact that collaborationist circles had also made great play with Orange Since then Orange flags and banners (with at the most, red, white and blue borders) have comfortably outnumbered the official red, white and blue at celebrations and sporting events. Orange has also become part of everyday life; it is no longer the colour of the monarchy or the national elites but of the whole Dutch nation. But though it has broken away from the specific figure of William of Orange, its present power still draws heavily on its historical connotations. One of its strongest features is that the colour orange can be associated with both sovereignty and resistance.

Orange in Belgian party conflicts

Whereas in the Netherlands the growing popularity of Orange has become a visible symbol of successful nationhood, in Belgium it has almost always led to discord. The simple fact that Belgian independence resulted from a struggle against the Orange dynasty obviously has much to do with this. The 1831 Constitution laid down that no descendant of the House of Orange-Nassau could ever ascend the Belgian throne and the first version of the Belgian national anthem made no attempt to disguise the hatred for Orange. Anyone who still dared to profess himself an 'Orangist' was automatically accused of being a traitor. However, this Belgian Orangism was only partly based on active sympathy for the Orange dynasty, past or present. Much more important was fear of the negative economic or cultural consequences of the split with the Netherlands. So, as the Belgian state became consolidated, such Orangist sympathies became more marginalised. A working-class variant of Orangism lived on for a long time, however; it surfaced, for instance, in early Ghent socialism. Even the present Socialist Mayor of Leuven, Louis Tobback, is still happy to label himself an Orangist. Although he too regrets the missed economic and strategic opportunities of the United Kingdom of the Netherlands more than the loss of the Orange dynasty.

Only from the 1860s on can one observe any active affection for Orange in Belgium. But then it was to be found exclusively among the Liberals who saw their battle with the Catholics as a continuation of the 16th-century Protestant resistance to the Catholic ruler Philip II. In Antwerp the Liberals set up a

Beggars Society (*Geuzenbond*) at which they enthusiastically sang the anti-clerical Beggars' Song (*Geuzenlied*); in 1876 the 300th anniversary of the Pacification of Ghent was celebrated in Ghent with great pomp. The Brussels Liberals also joined in to extol the Revolt. When planning the Kleine Zavel park in the 1880s the Brussels City Council chose an iconographic design that had the Dutch Revolt as its theme. The large statues of Egmont and Hoorne are surrounded by a series of smaller figures representing Belgian scholars and politicians from the Renaissance. Among them are Mercator and Ortelius, but also Marnix van Sint-Aldegonde and, as the French inscription puts it, 'Guillaume le Taciturne' [William the Silent].

The Kleine Zavel statues tell us a great deal about Belgian liberalism's relationship with Orange in the late nineteenth century. Firstly, William of Orange was only one small part of the broader cult of the Revolt or the Beggars. In the process of image-forming he was no more prominent than, and indeed sometimes subordinate to, figures such as Egmont, Hoorne or Marnix, all of whom had played important roles in the context of the Southern Netherlands. Furthermore, Belgian Liberals tended to use the epithet 'the Silent' rather than the noble title 'of Orange'. After all, to patriotic Liberals in the 1880s 'William of Orange' meant in the first place the despot to whom they had shown the door fifty years earlier. The William the Silent they extolled had been a hero in spite of, not because of, the dynasty to which he belonged – a hero of foresight and liberal thinking.

By detaching William the Silent from his dynasty, the Belgian Liberals also showed that they were not seeking reunification with the Netherlands under the House of Orange. Even in the cultural movement for a Greater Netherlands which Liberal Flemish militants developed in the second half of the nineteenth century, any appeal to the actual House of Orange was virtually absent. Until the First World War, Orange remained a focal point for liberal sentiments, not for geopolitical change.

The colour of radicalism

The German invasion of 1914 put boundary change on the political agenda of a small group of radicals. For this heterogeneous group of Activists, creating an independent Flanders took priority over any ideological issues. That made cross-fertilisation between Liberal and Catholic Flemish radicals possible. A striking instance of this was the way that Catholic activists adopted the rhetoric of the Beggars and associated it with a Greater Netherlands programme. Incidentally, that programme was very different from that of the 19th century Liberals because it was based on their common language. In other words, francophone Belgium would have been excluded from the Netherlands.

This 'common language' variant of the Greater Netherlands movement had absolutely nothing in common with William of Orange's dreams. And yet during the interwar years (paradoxically enough the period when the radical Flemish movement was becoming increasingly Catholic) it would become firmly rooted in the imagination of the radical Flemish nationalists. More than that, by appealing to Orange the interwar Flemish nationalists seemed to be trying to show that their radicalism was different from the pre-war Flemish Movement, which had been accused of provincialism and romantic extravagance.

Flemish nationalists showed their devotion to William of Orange not only by participating enthusiastically in the Orange commemoration of 1933, but also by giving the colour orange a prominent place in their own heraldry. It was no accident that this development was most apparent in the ranks of the fascist *Verdinaso*, the 'Union of Diets [Dutch] National Solidarists', founded in 1928 with the aim of forming a 'Diets' empire of Belgium, Luxemburg and the Netherlands. In 1932 the party introduced a new flag, showing a blue sword, plough and cogwheel intertwined on a white and orange ground. There was no reference to traditional Flemish nationalist symbolism. From 1934 on, Verdinaso's leader Joris van Severen began to campaign actively for a return to the Seventeen Provinces of William of Orange, and attempted to gain support for his movement in the Netherlands and Wallonia. After his violent death in the summer of 1940 his party honoured him as the 'Father of the Nation'.

Sharing some of Verdinaso's views, but more traditionalist in its imagery and approach, was the Flemish National Union (VNV) which was founded in 1933. Its orange flag with a blue and white delta symbol in the middle was adopted in 1935, but the party also continued to use the traditional Flemish lion and the

Kinderdijk (from *Maxima on tour)*, 2001. Photo by Raymond Rutting.

nationalist fulmar symbol. Even after the party chose to collaborate with the German occupiers during the war, its magazines often featured illustrations in which the 'Father of the Nation' overshadowed the historical and living heroes of Flemish nationalism.

The status of Orange in this Flemish Nationalist propaganda was highly ambiguous. On the one hand it seemed to justify far-reaching collaboration that looked beyond narrow Flemish interests; but on the other, the references to the 16th century Dutch revolt always contained an element of 'internal resistance'. This was due not just to the revolutionary sentiments they could arouse

Cornelis Lely, architect of the Zuiderzee works, on the Afsluitdijk dam inspecting the busses provided by the sponsor of Jong Oranje, the national under-21 football team during the Olympic Games in Beijing, 2008.

but also to the fact that in February 1941 the German occupiers had banned any reference to a political Greater Netherlands. Growing discontent in Flemish Nationalist circles with the VNV's excessive collaboration was expressed largely through references to the Dutch Revolt. The 'One Netherlands' group which developed within the VNV also used the name 'the Beggars'.

It was probably because of this 'resistance' connotation that Orange played an important role in the post-war revival of Flemish nationalism. By rallying behind Orange, various youth movements, student organisations and intellectual think-tanks were able to retain the radical nationalist elements that had justified collaboration while at the same time basking in the reflected glory of the Resistance. In 1952 the Orange Flag was carried into the Flemish Nationalist Song Festival to loud cheers, and to this day the annual festival closes with Netherlands' national anthem, the *Wilhelmus*.

However, as the years passed and Flemish Nationalism regained political credibility, Orange elements seemed to have been relegated to the intellectual margins. In 1955, the same year that the Flemish nationalist party called the Volksunie (People's Union) held its first congress (and opted firmly for yellow and black), the Order of the Prince was founded in Kortrijk. To this day the Order still operates under William the Silent's motto of 'Amicitia et Tolerantia' but more as a Greater Netherlands Society Club than as an active political organisation. The orange-white-blue heraldic shield of the Free University of Brussels which was established in 1970 reflects a similar intellectual strand of Greater Netherlands intellectualism, though it might also be seen as a return to the liberal Sea Beggars romanticism of the late 19th century. But even such a radical right-wing think-tank as the Delta Foundation has opted for an orange design, and despite its professed pagan beliefs sees William of Orange as a shining example.

When in July 2008 the Dutch right-wing populist politician Geert Wilders tried to win support for his Greater Netherlands project in Flanders with a newspaper campaign, he frequently referred to William of Orange's dream of a Greater Netherlands. In so doing, he undoubtedly over-estimated the resonance of Orange in Flanders today. While in the Netherlands the historical figure, and more especially the colour, developed during the last century into universally recognisable symbols of unity, in Belgian history they have always served as a vehicle for particular, concrete political objectives. Orange was used by the Liberals against the Catholics, by radical Flemish nationalists against the cultural nationalists, by the conditional against the unconditional collaborators. In the Belgian imagination William of Orange has never become part of a shared heritage.

But perhaps it is in itself remarkable that since the end of the 19th century William has hardly aroused any negative feelings in Belgium. After all, was he not the founder of the dynasty against which Belgium fought for and achieved its independence? And is not the colour with which he is associated also the colour by which its neighbour constantly and self-confidently presents itself to the outside world in a way that can only highlight Belgian disunity the more strongly? ■

Translated by Chris Emery

FURTHER READING

De Negentiende Eeuw, vol. 23 (1999) no. 1. (Themed issue on Orangism).

E.O.G. Haitsma Mulier& A.E.M. Janssen (eds.), *Willem van Oranje in de historie, 1584-1984. Vier eeuwen beeldvorming en geschiedschrijving*, HES, Utrecht, 1984.

T. van der Laars, *Wapens, vlaggen en zegels van Nederland,* Uitgeverij Jacob van Campen, Amsterdam, 1913.

U. Vermeulen, "Katholieken en liberalen tegenover de Gentse Pacificatiefeesten (1876)", *Handelingen der Maatschappij voor Geschiedenis en Oudheidkunde te Gent,* no. 20 (1966), pp. 167-185.

K. van der Wee & E. De Maesschalck, *Vlaanderen ontmoet Nederland. De Geschiedenis van de Orde van den Prince*, Lannoo, Tielt, 2003.

How North and South in the Low Countries Switched Religions

Catholic and Protestant

[WILLEM FRIJHOFF]

'The Protestant South and the Catholic North'. It could have been the title of a book printed 450 years ago, just before the Dutch Revolt. But it would have contradicted currently held views about North and South. The common assumption is that the Protestant North rose up against the anti-Protestant policies of the Spanish king and his representatives and that the villain of the piece was the Duke of Alva with his Council of Blood. In their struggle the Northern rebels, united by the Union of Utrecht in 1579, won independence as a Protestant commonwealth, as opposed to the Southern Union of Arras which remained Roman Catholic and loyal to Spain. It was also at this time that the North laid the foundations of intellectual independence and freedom of religious enquiry, which would lead to an unprecedented flowering of the arts and sciences. The South saw itself subjected to the combined yoke of throne and altar while the North tasted the fruits of political democracy and spiritual independence. It was there that the Reformation became the basis for what recent historians have called the Radical Enlightenment, that process of 'demystification' in which magical thinking and the spiritual power of the church were replaced by modern rationalism.

In the divided Netherlands, religious polarisation became the basis of two opposing self-images. The South remained Catholic. It even felt itself to be uniformly Catholic. The South's Catholicism became one of the factors in the Belgian Revolt of 1830 and for a long time national politics revolved around it. In the North, Protestantism in all its variants, even the most orthodox, still sees itself as a religion of freedom. It opposes the oppressiveness of Catholic dogma, hierarchy and morality under which it believes the South is suffering, even though it no longer describes the Pope as the Anti-Christ. On the other hand, the South enjoys a quality of life that it would never wish to exchange for the sombre, strict and hypocritical Protestant culture of the North. At least, that was how things stood until public life was secularised and the system of social 'pillars' came to an end after the 1960s.

Protestant Cemetery, Sint-Maria-Horebeke, Flanders. Photo by Jonas Lampens.

Religion or culture?

The contrast between a Catholic South and Protestant North is probably the best-known and most deeply-rooted distinction between the two halves of the Low Countries, but it is also one of the most surprising. After all, the North is far from being uniformly Protestant. On the contrary, entire districts in North and South Holland as well as the inland provinces have remained predominantly Catholic, and the big cities have always harboured their own solidly Catholic minorities. Merchants and ministers dominate the classic self-image of the North, but while the minister defined morality it was the merchant who governed society and the merchant was not necessarily a Protestant. He was often Catholic or Jewish. According to the most recent religious survey of Europe, published in 2003, at 31% the Roman Catholic community in the Netherlands is 50% larger than the 21% of the combined Protestant communities. The rest of the population is Moslem, Jewish, non-churchgoing or belongs to some other religious group. In strictly numerical terms, the North seems to have become a Catholic country.

Is the opposite true of the South? There are certainly more Protestant communities now than in the eighteenth century before the French occupation (1792-95), and there have always been a few more or less clandestine communities 'under the cross', but their numbers were nothing like that of the Catholics in the North. Although Protestant missionaries (Van Gogh!) have since rediscovered the South, and Protestant churches there have grown exponentially, it is still universally regarded as a Catholic country. Although liberalism and other ideologies have made inroads into the moral primacy of the Roman Catholic religion, the cultural base remains 'Catholic'.

And yet ... Although numerically the North may have become more Catholic than before, any self-respecting Catholic Northerner will invariably point out the Calvinist bias of his culture. Here, the contrast between Catholic and Protestant cuts across the stereotypes of the sombre, gaunt, plain-spoken and deadly serious Northerner and the refined, Burgundian *bon vivant*, flexible and occasionally hypocritical Southerner. The average Northern Catholic does not associate himself with the baroque South; rather he sees himself as a Catholic with a Protestant tinge. In their struggle since the 1960s to modernise the Catholic Church against the moral conservatism of the Vatican, Dutch Catholics invariably point to their unique history which has brought them into the sphere of Calvinist culture: the work ethic, rejection of hypocrisy, moral purity, individualism, sobriety in the expression of one's faith, with a liturgy close to one's everyday experience. In their contacts with Catholics from other countries, Dutch Catholics often feel decidedly Protestant, and certainly non-Vatican. The fact that they previously lived through a century of militant ultramontanism, as unashamedly loyal to Rome as the South, is now brushed aside as a product of a particular political and social period and no longer relevant. After all, at that time they needed an international protector in order to free themselves from Protestant domination.

A protestant soul?

In the sixteenth century Western European Christendom split in two. On one side were those who, with however many reservations, remained loyal to the established church. Their opponents described them scornfully as Romanists or Romish, as did, for instance, the Protestant mayor of Antwerp, Marnix van Sint-Aldegonde (1540-1598), in his satire *The Beehive of the Holy Roman Church* (De Byencorf der H. Roomsche Kercke, 1569). Those 'Roman' Catholics snapped back by calling the Protestants 'heretics' or, in the North until the 18th century, *geuzen* [beggars]. On the other side were those who *protested* against Rome's pretensions and claims to absolute truth. From Luther and Zwingli to Menno Simons and Calvin they wanted a more or less radical reform of the church. But the Roman Catholic Church also had its reformers. In opposition to the Protestant Reformation they almost immediately set up their own reformation, the Counter-Reformation, or what is now considered a more appropriate term since they ran in parallel, the 'Catholic' Reformation. The call for a better trained ministry with higher moral awareness, and a church organisation which was less obsessed with money found a response in the resolutions of the reforming Council of Trent (1543-1563). Their implementation finally began a process of internal reform.

Already early in the sixteenth century, 'Protestant' became the collective term for all those who wanted church reform without the Pope. Adopted by the reformed churches to mark their opposition to the Catholics, it was a political and public catchword that said more about what people disliked than what they actually wanted. Protestants were the persecuted victims of the Catholics, like the Huguenots in France, the Lutherans in Austria or the Waldensians in Italy. But on days of prayer for protection against disasters or war, the Dutch state was reminded of its Catholic soul. The designation 'Protestant' was what united many communities in this deeply divided land and, when in the nineteenth century the Roman Catholics also demanded their place in Christian society, confessing Protestants started to call themselves – somewhat tautologically – 'Protestant-Christian', a term that is still used among the more traditional or orthodox sections of Dutch Protestantism.

The process of national image formation has tried to project the North as the original Protestant country, the cradle of the Reformation in the Netherlands. It was intended to underline and strengthen the Protestant character of the Dutch nation in the face of the struggle for emancipation by Catholics and other religious groups. Yet in the sixteenth century it was in fact the South which initially and most fiercely embraced Protestantism, first in its Lutheran and later in its Calvinist form. The iconoclastic riots of 1566 began in Steenvoorde, now a commune in French Flanders, and spread through the rest of Flanders before reaching the Northern provinces. Even after the Revolt the North remained Catholic for a considerable time. Calvinism progressed in fits and starts and usually only because of the influence of preachers who had fled from the South and were the real Catholic-hunters. Only in the final decades of the sixteenth century did Calvinism become the dominant and official church in the newly independent North, and also briefly in Flanders and Brabant in the Calvinist urban republics of Ghent, Antwerp, Brussels and Mechelen, until the Duke of Parma restored Catholic order in 1585.

In the North there was no question of a theocracy. Although reformed, the civil government insisted on retaining responsibility for a republic which was religiously divided. They did not tolerate religious coercion, even from the Reformed who thought their claims should be honoured in recognition of their role in the Revolt. It is true that the Reformed church was the only publicly recognised and privileged church, but in the private sphere other faiths were tolerated, including Catholicism. So long as Christendom, the basis of Christian society, was not directly attacked, all churches could continue to profess their faith quietly behind the closed doors of private dwellings. Some places were freer than others, but nobody in the North was persecuted solely for matters of conscience.

And yet the North called itself Protestant. The Reformed communities saw themselves as a new, divinely-appointed second Israel, "Neêrlands Israël". This sense of Protestant nationhood had much to do with the enormous influx of refugees from the Southern Netherlands after 1585. At least 100,000 of these, and probably more, constituted between 5% and 10% of the North's total population, and up to 50% locally in places like Leiden. However, these immigrants were by no means all Calvinists. They could be Lutheran or Baptist, like the parents of the prince of Dutch poets, Joost van den Vondel (1587-1679), or even Catholic, since economic motives were certainly as powerful as religion. The Mechelen shipowner and herring trader Johan van der Veken (1548-1616) was

Catholic Beguinage, Amsterdam. Photo by Jonas Lampens.

related to the leading families in Antwerp but moved to the Reformed city of Rotterdam. He was one of the founders of the Rotterdam Stock Exchange, and with a fortune of at least 900,000 guilders he lived in the largest house in the city and was by far its wealthiest resident. In fact he was one of the three richest men in the entire Republic. But throughout his life he remained a practising Catholic who actively supported his co-religionists and in his country house at Capelle built and funded a private chapel with a full-time priest.

A Catholic bulwark?

So we should not fall back too quickly on clichés. In the South, the restoration of Catholicism proceeded faster and more forcefully than in the North. When the Twelve Year Truce was agreed in 1609 and Northerners were again allowed to travel to the South, an edict was issued strictly forbidding the spreading of heresy. But in practice the authorities were slow to prosecute those who transgressed. Just as in the North, harsh words and the occasional conviction could not disguise the fact that in general people disliked persecuting their fellow citizens, neighbours and relations or their fellow guild members. Contrary to what the language of the edicts would lead one to expect, after the gruesome death of Anneke Utenhove, an Anabaptist who was buried alive in 1597 on the express instructions of the Archduke, no more heretics were executed. Antwerp in particular was concerned that the persecution of heretics would damage the economic interests of the city. And in both North and South, the fight against heresy was tempered by the fear of reprisals against co-religionists over the border.

However, the South did go its own way. The prince-bishopric of Liège naturally remained entirely Catholic. But it was the Archdukes Albert and Isabella, whom Philip II appointed to govern the Southern Netherlands in 1598, who set out to be recognised as Catholic rulers in sharp contrast to the Protestant North. For them Catholicism was not merely a set of values but a means of giving the South a clear identity as a bulwark of Catholicism. They made every effort to achieve a theocratic ideal of a homogeneous Catholic community with renewed discipline, morality and spirituality. This re-Catholicisation became a grand programme that also re-energised numerous sectors of the economy: the building of monumental churches with flamboyantly Catholic decoration (such as the Jesuit church in Antwerp which cost an absolute fortune), the foundation of new monasteries (Jesuit, Capuchin, Augustinian, Carmelite, Oratorian, as well as numerous sister convents), the reform of ancient abbeys, high standards of training for priests in new seminaries, the reorganisation of education (in particular the colleges and the University of Leuven), the deliberate resourcing of saints' cults and the promoting of major centres of pilgrimage such as Halle and the brand new Scherpenheuvel (Montaigu) in 1606. Seminaries were also set up for missionaries to Protestant countries like the Dutch Republic, England, Scotland and Ireland.

The Jesuits in the South, with many recruits from the North and led by razor-sharp polemicists like Charles Scribani and Cornelius Hazart, organised an intellectual, theological and moral offensive designed to revive Catholicism in the South and provide support and encouragement to Catholics in the North. Altarpieces and paintings from the workshop of Peter Paul Rubens and his pupils gave form to a world of Catholic imagery which in its emphasis on the sacred, even heavenly, significance of the body and the merits of virtue distinguished itself from the sober Protestant emphasis on the Word, its rejection of merit, and its fear of God's judgement. In this way, a social and mental framework was created that for centuries made the Southern Netherlands a homogeneous 'Catholic nation'.

So the North's Protestant self-image gradually came to stand in opposition to a South that increasingly felt itself to be Catholic. When they first split in the late sixteenth century, they therefore traded places. It explains why the South for so long displayed the grim-faced traits that we now associate with Calvinism while the Protestant North showed sometimes surprising tendencies towards ecumenism and Catholicity. This brings the religious dimension of the development itself into the debate. Is it not therefore more of a cultural than a religious distinction? After all, cultural anthropology has shown that every country constructs its own North and South. In our hemisphere the North intuitively represents coldness and the South warmth. In the Netherlands there is also a cold North and a warm South. Catholicism, which dominates in the south, represents the smells of home, *laissez-faire*, high spirits and warmth while Protestantism in the North stands for individualism, the work ethic, prudishness and coolness. Carnivals, pilgrimages and festivities are Catholic and belong in the South; strict observance of the Lord's Day, moral agonising and teaching the Bible in school are Protestant and characterise the North.

Emile Claus, *Girls at their first Communion*, 1893. Oil on canvas, 82 x 117 cm. Collection Dexia, Brussels.

After 1815

The rise of the antithesis between Catholic and Protestant is therefore closely tied up with the self-definition of North and South as separate cultures and subsequently as separate states. Religious belief became a hallmark of national identity. Although religious minorities in the North played an active role in the Patriot movement of the 1780s and the Batavian Revolution of 1795, Protestantism did not become an issue. During the eighteenth century a broadly Christian form of religiosity had developed within the Protestant churches, which was moderate and enlightened. This had watered down the Calvinist nature of the official church to a broad-based Protestant culture that gradually turned the original Protestant *state* into a Protestant *nation* with a sense of solidarity in which, in fact, only the Catholics felt uncomfortable. In that sense the Dutch nation in the nineteenth century was more 'Protestant' than the old Reformed republic had ever been. But in the uniformly Catholic South matters were very different. A conservative movement led by popular orators and intellectuals such as Hendrik Van der Noot and F.X. de Feller whipped up the population to regard traditional Catholicism as the hallmark of the nation and to defend it against the Enlightenment and the supporters of political modernisation. Resistance to the French invasion with its anticlerical radicalism revolved around the Catholic clergy who, because of the political circumstances, became increasingly conservative and ultramontane.

The short-lived United Kingdom of the Netherlands (1815-1830) again pushed relationships to the limit. The two communities were thrown back on their carefully nurtured individual identities: in the North, religious plurality but with

Protestant dominance, and in the South a Catholic monoculture, though with deep-seated differences between an arch-conservative hierarchy with theocratic tendencies and a liberal political and cultural elite that wanted to subject the Catholic Church to the state. In 1815 the reactionary bishop of Ghent, Maurice de Broglie, began a successful crusade against the new constitution because to him its acknowledgement of the freedom of religion clashed with the legitimate claim of the Catholic Church to absolute truth. So Catholicism became entangled in the politics of identity in the Southern Netherlands and inflamed a reflex reaction of Protestant identity in the North. The clash between Catholic and Protestant became a weapon in the political conflict and ultimately one of the decisive elements in the separation of North and South. The Protestant North and Catholic South could simply no longer co-exist.

The unnatural alliance between the Southern Catholics and Liberals in 1828 meant that unionism became the dominant political formula after the new Belgian state was established in 1830. But after Belgian independence was recognised in 1839 the alliance fell apart and after 1857 it ended definitively as Liberals and Catholics took up sharply opposed positions. Clerical ultramontanism and political conservatism worked hand in hand. Worse still, the Catholic leaders in the South with their baroque legacySS looked down on their humble coreligionists in the North, even though they had absolutely no justification for harking back nostalgically to the *Ancien Régime*. On the contrary, the Northern Catholics, who represented nearly 40% of the population, were trying to build a new position as a modern national movement, equal in status to the Protestants. This did not always run smoothly, as was shown by the Protestant April Movement of 1853 against the restoration of the Catholic hierarchy. But in spite of the 'Protestant character of the nation' they were ultimately, in L.J. Rogier's famous formulation, 'reborn in freedom'. ■

Translated by Chris Emery

Pieter Brueghel the Elder, *The Preaching of St. John*, 1566. Oil on panel, 95 x 160.5 cm. Szépm vészeti Múzeum, Budapest. Was the painter portraying a contemporary protestant preacher?

Rich Cities, Deep Dykes

Burgundians and Calvinists

[WIM BLOCKMANS]

To what extent are the striking cultural differences between Flanders and the Netherlands rooted in their divergent political and religious backgrounds, commonly described as 'Burgundian' and 'Calvinist'? They involve many aspects of their respective life-styles: differences in the way the day is divided up, in eating habits, appreciation of the role that fine food and drink plays in social intercourse, etiquette, negotiating tactics and, ultimately, values in general. In fact, one might wonder whether what is at issue here is not rather the contrast between Northern and Southern Europe.

Gastronomic culture

What one eats, in what circumstances and at what times, is a cultural characteristic. That is not surprising. In most cultures, meals and drinking sessions serve as markers and affirmations of life's important events. The Dutch are constantly amazed at the elaborateness of what Belgians refer to as 'lunch', while the Flemish never tire of talking about the two sticky rolls and one currant bun with a glass of buttermilk, and, on a good day, a greasy croquette, that they are so generously given when they were expecting a proper dinner. The Dutch lean towards the British tradition of providing sandwiches during a short lunch break in the middle of the day. In the Southern Netherlands, and in this respect there is little difference between Flanders and Wallonia, they follow the customs of Southern Europe where people will happily take the time to enjoy an elaborate cooked meal. If one is entertaining guests, it provides a perfect opportunity for pleasant and relaxed conversation. If it is a business lunch, calculations of profit and loss are put to one side. Rather, it is seen as an opportunity to get to know each other better and create a relationship of trust. If one really wants to strike a good deal and create a durable relationship, then building up trust is more important than pressing for a quick decision. The Flemish enjoy the culinary experience quite as much as the social, and are prepared to invest in it with an eye to the long term. Of course they hope it will be reciprocated. They want to get to know the person behind the business partner, so that they

Members of the Old Reformed Congregation at Ederveen go to Sunday service, 2006. Photo by Marcel van den Bergh.

can accurately assess his way of working. In this process, subjective considerations can sometimes gain the upper hand. The Dutch are always inclined to give precedence to business considerations, and regard elaborate dinners as a waste of time and money. They prefer to do their negotiating over a cup of coffee, relying on thorough homework and rational calculation. Southerners often find that approach narrow-minded, cold and opportunistic. It is surprising how these cultural differences, which are so well-known, still create problems in negotiations between North and South, whether it has to do with large-scale business mergers or simply the working of bilateral agreements. Drinking each other's health is a solemn moment that seals a relationship. Socialising is pre-eminent in providing the opportunity to confirm good relationships and create new ones. A century ago, the sociologist Max Weber described these fundamentally contrasting ways of seeing, being and doing business as goal-oriented versus means-oriented rationality. Both attitudes are rational in their own way, but the first focuses on the desired objective and the second on the method of achieving it. How can two such close neighbours differ so fundamentally from each other?

During the last few decades the Flemish and the Dutch have become more oriented towards each other. Nevertheless, in the profiles outlined above the Flemish still have more in common with the Walloons than with the Dutch. In so far as those patterns of behaviour are linked to eating and drinking habits, they point to the material origins of their cultures. Since when have we been eating and drinking in the particular way that we do on everyday or ceremonial occasions? The most important characteristics of our material culture are not much older than the nineteenth century, though some parts are older and others more recent. And how did these obviously different cultural features develop which the Dutch and the Flemish now consciously use to distinguish themselves from each other? In my opinion neither the Dukes of Burgundy nor Calvinism played a decisive role. What is eaten and drunk every day depends on the food that is available in a particular environment. In Europe there are regions that produce wine or beer, olive oil or butter, fish or meat. The environment provides opportunities which people then develop using the technical means available to them.

In the fourteenth century Holland developed herring fishing and beer brewing into important export industries. Using techniques they had learned on the Kattegat, between Sweden and Denmark, they improved their method of gutting herrings, removing the head and entrails from the fish and then salting and storing them by the thousand in barrels. Initially the salt was extracted from peat lands, but very soon better quality salt was transported in much greater quantities by ship from salt pans and marshes along the Atlantic coast between Brittany and Portugal. Shipmasters from Holland and Zeeland made a good profit as the salt was the return freight for bulk goods like grain, wood and wine. The salted fish could be transported long distances by water, up the Rhine, Maas and Scheldt rivers and along the Atlantic seaboard. When herring stocks in the Kattegat became exhausted in about 1400, the fishermen of Holland, Zeeland and Flanders found new fishing grounds around Scotland and later on near Iceland. The Dutch still exploit this rich source of vitamins to feed themselves, and they also export the processed young fish known as

Pieter Saenredam, *Saint Odulphus Church at Assendelft*, 1649. Oil on panel, 50 x 76 cm. Collection Rijksmuseum Amsterdam.

maatjes to the rest of Europe. And they have done the same with beer. Almost every village in Northern Europe has always brewed some form of beer. The big leap forward, however, was made in North-West Germany where they discovered that adding hops improved the brew's taste and also its storage life. Beer production no longer had to be limited to local consumption. In Holland the raw materials were readily available, and from the fourteenth century on beer was produced for export. It was the lighter grains, especially barley, that were needed, and they grew better on the thin soils of the polders than did the bread grains, wheat and rye. Hops, clean water and peat were also plentiful. In all this the omnipresent navigable waterways played a major role in shipping the beer barrels to the cities of Flanders and Brabant. Hollanders also shipped dairy products to the South. So from the fourteenth century they developed not only their own patterns of consumption but also an export economy which dominated maritime transport between the Baltic and Portugal. Today *maatjes* herring and cheese are typically associated with Holland, and one of the largest brewers in the world is Dutch. The long coastline, the favourable situation on the great rivers and a soil unsuitable for growing bread grains created both the need and the opportunity for Holland to develop into a great economic power. Their difficult environment, producing few luxury items and constantly in need of new investment to keep the sea at bay, forced them to look overseas for new possibilities and to be very conscious of costs and benefits.

Water management

And this brings us to another geographical feature without which it is impossible really to understand Dutch culture: for centuries, about half the land now occupied by the Netherlands has been engaged in a life-and-death struggle against flooding. All the coastal provinces were involved, as well as the regions along the great rivers. The story is well-known: cultivating the layers of loam on the peat lands required drainage through the construction of ditches and canals which in turn needed dams, dykes, sluices and, from about 1400, windmills. Arable farming quickly impoverished the soil and the drainage led to soil compaction and a rapid drop in the level of the land, resulting in an ever-greater need for more drainage and protection against flooding. As early as about 1400 arable farmland had to be converted to pasture on a massive scale, which though less labour-intensive also needed to be connected to a marketing system. Over the centuries these problems became steadily greater and the small-scale solutions of the early years were no longer adequate. But from as early as the eleventh century, it was always the local communities who found and implemented methods of draining their land and keeping it dry in increasingly difficult circumstances. There were no great landowners involved, unless the problems extended across the borders. This did indeed happen more and more frequently, but even then every solution ultimately depended on the experience and skills of the local population and their willingness to invest their time and effort. Every decision therefore required the agreement of the inhabitants, who were well aware that only by cooperating would they be able to protect their property against the threat from rivers, inland waterways and the sea. The development of an increasingly extensive system of water management relied on the voluntary input of labour and resources from everyone whose land needed protection. Furthermore, the infrastructure itself needed to be constantly inspected and maintained. All of which required a great deal of organisation and consultation. This was provided by the local, provincial and regional water boards. The small scattered units set up almost a thousand years ago to meet local needs have gradually merged into ever-larger organisations. The invariable principle was that everyone should contribute to the common defence in proportion to the size of their land, whether leased or freehold. In return, they would have a say in whatever decisions were made. The water boards had the authority to carry out public works, raise taxes to pay for them, to lay down regulations for their maintenance, ensure these were complied with and punish any negligence. For serious failures that could harm the whole community, the dyke reeve or the dyke boards and their bailiffs could even impose the death penalty.

The community's survival depended on collective decisions, on communal work that might also be contracted out, and communal sharing of the agreed costs. The constant threat from the environment encouraged a strong sense of community; it went hand in hand with collective action and the realisation that strict supervision of all the agreed measures was essential. Awareness of one's duty was closely linked with participation in the decision-making process. Everybody knew that the negligence of a single landholder might lead to the collapse of a dyke with disastrous consequences for the entire community. So as early as the Middle Ages, a rational approach to land management led to careful administration and a management culture imbued with a consciousness of the collective interest and the need to involve every inhabitant. In that sense, political participation in the water boards is more deeply rooted in society than is urban political participation. Town and country, however, were closely connected through the market, and the ownership of land by townsmen.

The wealthy South

In the Southern Netherlands the water problem was much less serious; the organisations set up to deal with it were never as important as in the North. Only in the most north-westerly parts of Flanders and Brabant, along the coast and the Scheldt, does one find peat bogs and infertile sandy land. Further south, layers of loam and chalk make the land fertile. In Hainault, Artois and Picardy it was possible to grow wheat on a large scale, much of which was transported north along the coast or down the Leie or Scheldt rivers. This led to the rapid growth of an urban population as early as the twelfth century, three or four centuries before Holland. In around 1300 Artois and Flanders had seven cities with more than 20,000 inhabitants, while Bruges and Ghent probably already had twice and three times that number respectively. Nowhere else in the Low Countries did such high urban concentrations appear so early.

While these townsfolk were supplied with food by the fertile hinterland with its good system of navigable waterways, they earned their bread through trade and industry. The most important sector was textiles, with a Europe-wide reputation for high quality. During the fourteenth and fifteenth centuries Bruges was the undisputed centre of a network that linked England, the Baltic and the Rhineland with the then much more advanced Mediterranean area. The cities of Northern and Central Italy formed the core of a trading network that brought a wide range of such high-value products as wines, silk, spices, sugar, fruits, precious stones and dyes from the South and the East as far as to Bruges, where merchants from all over the known world established their offices, warehouses and residences. In about 1560 when Antwerp was at the peak of its economic and cultural power with about 100,000 inhabitants, the population of Amsterdam, the largest city in the North, had reached 30,000: smaller than Ghent and Bruges and comparable to Brussels, Mechelen and 's-Hertogenbosch. In 1581, a third of Antwerp's population declared themselves to be Protestants of one kind or another, while no more than another third openly claimed to be Catholic. So it is likely that a small majority of the city's residents had converted to Protestantism. The city council would also fall into Calvinist hands, as had happened in the other great cities of Brussels, Mechelen, Ghent and Bruges. So Calvinism as such should not be necessarily or solely associated with the sobriety and puritanism traditionally attributed to the rulers of the Dutch Republic.

Burgundian? Calvinist?

For convenience' sake, in the foregoing I have set North against South. But on closer examination we should perhaps also emphasise the differences between West and East, seeing that the greatest concentrations of population, wealth and creativity were in the coastal provinces and less in those inland. Moreover, my analysis thus far has been fairly materialistic, focusing on the quality of the land, hydrography, geographical location, merchandise and eating habits, to which I linked such factors as population growth, urbanisation and social organisation. And I am indeed convinced that what is called 'the Golden Age of Burgundy' was to a large degree determined by and found in the great cities of the Southern Low Countries. Long before a Duke of Burgundy was proclaimed Count of Flanders in 1384, Bruges' annual fairs were bulging with all the expensive products to be found in Europe. From there some of them would find their

Hieronymus Bosch, *Gluttony*, ca. 1485, detail from *The Seven Deadly Sins*. Oil on panel, 120 x 150 cm. Prado, Madrid.

Jacob Jordaens,
The King drinks, ca. 1640.
Oil on canvas, 156 x 210 cm.
Royal Museum for Fine Arts, Brussels.

way to purchasers elsewhere in Europe. The splendour we associate with the Burgundian court was made possible by the wealth and highly specialised skills of craftsmen and artists in the great cities of Flanders, Brabant and Artois. The wide range of artistic skills to be found there did not exclusively serve an itinerant court but also supplied a regular clientele of wealthy burghers, merchants and churchmen at home and abroad. The better-known painters, illuminators, gold- and silversmiths, sculptors and tapestry-weavers had clients throughout Europe. They had moved to these vibrant centres to find inspiration from fellow-artists and a market for their own work. On occasion they received commissions from the dukes, but none of these artists was entirely dependent on the Court. The Court rarely appeared in the Northern provinces and its ceremonial entries / processions there were a great deal more sober than in the South. In general, the absence of a Court can be seen as another fundamental difference between North and South. The influence of courtly culture had already disappeared from The Hague by about 1425, from Utrecht in 1527 and Guelders in 1543. Under the Republic there was even a fundamental aversion to it. In Mechelen, Brussels and Liège, by contrast, the courts continued to provide extravagant role models until the end of the 18th century. The sovereign Habsburg princes Albert and Isabella (1598-1621) maintained a courtly way of life that was mirrored by the nobility and became a role model for the rest of society.

The 'Burgundian Netherlands' is a term coined by modern historians. The dukes themselves spoke of 'the lands around here' as opposed to those 'around there' referring to the Duchy of Burgundy and the Franche Comté. Shortly after the duchy fell into the hands of the Kings of France in 1477, the dynasty became formally described as Habsburg through the marriage of Mary of Burgundy to Maximilian. Nevertheless, the splendour of the Burgundian dynasty continued to be an important source of imagery, even though it had ruled only a part of the Netherlands and that for less than a century. The Emperor Charles V retained the symbols of the Burgundian dynasty, such as the Order of the Golden Fleece and the organisation of his court. The 'Burgundian Circle' which was intended to give the Low Countries a regular status within the Holy Roman Empire from 1549 was yet another reference to the imagined illustrious past.

The label 'Burgundian' that is now such a popular sales tool of the Dutch catering industry, which describes a rotund, good-natured man who fully enjoys the pleasures of life, is a twentieth-century invented tradition. It is popularly contrasted with Northern Calvinist sobriety, but neither has much to do with dynasties on the one hand or religious persuasion on the other. I hope that I have shown that both were grafted on to cultures that had been formed much earlier. Willem Frijhoff's contribution elsewhere in this volume shows that during the Reformation Calvinism spread earlier and more strongly in the South and that it never appealed to a majority in the North. Nevertheless, in the Republic it proved possible to tack a rigorous interpretation of Calvinism on to the much older administrative culture that was characterised by the rational use of scarce natural resources, collective decision-making, a sense of duty, and communal solidarity. It was the absence of a genuine princely court and of a widespread aristocratic culture which led to ordinary respectability becoming the standard and extravagant enjoyment being regarded as alien. ▪

Translated by Chris Emery

A Country of Bores and Windbags

The Netherlands Seen Through the Lens of *Max Havelaar* and *Turkish Delight*

During the last years of his life Jan Wolkers (1925-2007) resembled nothing as much as a friendly grandfather. With his unstoppable delight in story-telling, his somewhat high-pitched, drawling voice and singsong diction, he was a welcome guest on just about every television show. Apart from his eternal bright red or blue t-shirts with the logos of American universities, there was little to remind one of the one-time provocative scourge of the bourgeoisie. It is true, he could still come out unexpectedly with some candid erotic tomfoolery, but more often than not this now concerned the slugs and froghoppers in his overgrown garden among the dunes of Texel. Only rarely would he still get a rise out of small-town churchgoers. Many young people would not even have known that this man was first and foremost a writer and an artist.

Yet it was Wolkers probably more than anyone else who fixed the image of the Dutch sixties (should one really add: of the twentieth century?), or rather the image that we, the Dutch, love to have of ourselves and which also exists in many foreign countries, especially in America. To many it is a horrifying image, but we are proud of it. Or rather, we *were*. And even at that time, this united front was actually a myth. Now it has definitively been shattered and many no longer wish to be reminded of their former enthusiasm. During the past decade – with the attack on the Twin Towers as the obvious turning point – the sixties have become more and more discredited, even though at the same time the grumbling, dissatisfied populace is increasingly showing an alarming contempt for authority, that has its roots in precisely that period.

The Netherlands was a permissive country. Here all God's prohibitions were trampled underfoot. Even God Himself was made fun of. Only in the Bible Belt – a ribbon of Dutch Reformed villages diagonally connecting the islands of Zeeland with North-Eastern Groningen – did His Word remain sacrosanct. In the eyes of God-fearing America, and not only there, Amsterdam was the Sodom of our time. Promiscuity was the rule there, abortion and euthanasia were generally accepted, prostitutes and heroin were for sale on every street corner, while the police just stood there and looked the other way by order of the authorities.

This image was grossly exaggerated, but not entirely untrue. It brought hordes of curious tourists to the capital, and for that reason alone the administration and other interested parties would have been little inclined to correct it.

Shameless and contagiously physical

Jan Wolkers and his wife Karina. Photo by Stephan Vanfleteren.

Wolkers was already a well-established author when in November 1969 he published *Turkish Delight* (Turks fruit). Trained and working as a sculptor, his first publication had been the collection of short stories *Serpentina's Petticoat*, after which more short story collections, novels and a play followed in quick succession. His work immediately attracted attention, also and especially among literary critics, and immediately sparked controversy and outrage. He showed himself to be a stylist of great expressiveness, with an original and sharp eye for detail and a leaning towards morbidity. But also, to put it mildly, with little respect for the force of tradition.

In his stories from the early 1960s, which are generally – and rightly –regarded as his best, he subtly pictures the taboos, the shortsightedness and the fears of an orthodox Christian boyhood in pre-war Oegstgeest and, even more,

Turkish Delight (1973).
Film by Paul Verhoeven with Monique van de Ven and Rutger Hauer.

the sensation of the bound-breaking and sometimes sneaky game played with it. Against the crushing, life-denying sombreness of an orthodox Christian background, his work shows the development of a child with a feeling for language, a mocking and sharply observing child, the like of which Dutch literature hadn't known before.

Wolkers' prose, also in spoken form, testifies to an original, shameless and contagious physical presence, an indomitable, earthly primal force that brutally silences the depressing spirit of lowland Calvinism that is forever saying no. Wolkers is the incarnation of the rejection of all authority, not so much for political reasons, although that too plays a role, but mainly because of an unbridled and unambiguous love of life, including all its dark and ominous aspects. *Turkish Delight*, his ninth novel, is the jewel in the crown of that liberating work, even though it is far from being the highpoint of his literary oeuvre.

Turkish Delight is a love story. Or rather, a novel about a turbulent love affair that is unilaterally brought to an end. The girl, the young, voluptuous Olga, takes up with someone else; the man she has dumped, consumed with impotent rage, is still obsessed with her even when, a few years later, she wastes away before his eyes as a result of a brain tumour. These may seem like the ingredients of a soap opera, a tried and tested recipe, but Wolkers turns them into much more.

The story is told by the (nameless) man, retrospectively and in a raw and hurried style, for he has landed in `quite a mess' after Olga's departure. This does not lead to melancholy memories of moonlit nights, nor to a well-considered, introspective search for the reasons for their parting; this book's power lies precisely in the primarily physical, and therefore vehement, reactions of the narrator.

Unable to distance himself, the man is driven by an almost uncontainable, regularly exploding mixture of rage, frustration and vindictiveness. The book may be divided into chapters, but these follow, jerkily, the emotions of the narrator rather than any chronological sequence. Likewise there is no division in paragraphs, with reason, for there is no quiet and space in the man's head

for any detailed descriptions, dialogues or meditations – as if in delirium he rushes, pursuing associations, through the archive of his anguished memories.

In doing so he displays an unprecedented spontaneous inventiveness as regards pejoratives, invectives and gutter language. The course language is certainly one of the reasons why the book became so popular. Consistently and as a matter of course the narrator uses street jargon; he avoids discreet alternatives with verve and abhors undergraduate vocabulary. This wasn't exactly unique; *Turkish Delight* was not the first book in modern Dutch literature with so much undisguised, not to say exhibitionist and voluptuous sex in it. That honour goes to the `runaway bestseller' *I Jan Cremer* (Ik Jan Cremer, part 1, 1964). But in that book the rough language is used to support the tall stories of a working-class boy with a taste for provocation – later on the term `picaresque novel' came into fashion for stories like this. Wolkers too was working-class, his father had a run-down grocery store, but he undoubtedly had more talent and ambition than Cremer. *Turkish Delight* was also a great success commercially. Reprint followed reprint at breathtaking speed: in four years three hundred thousand copies of the book were sold. The sales were given a new boost in 1973, when the film based on the book, directed by Paul Verhoeven, was released. The film's success was proportionally if possible even greater. Three and a half million people bought tickets to see it, a multiple of all earlier and later box office hits.

On an artistic level, too, the film was a great success. Film buffs see *Turkish Delight* as the beginning of modern Dutch cinema; everything before it is regarded as prehistory, while all later work was and still is measured against Verhoeven's film. Apart from Wolkers' taboo-shattering story this is due to the beautiful cinematography, especially during the sex scenes (the cinematographer fell madly in love with the young actress Monique van de Ven, who right at the beginning of her career was playing the role of her life) and the `American' style of shooting and editing, based on the new television conventions. Verhoeven told the story in the same rushed tempo as Wolkers, with the then unheard-of average of six seconds per shot.

It's impossible to say how far *Turkish Delight* was responsible for the cultural upheaval that Holland experienced around that time. What is certain, though, is that both book and film were perfect expressions of that upheaval. Europe was, in Nietzsche's eyes, `an ascetic star' and The Netherlands, until the beginning of the sixties, were no exception. But then, within a very short time, all caution was thrown to the winds, as if people had suddenly and painfully realized that all those self-imposed restrictions and standards no longer served any reasonable purpose. Suddenly, to use a title by Remco Campert, it was `every day a party'.

The Netherlands – or at least an urban, intellectual vanguard in the Netherlands – was transformed into a hedonistic paradise. Everything was allowed. And what wasn't allowed, was tolerated. An unprecedented wave of informality blurred the traditional divisions and undermined hierarchies of every kind. The difference between `*u*' en `*jij*', the polite and familiar forms of address, disappeared, and with it the invulnerability of the authorities that was largely based on this division. Thresholds were abolished, and with them the inaccessibility of persons and institutions.

But this society without thresholds also fostered a catastrophic egalitarianism. Along with each hierarchy the sensitivity to contextual differences in attitude, behaviour and language also disappeared, even the very notion of standards and differences in quality as such. That thus the seeds were sown for an anti-intellectualism that at first proliferated mainly underground but would soon manifest itself in all its brutality, seemed to worry hardly anyone. For the time being only the liberating aspect of the change was being celebrated.

Seen from a broader historical perspective, though, this development may seem surprising. For hadn't the Netherlands always been an egalitarian society, flat and boring and everywhere the same, just like its reclaimed land? Hadn't the Netherlands been a country in which for centuries meritocratic principles had won out over class privilege? The country in which it was not the irresponsible aristocracy but a proud bourgeoisie – see our seventeenth century art, headed by Rembrandt and Frans Hals – that called the shots? A country in which openness went so far that, much to the astonishment of foreign visitors, people didn't even deem it necessary to screen their private life from the curious glances of passers-by with curtains?

All this is certainly true, but at the same time it is only a part of the truth. For the Netherlands was not just a proud and self-confident bourgeois country; during large periods of history it was also and especially a parody of itself: a country of small-minded, stingy money-grubbers (something that already struck foreigners during the glory days of our history), timid moralists, hypocritical self-appointed moral censors, unimaginative, joyless drudges, ascetics who despised all pleasure from fear of the wrath of God – in short, the types our literature teems with..

In *Turkish Delight* we have Olga's parents, her sad-sack, hen-pecked father and `that lousy sly bitch', also described as `that pale, sickly witch of a mother of hers'. But we should especially consider a book that is twenty years older, the novel *The Evenings* (De avonden, 1949) by Gerard Reve, which paints an incomparable picture of the darkest and most depressing narrow-mindedness of the post-war period , the same narrow parochialism savaged by Wolkers and many of his generation.

Multatuli, Amsterdam.

It should be added that *The Evenings* is typically Dutch in a more exclusive way than *Turkish Delight*. Reve's book, which in the Netherlands is generally more highly esteemed than Wolkers', may have been a cult book for decades in our country, but even for Flemings it is virtually incomprehensible. That, unlike *Turkish Delight,* it has been little translated is therefore not surprising. It can hardly have contributed anything to the image that foreigners have of our country.

The ultimate petty bourgeois

The literary prototype of the Dutch bourgeois, however, comes from a much earlier time. It dates from the nineteenth century: a personage named Batavus Droogstoppel. Until recently nearly every Dutch person with a secondary school education could add to the name: `I am a coffee broker, and I live at No. 37 Lauriergracht'. Droogstoppel – as one of the narrators of *Max Havelaar* (1860), Multatuli's phenomenal novel – was so universally known that his name became generic and needed no explanation.

Van Dale's Comprehensive Dictionary of the Dutch Language still gives a euphemistic definition: a `boring, tiresome person', or `someone without higher aspirations or idealistic tendency, a dry, prosaic person'. But when we consider who gave him his name, this is much too positive. Droogstoppel – which means 'Dry stubble' – is the ultimate petty bourgeois. He is narrow-minded, egocentric, sexist, and above all a hypocrite and a liar, as gradually becomes apparent to the reader. For Multatuli has Droogstoppel introduce himself, right at the beginning of the book, and he does this with total immodesty. He boasts of his healthy outlook and his principled love of truth, in which he makes an exception only for 'Holy Scripture'. But he soon gets entangled in his contradictions and thus shows himself to be a liar. This boastful self-portrait is at the same time a very clever satirical portrait of a braggart.

Robert Voûte, coffee broker (1810-1871), model for Droogstoppel/Drystubble.

Heden beviel van een' Zoon J. M. H. Buys, Echtgenoote van R. Voûte.
Amsterdam, 1 Sept. 1842.
Eenige Kennisgeving.

For his thoroughly corrupt love of truth Droogstoppel relies on his ideological spokesman, the Reverend Wawelaar, whose name probably did not become a prototype in Dutch because it was already based on an existing verb, 'wauwelen', to blether or drivel. But the name also has an echo of Havelaar, his opposite in matters of mentality and truth.

In his sermon about 'the love of God apparent in His wrath towards unbelievers' Wawelaar does not present colonial policy in the Dutch East Indies as the institutionalised trampling on human rights, maltreatment and exploitation, as Havelaar does, but as altruistic beneficence towards the native population. Holland has been chosen to bring those wretched 'Javanese and other heathens'

Multatuli.

`civilisation, religion and Christianity' and thus save them from eternal damnation. Consequently it is our Christian duty – and this explains the enthusiasm of Droogstoppel, coffee broker and thus dependent for his income on colonial profits - `to require that the Javanese shall be brought to God through his *labour*.'

Among lovers and scholars of literature *Max Havelaar* is considered to be an absolute masterpiece, even the most important book in the history of Dutch literature. This is true for purely literary reasons, as far as those exist, although Multatuli certainly wasn't interested in literary praise – as regards literature and especially poetry, he wasn't without his Droogstoppel-like traits – what counted for him was the political effect of his work.

But with its repeated changes of perspective and register, its countless references to literature and current events, its complex play with reality and fiction, it is also a distinctly difficult book, too difficult for many readers in 1860 and much too difficult for the barely cultured or completely uncultured reader of today. Until a few decades ago the book was on the reading list of every secondary school student; in today's education literature starts, if it starts at all, at best with *Turkish Delight*.

In those circumstances the question of the Dutch self-image in *Max Havelaar* becomes purely hypothetical, even though the rather unflattering picture Multatuli paints of his fellow Dutchmen has lost hardly any of its truth and sharpness. It's not hard to recognise the spiritual heirs of this ultra-Dutch duo of Droogstoppel and Wawelaar, the merchant and the minister, in the contemporary public and not-so-public life of the Netherlands. The hypocrisy, the self-importance, the lack of imagination, the self-interest, hidden by idealistic talk, the paradoxical combination of pedantry and lack of backbone, all those traits, denounced by Multatuli, seem more than ever to characterise the average Dutchman of today. And what is worse: people who do not resemble this average Dutchman, people like the brave, upright civil servant Max Havelaar and his alter ego, the penniless non-conformist writer Sjaalman, are becoming harder and harder to find. Unconventional behaviour is not appreciated, willfulness is discouraged.

Of course Holland is still a superbly organised and equipped country; according to *Newsweek* (August 16, 2010) it is the eighth most pleasant country to live in – captured Somali pirates recently declared happily that their lives had never been as good as in their Dutch prison and that they wished they could stay there for the rest of their lives. Even in times of economic crisis the standard of living is still high and unemployment low. Social contrasts are a lot less harrowing here than in almost any other country and in the cities there are still large enclaves of enlightened sophistication where the old Dutch democratic traditions are cultivated.

But since 2001 increasing strain and hardening of attitudes can clearly be felt in broad sections of the population. Foreigners are surprised at how unrecognisable the Netherlands has become in such a short time, how fearful, small-minded, rude and introverted the once so open, progressive, tolerant and freedom-loving public atmosphere has become. But perhaps this surprise is indicative of a certain historical shortsightedness – the influential journalist, columnist and historian Jan Blokker (1927-2010) was convinced of it – perhaps the sixties were only an intermezzo, an oasis of frivolity in an endless desert of joyless conformity. In his own time Multatuli didn't exactly have a lot of support either.

That rapacious sweaty animal

To prevent possible misunderstandings: Jan Wolkers is certainly not to blame for this existential change in the climate. He may have garnered the sympathy of a largish television audience during the last years of his life, but in no way did he ever conform to the new morality, the revival of the 'standards and values' of the Droogstoppels and Wawelaars.

Even when his hair was thinning, he still provided the convincing proof that one could brilliantly withstand daily indoctrination with the Holy Book. He was still the man who had resolutely turned his fascination with the biblical miracles of his childhood into an uncensored fascination with the wonders of life. He would still, when the spirit moved him, deliver a baroque hymn to the magnificent buttocks of his wife Karina, or fulminate in no less impressive imagery against those rogues of politicians, especially the ones with a Christian background, who almost by definition were screwing everyone to their own advantage.

Swipes of this kind are also regularly found in Wolkers' books, although he lacked the messianic drive of Multatuli. Still, there is one book that does seem to have been written in the dark shadow of *Max Havelaar*: *The Dodo* (De walgvogel), his most substantial novel, from 1974. Its subject is the `police actions' as the war against the Indonesian anti-colonial independence struggle in the late 1940s is still euphemistically referred to in the Netherlands – a black page in the political history of our country, stripped by Wolkers of all false pretence and heroism.

Multatuli's *Ideas* (Ideeën) is on the bookshelf of Uncle Hendrik, the non-conformist model of the protagonist in *The Dodo*. Wolkers doesn't leave his readers guessing where his sympathies lie. Already on the first page `out of the ghostly greyness of the depression of the Thirties' – beautifully described in, especially, *Back to Oegstgeest* (Terug naar Oegstgeest, 1965) -appears `the election poster of the Anti-Revolutionary Party.' On it Colijn, the government leader at the time, who had become immensely rich from oil and was making eyes at Hitler, is depicted `in a southwester at the helm of the ship of state. But' – Wolkers' style soon takes on its familiar hyperbolic character - `My God, those aren't waves of unsullied sea-water breaking against the bow. It's pure petroleum. Stolen from under the feet of the brown peoples who languish in illness and hunger under the suction caps of that rapacious sweaty animal in tails and a three-cornered hat.'

I don't find it hard to read into these explosive words, the beginning of a much longer tirade, a tribute to Wolkers' great nineteenth-century colleague as well. Nor to see in this `rapacious sweaty animal' an angry and prophetic pointing ahead to the power-hungry Dutch right-wing Liberals and Christian Democrats, ideological heirs of Droogstoppel and Wawelaar, who have, without embarrassment, forged a pact with the Devil with an extremist, anti-democratic, crypto-racist movement. ■

Translated by Pleuke Boyce

Become What You Are – Between Lavish Living and Piousness

Notes on *The Sorrow of Belgium* and the *Legend of Ulenspiegel*

Greedy sensuality and mysticism: the dichotomy between the two provides a fruitful cliché for evoking the identity of the Southern Netherlands – or its *pars pro toto* Flanders, or even Belgium as a whole. It is a cliché that has long been widespread in the German and French worlds.

After seeing the procession of the penitents in Veurne in 1906, the poet Rilke characterised it as 'Busse und Kermes' (penitence and carnival), while Stephan Zweig, in the chapter on 'The New Belgium' in his book on Emile Verhaeren (1910), spoke of 'Lebensfreude und Gottsuchertum' (*joie de vivre* and the search for God). Two constantly recurring names in the language-game between earthy vitality and religious devotion are those of the mystics Hadewych and Ruusbroek; the uncouth Brueghel is contrasted with the refined Van Eyck, the ethereal Memlinc with the exuberant Rubens.

Later, 'Burgundian' became fashionable as an alternative to 'greedy sensuality', this time as the opposite of all that was rigidly sober and 'Calvinist'. In this sense it is heard mainly in the Dutch language area itself, and specifically in the

North, where even today Belgians and Flemings are referred to with some envy as 'Burgundians', who know how to live, or at least to eat, drink and be merry. The term should never be used in French, for there it refers solely to an area of France that was once a duchy; nor will the word be fully understood in English or German.

In one of his poems the Flemish writer Hugo Claus formulated the cliché aptly and concisely as 'lavish living and piousness':

Anthropological

This people that, so it's said,
moves between opposite poles,
lavish living and piousness,

believes less in the life to come
than in its daily grub.

This people will give Sunday alms
for the pope or for the blacks,

or burn incense to honour the statue
of the curé of Ars who stank of the poor

but mostly this people, fearing the lean years,
cajoles with cash and prayers
its docile rulers, the brokers.

Claus, however, gives a polemical edge to the cliché: in his paraphrase mysticism has degenerated into sanctimonious piety and cowardly subservience. Lavish living has become humdrum materialism. And there you have the Flemish national character.

In this article I shall examine the extent to which this image of Flanders is projected, if at all, in two books: *La Légende et les aventures héroïques, joyeuses et glorieuses d'Ulenspiegel et de Lamme Goedzak au pays de Flandres et ailleurs* of 1867 by Charles De Coster (1827-1879) (*The Legend of Ulenspiegel and Lamme Goedzak, and Their Adventures Heroical, Joyous and Glorious in the Land of Flanders and Elsewhere*, 1922) and *Het Verdriet van België* by Hugo Claus (1929-2008) of 1983 (*The Sorrow of Belgium*, 1990). I cannot avoid mentioning Belgium, since the Flemish movement only developed within Belgium, which came into being in 1830 when it seceded from the North. The young state felt a need for legitimacy, and in order to acquire this, and above all to differentiate itself from France, it opted to cobble together a glorious history of its own. The elements

Young Hugo Claus.

of that past were readily available, namely in the heyday of wealthy Flanders, often seen as synonymous with the whole of the Low Countries. However, it was expressed exclusively in French. Even Hendrik Conscience's historical novel *De Leeuw van Vlaanderen* (1838; English translation *The Lion of Flanders*, 1855) was written in (rather stiff) Dutch in order to secure a place for Flanders ...within Belgium. Only towards the end of the nineteenth century did it become clear that the attempt to continue presenting a Flemish past in what was officially an exclusively French-language state was doomed. As an "imagined community" Belgium was a failure. The invented traditions no longer united the country, if they ever had done, and the centrifugal forces were unleashed that are still at work to this day.

'Lourde beauté'

Yet the defining image of Flanders persisted for a long time in French. There is a line that runs directly from the Francophone 'Flemish' poet Emile Verhaeren (1840-1916) to the equally 'Flemish' *chansonnier* Jacques Brel (1929-1978).

Brel was the last to give voice to the commonplaces – and brilliantly too. So what was Brel? A Fleming, or at least a misunderstood lover of Flanders,

Ulenspiegel.

a Belgian or a Frenchman? Certainly France annexed him, and after the initial years of frustration he scored huge triumphs there. Venues like Olympia in Paris were his to command. Paris appeared as a backdrop in his songs, and it was there that he eventually came to die. But his accent marked him out as a Belgian. 'Belgian' remained a label that he made use of when it suited him and then discarded, like 'Fleming'. 'Flamingant' on the other hand was anathema to him. For someone from Brussels, a member of the Gallicised Flemish middle class, the term meant nothing more or less than a narrow-minded, fanatical Flemish nationalist. Brel had little sympathy for the social and cultural emancipation of the Flemings. That robbed him of his mythical Flanders, in the tradition of Emile Verhaeren and Georges Rodenbach: a Flanders where the Dutch language is replaced by a warm, folksy and hence harmless 'Flemish', to which one is deeply attached because it is the *langue des choses,* while French of course remains the *langue de culture.* Given the irrevocable evolution towards monolingual areas within Belgium, Francophones who have remained in Flanders have fallen between two stools. They feel that Flanders has been stolen from them, and respond in different ways. But they share the same nostalgia, a nostalgia for a Flanders that never was, which often makes the books and songs of French-speaking Flemings so poignant, for in many cases it is they who have sung Flanders' praises most memorably. Take the song 'Le plat pays', for instance, in which Brel conjures up a non-existent country out of sky, rain, fog and wind; take 'Mon père disait', in which the father calls London a suburb of Bruges (a mythical Flanders if ever there was one!) or sigh sympathetically at 'Marieke', the Flemish girl who lives somewhere among the towers of Ghent and Bruges. For that matter, Brel did the same thing with the port of Amsterdam, which he celebrated as a kind of mythical harbour where lonely seamen with pent-up longings eat, drink, dance and empty their bodily fluids into women and the gutter. And then of course there is 'ça sent la bière de Londres à Berlin': the bacchanalia of Brueghel and Teniers are never far away, and form part of Brel's clichéd image of the past of the Low Countries.

In 1959 his 'Les Flamandes' sparked a controversy that now seems very distant. Compare it with Verhaeren's 'Aux Flamandes d'autrefois' from his first collection of poetry *Les Flamandes* (1883). In Verhaeren the Flemish women, with their 'chairs pesantes de santé' (flesh heavy with health), have a 'lourde beauté' (ponderous beauty). For the bard with his wild moustache they embody 'notre idéal charnel' (our carnal ideal). Brel paints a grimmer picture of the healthy Flemish wenches' passion for dancing. Ultimately they are dancing to the tune of the clergy, who keep them pious and industrious, true to the gospel of reproduction and the maintenance and increase of material prosperity. He chastises the Flemings because he feels he is one of them. As always, the opposite of love is not hate, but indifference. The women in Auvergne and Brittany were just as bad, he once remarked, but since he happened to be a 'Fleming' he satirised *his* women. Towards the end of his life Brel fled to the Marquesas Islands. When he did return to the subject of Flanders, he was deliberately provocative: 'Les F.' (by which he meant 'les Flamingants') receive a final rebuke: 'Nazis durant les guerres et catholiques entre elles' (Nazis during both wars and Catholics in the interim) – one has to overlook the fact that it was difficult to be a Nazi in the First World War. People usually forget, though, to quote the agonised lines from this 'chanson comique' that sum up the hybrid identity of Jacques Brel (and many Belgians, somewhat embarrassed about their *belgitude* and hesitating between their languages):

(...) quand les soirs d'orage des Chinois cultivés
Me demandent d'où je suis, je réponds fatigué
*Et les larmes aux dents: "*Ik ben van *Luxembourg".*

[(...) when on stormy nights cultured Chinese
Ask me where I'm from, I answer wearily
And with tears in my voice : "*Ik ben van* Luxembourg".]

A carnival at the foot of the stake ?

Charles de Coster's *La Légende et les aventures héroïques, joyeuses et glorieuses d'Ulenspiegel et de Lamme Goedzak au pays de Flandres et ailleurs* appeared in 1867.

In his book on Emile Verhaeren Stefan Zweig wrote that De Coster's *Légende* signals the beginning of Belgian literature, just as the *Iliad* marks that of Greek

Charles de Coster.

literature. The story of Ulenspiegel was acclaimed as a prose epic in which the blood flows as freely as the beer, as a carnival at the foot of the stake.

Since De Coster's death in 1879 the novel has gone through over twenty editions in French and a hundred or so in other languages. The book eventually became better known outside Belgium and the French-speaking world, especially in Russia, where a translation appeared in 1915. Actually, for a long time many French-speakers thought that the book had originally been written in 'Flemish', and had been translated into French by De Coster. Understandably, since the book has nothing to do with France, but is all about ... Belgium. De Coster placed the Low German medieval hero of folklore against the backdrop of the sixteenth-century Southern Netherlands. His Ulenspiegel is born in Damme near Bruges, the son of Claes and Soetkin. At the same time, in faraway Spain Philip II first sees the light of day. A greater contrast than that between Ulenspiegel, growing up in open, free and easy surroundings and the lonely, gloomy and cruel royal child in a Spanish palace is scarcely imaginable.

These are dark days in Flanders. De Coster evokes an apocalyptic land of terror and fear, cowardice and betrayal, greed and hypocrisy; a country of torture and scaffolds, gallows and burning at the stake. Claes meets his end on one such pyre, and his son rescues a handful of ash to hang around his neck in an amulet. 'Les cendres de Claes battent sur ma poitrine' (Claes's ashes beat upon my breast) becomes the story's mantra, Ulenspiegel's spur to action. As recently as the late 1980s this ominous sentence was quoted by Eduard Shevardnadze, the Soviet foreign minister, during a visit to Belgium.

From the picaresque rogue of German folklore Ulenspiegel is transformed into a freedom fighter and a herald of justice, a patient avenger who never forgets, a wanderer among ruins who wades through blood and tears. He embraces the revolt against Spain and joins the Beggars' resistance movement.

He is the spirit, the intellect of Flanders ("*Esprit de Flandre*"), while his sidekick Lamme Goedzak is its stomach. Goedzak glistens with fat, but it is an honourable fat: 'ma graisse de Flamand, nourrie honnêtement par labeurs, fatigues et batailles' (my Flemish fat, nourished honourably by toil, fatigue and battles). After hard toil, the Fleming may gorge. Lamme also embodies the longing for everyday and domestic happiness.

Ulenspiegel's sweetheart Nele is the heart of Flanders, to whom he remains true in spirit, without that preventing him from having carnal relations with other women.

At the end of the book De Coster despatches him to eternity by contriving a splendid vanishing act. Ulenspiegel awakens from a deep sleep that everyone had taken for death. He shakes off the sand that has been thrown over his body: 'Est-ce qu'on enterre, dit-il, Ulenspiegel, l'esprit, Nele, le coeur de la mère Flandre? Elle aussi peut dormir, mais mourir, non! Viens, Nele.

Et il partit avec elle en chantant sa sixième chanson, mais nul ne sait où il chanta la dernière.'

('"Can any bury," said he, "Ulenspiegel the spirit and Nele the heart of Mother Flanders? She, too, may sleep, but not die. No! Come, Nele."

And he went forth with her, singing his sixth song, but no man knoweth where he sang the last one of all.')

Ulenspiegel.

Few books or characters have taken on more of a life of their own than De Coster's Ulenspiegel. Of course the writer was an anti-clerical liberal, who was not focusing on the Flanders of his time, but wanted to give his country, Belgium, an icon of freedom. But that icon very quickly transcended Belgium. In the Soviet Union Ulenspiegel was admired as a right-thinking hard-line guerrilla. The good-natured Lamme Goedzak became the prototype of the jovial Fleming. Die-hard Flemings in turn saw Lamme as the incarnation of the spineless good nature that had to be written out of the national character if that nation was ever to amount to anything. Ulenspiegel became a model for that Flemish nation and an all-purpose banner for the Flemish Movement. In the end Left and Right were able to unite around him, and even Catholic Flemish Nationalists forgot that he had fought on the side of the Protestant Beggars.

'Nazis durant les guerres et catholiques entre elles'

The Sorrow of Belgium is the magnum opus of Hugo Claus, or is regarded as such by foreign critics: at any rate the French, German, Spanish, English and Italian translations met with great acclaim.[1] The book was seen as the definitive interpretation of an incomprehensible country. The Great Flemish/Belgian novel had finally arrived. Claus himself called his book a family novel, but it is also mythologised autobiography, a picaresque novel and a *Bildungsroman.* He had previously said of it: 'It's intended to be a book about life in Flanders as I knew it, but which now no longer exists.' By this he meant a Flanders where the Catholic church was still all-powerful, a Flanders fascinated by the New Order whose highly-disciplined troops had marched into Belgium in 1940. To make matters worse, part of that Flanders expected help from that New Order in its own struggle for liberation from the Belgian state, and 'collaborated' in spirit and/or in deed with the German occupier.

The hero of the story is an eleven-year-old boy, Louis Seynaeve, a pupil in a Catholic boarding school and later in a Catholic high school. Confusion, vague longing, friendship and betrayal are his lot. Reality is incomprehensible, perception murky, the world of adults unreliable, and so he constructs his own reality, a world of his own.

And then the German armies invade his world. 'The arrival of the Germans was dazzling for a boy of eleven,' the author commented. Louis' father is a German sympathiser, his mother flirts with an officer whose secretary she is, and the son joins the National Socialist Youth of Flanders. A boy tries to find his way amid gossip and rumour, words that have lost their meaning, if they ever had one.

A priest who teaches him in high school tells him – quoting Baudelaire – that there are only three respectable professions: priest, soldier and poet. Naturally, as a child he had dreamed of heroic missionaries; now he looks up to the knights in high boots with death's heads on their caps. Ultimately, though, it is words and sentences that prove to exercise the greatest seductive power.

When he comes across books by 'degenerate' writers hidden in a cellar, he discovers his true vocation: if he belongs anywhere it is with these Cubists, Expressionists, all the other –ists. Louis learns fast. The New Order crumbles before his eyes and in his heart. After the liberation his father is arrested, the son now hangs around with the Americans, and an aunt initiates him into love.

At the end of the war Louis learns of the suicide of his friend from boarding school. Eternal loyalty has long since been smothered by time. From now on the protective crust around his soul will be called literature. It will save him, or at least give him something to hold on to. He writes a book called 'Sorrow', which is published. A child dies, and a writer is born.

'It's the language, stupid'

The *Légende* and *The Sorrow of Belgium* have become the idiosyncratic national epics of a country that is not a nation. A Flemish hero, borrowed from Germany and celebrated in French, and a Flemish boy struggling to find himself in a country called Belgium.

How do you find yourself in a hypocritical country where nothing is what it seems and people collaborate with the powers that be, be it in the sixteenth century or in the years 1939-1947? By 'lying the truth', by forging lies into art, by adopting the pose of the artist.

Ulenspiegel is a rogue, a jester and a smooth talker who gets away with everything, and a lady's man too. Louis Seynaeve positions himself amid the lies that surround him. He dreams up his own reality; the survival strategy becomes a pose, the pose a method. The final result is the story of his life, the book itself, the work of art. Claus rewrites his own genesis as a writer. From the publication of *The Sorrow* onwards, in his public life as a writer he will increasingly merge with the smooth talker and poser. In each interview he will methodically answer the same questions differently, play games with truth and with the interviewer, each time, like Ulenspiegel, like a jester, concocting a different image of himself. When every expression of reality fails, we must capture that reality in words in countless ways, ever anew.

The two books are first and foremost linguistic works of art. Their world is constructed of language and consists solely of language. De Coster's novel works best in French: the writer found a language of his own that was not a pastiche of sixteenth-century French, but has an epic, incantatory force, larded with Flemish words that give it just the right flavour. When translated into Dutch those Flemish words, which are intended to guarantee the *couleur locale* of the French original, lose their meaning. The incantatory repetitions do not impede the tempo of the narrative, quickness being one of the demands that Italo Calvino made of literature in his *Six Memos for the Next Millennium*.

The true splendour of *The Sorrow* also resides in the language. Claus wrote a multi-layered artificial language comprehensible from Southern Flanders to the northernmost tip of the Netherlands, but the substratum of that layered language is the dialect of Kortrijk, the town where the novel is set. As a native of Kortrijk myself, I can say with some authority that that substratum is accessible only to someone born and bred there. The British writer Tim Parks observed recently in an interview with the daily *NRC Handelsblad* that many contemporary writers strive to be "international": "Writers no longer focus on the local situation and local matters, since an international readership is not interested in them." In this context he mentions Claus: "A wonderful writer like Hugo Claus is not easy to understand for readers outside Belgium; you really have to make an effort to enter into his world." The fact is that Parks believes that a text is totally transformed in translation. Must I end with the depressing truism that books like those of De Coster and Claus can only be fully understood in their own language? Let us accept the fact that great books are always rooted in the local and the private, and that they always transcend their roots.

Do De Coster and Claus confirm the clichés of lavish living and piousness? No, as we have seen. Do they play with them? Yes, each in their own way, and according to their own rules.

At most they show how artists become what they are, how they manage to survive amid the lies and the horror, the hypocrisy, the vulgarity and, if you like – the lavish living and the piousness. De Coster sings the song of the liberation of the senses and the mind, freed by the imagination from all frustrating religiosity. Claus displays and celebrates reality in its submissive corruption, but as a master of the disappearing act he remains – *ni dieu ni maître* –out of range. ■

BIBLIOGRAPHY

Charles De Coster, *The Legend of Ulenspiegel and Lamme Goedzak and Their Adventures Heroical Joyous and Glorious in the Land of Flanders and Elsewhere*, translated by F.M. Atkinson, William Heinemann, London, 1922.

Hugo Claus, *The Sorrow of Belgium*, translated from the Dutch by Arnold J. Pomerans, Viking (Penguin Group), London, 1990.

NOTE

1. *Le Chagrin des Belges* (Julliard, Paris, 1985)
Der Kummer von Flandern (Klett-Cotta, 1986)
La pena de Bélgica (Alfaguara, Madrid, 1990)
The Sorrow of Belgium (Viking, London, 1990)
La sofferenza del Belgio (Feltrinelli, 1999)
Der Kummer von Belgien (Klett-Cotta, 2008)

Translated by Paul Vincent

Photo by Stephan Vanfleteren.

Railway line over the Hollandschdiep near Moerdijk, 1871.
Photo by Pieter Oosterhuis.

Modernity reaches the Netherlands: railway lines and bridges nestle tranquilly in a centuries-old landscape between motionless water and lofty skies.

Untitled, ca. 1936.
Photo by Paul Guermonprez.

Middle class couple on the beach at Scheveningen. The idyll of the interbellum?

Bloody Monday, Amsterdam, 7 May 1945.
Photo by Wiel van der Randen.

Two days after the capitulation of the German army in the Netherlands a crowd of celebrating people are getting ready to welcome their Canadian liberators on the Dam in Amsterdam. From a building on the corner of the Kalverstraat and the Dam German marines suddenly fire on the crowd. Nineteen people die and over a hundred are wounded. It is the bitter and absurd end of an occupation that was hard on the Netherlands.

Commemoration of the dead on the Dam, 4 May 1946.
Photo by Ad Windig.

THE image of the commemoration of the dead, the impressive two minutes silence that has recalled the memory of the victims of the Second World War each year since 1946.

On the beach, ca. 1947.
Photo by Emmy Andriesse.

Das Ewig Weibliche? Or the sturdy, athletic beauty of the Dutch woman? The picture exudes the self-confidence, the optimism and vitality of the years of reconstruction.

Turkish family in the Eerste Atjehstraat, 1953.
Photo by Ben van Meerendonk.

A smart foreign family parading in its Sunday best in a Dutch street.
In the 50s peace still reigns. Integration happens quietly and without problems. Glowing, the newcomers join the Dutch utopia. But nothing is what it seems. In reality the man was a civil servant drafted to the Netherlands temporarily.

Lijnbaansgracht, Amsterdam, 1963.
Photo by Frits Weeda.

The years of prosperity bring with them demolition and construction. The city goes under the shovel. Consumerism starts to leave its mark. The boy standing on his head heralds the joyful madness that will break out a little later in the decade.

Rotterdam Kralingen, 1970.
Photo by John Berwald.

In June 1970, on the grassy expanses of the Kralingse Bos in Rotterdam, the Holland Pop festival took place - Woodstock in the polder. This naked statue - Tadzio from Visconti's *Death in Venice* - is surrounded by good-natured and relaxed indifference. Everything's possible and everything goes. In the Randstad, anyway.

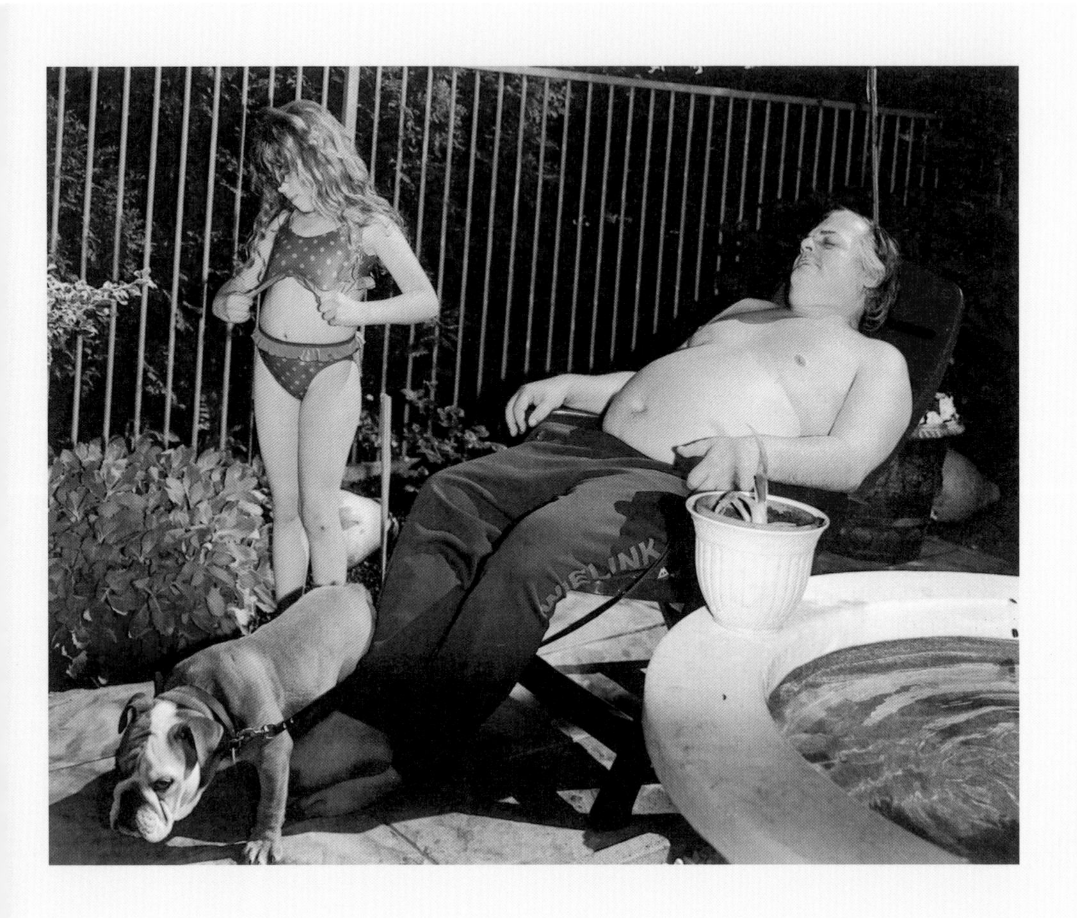

Bam Bam, Michelle and Henk, Tuindorp, Oostzaan, 1998.
Photo by Raimond Wouda.

In the working-class district of Tuindorp in Amsterdam, one of the last 'native' areas in the city, life is carefree and contented. This, too, is the Netherlands.

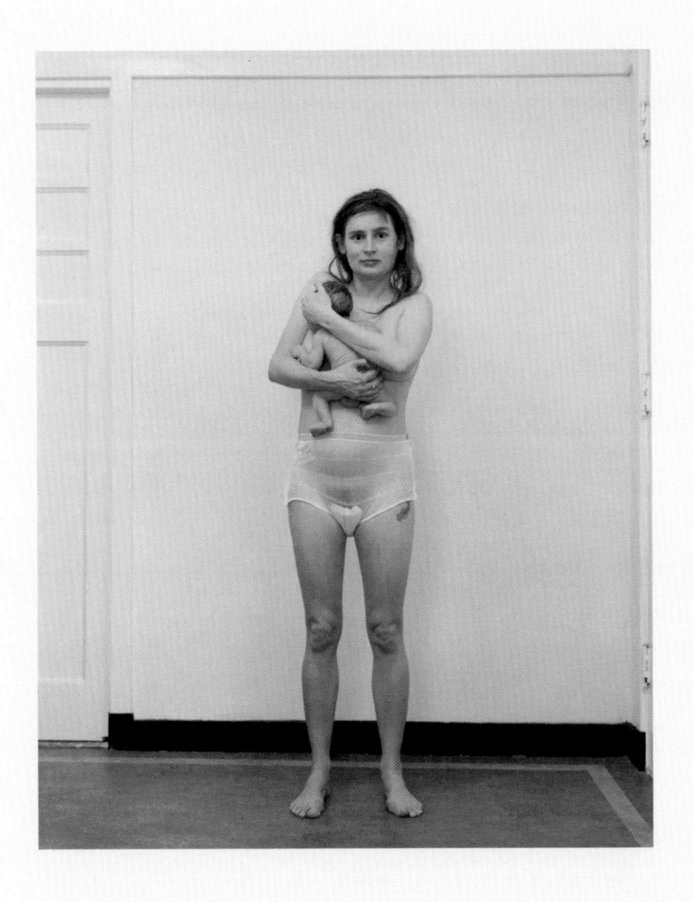

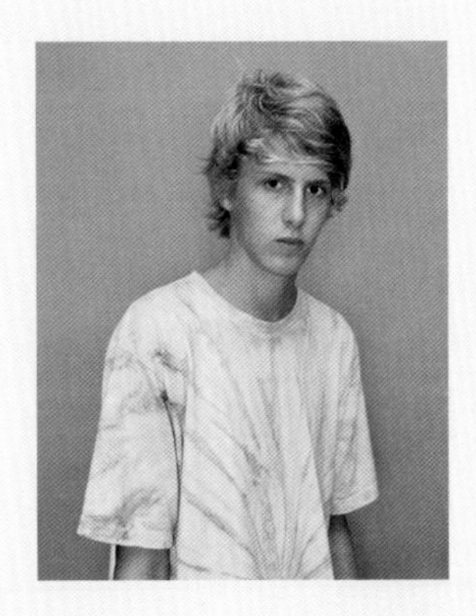

Julie, The Hague, the Netherlands, 29 February 1994 / Louis, The Hague, the Netherlands, 10 August 2010.
Photos by Rineke Dijkstra.

A young Dutch woman has just given birth to a son. Sixteen years later, in 2010, the son, Louis, says:
"I don't have to stay in the Netherlands. I think Barcelona's cool. It's livelier, livelier than Amsterdam. Sometimes I have to go to Zeeland. It's just dead there. The closest town is Middelburg. One street and you've seen it all. But the Netherlands is OK for working in. Everything's well organised."

Giving Form to the Fleeting

A Response to Leonard Nolens' Diary

Winterswijk, Sunday 29 November 2009

Poetry, love and alcoholism form a fatal triangle. It's a fact that they are related, but it's not that easy to pinpoint the source of their affinity or the reason they so often need each other. What does link them at any rate is the intoxication that takes hold unexpectedly and causes the helpless victim to wake afterwards with a hangover. This explains nothing. We should like to know what the essence of the rapture is and why it leads to physical and mental exhaustion. Are intoxication and hangover perhaps two ostensibly opposed manifestations of one and the same thing? Is what the poet, the beloved and the drinker are after not relief from the fundamental loneliness of the individual, escape, if only for an hour, from the feeling of being thrown into the world' (to use Heidegger's expression) that constitutes our deepest self? Language, lovemaking and alcohol offer the short-lived illusion that everything is interconnected, and this illusion presents itself as an aesthetic experience.

Does it follow from this that beauty is based on a misunderstanding? That would be a shame. But if it is true, let it be a fruitful misunderstanding. Two people who listen to Bach and each hear something different, but at the end are sure that they have shared something. In such a case mutual misunderstanding is not a problem, quite the reverse, it brings them together. Briefly, but even so.

'He put his mouth in the dust, to see if there were hope there.'

'We must take our solitude with us to others.'

Amsterdam, Friday 4 December 2009

No literary genre is as impossible as the diary. The author tries to strike up a conversation with someone he doesn't know, whom he *cannot* know because it is a derivative of himself that only comes into existence when addressed. The written other is a construction, a living being that may be constructed from words, but is not therefore any less real than its creator, who after all only takes shape in the conversation. The person keeping a diary wants to become himself. Once you've started on the project you can't stop, on pain of disappearing. Stopping writing puts a full stop after your identity. There are, though, cases where that is the best decision. Sometimes you don't make much headway with an identity.

Leonard Nolens (1947-).
Photo by David Samyn.

Becoming a person transports you from the frying pan into the fire, because it isolates you from the others. The very first word is a farewell.

'Every poem is a farewell to the poem. Longing to be delivered from the longing for the poem.'

Winterswijk, Thursday 10 December 2009

The function of writing, which is giving permanence to speech, seems obvious. The I reaches out to the other, both come to light only in that reaching out, writing tries to bridge an emptiness that did not exist before that writing. Poems and novels are written with an eye to a readership of strangers. Of course a poet may maintain that he writes his work solely for himself, but that is never true. You look for a form to make universal what is strictly individual. You want to contribute to the misunderstanding, perhaps to keep the world turning. That is your job.

But does this also apply to the diary? If you write it purely for yourself you have no need to take account of anyone at all. You can moan about your ailments, the insufferableness of those closest to you and your inability to put anything sensible down on paper, and no one worries if you constantly repeat yourself. And is repetition not the core of every diary, since its purpose is to make you who you already were? Apart from the continual flogging of dead horses the diary need have no structure. Quite involuntarily time forms a stream of fragments, ice floes in a wintry river, which do not need to be ordered. Ordering would be a betrayal.

Isn't ordering *always* a betrayal?

Amsterdam, Tuesday 15 December 2009

If you are writing with a view to publication, merciless honesty is scarcely sustainable, unless you are prepared to sacrifice yourself and your loved ones to your narcissistic exhibitionism. Are you prepared to pay that price? Do you want to show how life really is and so make it it more difficult than it already was? No, anyone who from the outset writes to reveal things to the outside world either exercises a certain degree of self-censorship, even if he is not aware of it, or knows that later publication will be preceded by a process of selection and editing. Unless it appears posthumously, the published diary is always a sophisticated form of fiction.

'Of all literary genres the diary is the least genre-like. But the danger exists that the initial impromptu character of these notes will turn into the everyday compulsiveness of other work (poetry, novel). I must go back to the poem or the novel to protect the diary from premeditated composition.'

Absence of composition as a formal principle.

Winterswijk, Monday 21 December 2009

How are you supposed to read a written life? The illusion of authenticity is created by phenomena that often make other texts unreadable: things not quite ripe for expression or incomplete, the duplications, the unbowdlerised obsessions, the general absence of direction that characterises everyday life. In addition there is the fact that what fills someone's daily life, a job for example, is often completely uninteresting to write about, with the result that it either does not find its way into the diary – which thereby loses authenticity – or reinforces its unreadability.

The only correct way to read someone else's book is to take as much time over reading as the writer needed to write it. The result is that you begin to merge with the writer. In order to understand him you have to repeat his life. That is quite simply impossible in a compressed form.

But perhaps you don't want to understand the writer. Perhaps you just want to use his work as a mirror.

Winterswijk, Friday 25 December 2009

In these past weeks, during which I've been reading the diaries of Leonard Nolens, I have felt drawn into a conversation. The work covers a period of almost thirty years, and at each date I try to remember what I was doing on that day, who I was in 1979, in 1992, in 2007. I slide my life across that of Nolens or vice versa, and realise that I *have to* write back. This diary is unreadable, like all diaries, since it provokes a response, since you want to put your own passage alongside every passage, your own aphorism alongside every aphorism. The reading is constantly interrupted because you realise that you are writing along with, or rather in opposition to, the author. 'Unreadable' is the wrong word. This is the most perfect form of reading. But to finish this book I shall need thirty years. I don't know whether I will be granted that many years. Or whether I want to fill them in that way.

'I'm a navel-gazer. But my navel is huge.'

In his diary Nolens, who – as he himself never tires of stressing – is a great poet, constructs an alter ego with which he is infatuated, although it repels him in equal measure. With unblinking frankness and an eye for the telling detail he imparts to me his dramatic union with Leen, his occasional disgusting drinking binges and the despair and triumph that the writing of poems entails, systematically asking himself what role he can play in the world as a poet. With panache (that is, authentically, because the emotions and gestures, as required by the stage, are enlarged), he performs the parts assigned to him of lover, drinker and poet.

'Every *I* is a construction, that's true, but one made by someone, by a human being of flesh and blood. Every *I* is a construction, that's true, and for that very reason that *I* is not a fiction. It has been worked on. It has become a reality. And if that weren't the case, no one else would be able to recognise themselves in it.'

Winterswijk, Wednesday 30 December 2009

Perhaps Nolens' love life is no more exceptional that that of most of us, perhaps his addiction reflects the battles we all have to fight to stay afloat, but it is difficult to argue that his work as a poet is an occupation like any other. With Nolens it is a matter of all or nothing. A poem for which you haven't put your life in the balance will find no favour with him. Probably that is the only way to deal with poetry. Poetry that is the not the product of blood sweat and tears has no right to exist.

Yet it is not Nolens' work as a poet that makes this diary a work of vital importance. The most important theme is the writing of the books themselves, writing to maintain the dialogue with oneself, writing as an existential act. This diary is to a large extent about itself. That sounds like incestuous fiddling, and deadly dull, but since for the *persona* Nolens living and writing coincide, it is neither. Writing oneself is a precondition to getting through the day. The diary can be read as an extended poem. What he presents here in the form of a well-nigh endless series of fragments does not differ essentially from what his poetry does in highly stylised form: give meaning to being thrown into the world.

'I believe [...] in the greatest possible concordance between my life and my writing, that is, I try not to lie. The poem that I write must have the value of a cheque, covered by what my life has in the bank. A poorly placed comma is a breathing problem; a wrong or redundant adjective implies that there's something wrong with my life.'

Nolens is style itself, and it goes without saying that the diary is also highly stylised. However modest or even mundane some observations are, every sentence is well-formed. Anyone who has ever seen Nolens' handwriting realises that for this poet every stroke of the pen is an aesthetic act, with the straining after beauty interpretable as a moral duty. Every sentence is an ethical statement. It follows that the interweaving of ethics and aesthetics, morality and prosody is a prominent leitmotif in the diary.

'If in 1998 the I no longer exists, then you must make it. Only that newly-made I can save you. Formal innovation and ethical principles always go hand in hand. The innovation you are after in your poems is a rehabilitation of the individual. And paradoxically that insight corresponds with the wonderful saying of Roland Barthes: 'Literature is the Utopia of language.'

Winterswijk, Saturday 2 January 2010

Nolens likes quoting frequently and at length from his extensive reading, which – as was perhaps obvious – includes besides poetry a great deal of life writing. The philosophical notes of Marcus Aurelius, the (fictional) letters of Seneca, the confessions of Rousseau, the reflections of Kierkegaard, the notebooks of Paul Valéry, the jottings of Elias Canetti, the autobiographical essays of Jean Améry. Nolens measures his thinking, his life and his writing against these authors.

"The diarist learns from other diarists how to formulate his intimacy. They provide him with the forms – and the potential of the apparently formless – within which he gives a shape to his fleeting presence."

Winterswijk, Sunday 3 January 2010

Giving shape to the fleeting is an aspiration doomed to failure, which nevertheless occupies our whole lives. What else can you do? Evaporate like alcohol? Be blown away on the wind like the cries of rooks or seagulls? Drain away like infertile seed? Beckett concludes *The Unnameable* with these words: 'you must go on, I can't go on, I'll go on.'

Most people opt to ease their progress by learning a trade, accepting a job, possibly making a career, reproducing, and, whenever the abyss comes in sight, enjoying themselves. Working, caring and having fun, don't think there's much wrong with organising your life like that. Work does not necessarily have to distract you from what really matters. You can undertake work that has to be done, for example, to make other people's lives better, or to preserve civilisation.

Nolens has always kept aloof from social activity. That is a courageous choice, which has enabled him to investigate the meaning of that very choice for more than forty years to date. Besides this impossible diary, it has produced an extensive poetic oeuvre, which is rightly counted among the best Dutch literature of the past few decades. But is it the only right choice? Would practising a profession have harmed his production? More than that, might a more profound contact with the world of institutions, money and ambition not have had a fruitful influence on his work, because it would in that case have been even clearer why we need poetry as a place of refuge?And might it not have spared the poet a great deal of suffering? Someone who has to go to work every day, who is responsible for the welfare of others, cannot afford to go on wallowing in his own malaise.

But this is purely hypothetical. Nolens has chosen this life because it turned out to have chosen *him*. We can never know what would have happened if he had become a doctor or a lawyer or a teacher. Just as well.

'Most people have a job, a real job, and hate the idea of dealing consciously day after day with their longing for the poem. Most people work for a living and rely on the evenings, the weekends, the days off when the spirit will move them. Forget *herbeigerufene Inspiration* (invoked inspiration), as Rilke calls it. No, they read and write by virtue of pure grace. I wish I could do that. I wish I could accept that not every day of my life can be poetry. But what was it René Char said? 'There is not one place for beauty. Every place is for beauty.' Yes, the daily fight for air.'

Winterswijk, Sunday 10 January 2010

Last night I sat talking with my lover for ages about Nolens' diary, my struggle with it, my fascination, the way it provokes me to respond and makes me take stock again of my life and writing. My poetic output is about as great as his, which of course does not imply that the quality is the same. What he does in his diary I do at least in part in essays and in teaching. Is my choice of poetry uncompromising enough? Do I still hanker too much for social recognition? Am I looking for an equilibrium between being a poet and serving society? Does the ultimate subservience manifest itself preeminently in seeking an isolation that affords scope for reflection on the human condition of being thrown into the world, for the creation of consoling beauty? I haven't reached a conclusion.

I drank too much, slept too little and wrote this piece this morning in one fluid motion. ■

Translated by Paul Vincent

Extracts from A Poet's Diary 1979-2007

By Leonard Nolens

Berchem, Friday 17 September 1993

How can the intelligence stay flexible when year after year at school it is pulled taut by parroting?

Does intellectual freedom disappear when at the age of thirty it has to dress in three-piece suits?

Does sufficient blood flow into a married penis?

Can you stay a child if you have children?

Can a child father? Can a child mother?

Can you stay a wanderer if you've got houses, cars and studies to pay for?

How can I regain my innocence after I have put a thousand closely printed pages into the public domain?

How can I regain the passion that for twenty years has made, sustained, given birth to me and my poetry?

How can I regain the intoxication of alcohol, which for almost thirty years has spelled my death?

Is it still possible with this clear head to do something wonderfully stupid?

Will thoughtful sluggishness finally win out over racing thoughts, flashes of imagination, the boundless impulsiveness of the adolescent that you were and want to remain?

Can the pure intellect regain through cunning the state of grace that issued from sorrow, melancholy, the pain of birth?

Do I write only because I have written?

Do I speak only because I was taught to?

Do I live only because I am incapable of not living?

Do I stay with you for fear of my absence?

Is it possible to write poems in exchange for government money?

Is this desperate asking of questions only bearable because your body is not desperate? How can that be squared with the fact that your thought says: there is no hope, and your flesh quite calmly consumes a tartare roll?

Why do you buy yet another book? Won't you ever have read enough? No, the same way a person has to eat every day to stay healthy. (Healthy?!)

Aren't you ashamed to be looking forward so much to the evening of readings to be given shortly? So, are you so turned on by your own texts?

Don't avoid the cat. It's your own flesh that nuzzles.

Fear power and do not wish for it. Whoever has it can never escape it again.

Missenburg, Wednesday 18 September 1996

Poets know with statistical certainty that almost no one is interested in what they make, therefore in what they are. That realisation determines their view of life: they rightly work on the assumption that the man or woman sitting opposite them, with whom they are having a fascinating conversation, sharing a drink and possibly afterwards going to bed, has no interest in their true intimate self. To begin with, that lack of interest provokes anger, sorrow, helplessness and even bitterness, but finally leads the poet, when poetry wins the day, holds its own in the midst of so much indifference, to project his reader into the future and essentially to write for posterity. That is what I mean by the old adage: 'Writing, real writing is always writing for eternity.' That eternity is by definition not quantifiable and only points to the future. The future is: tomorrow, next year, the contemporaries of my children and grandchildren. Writing for eternity is writing in such a way that the letters are still clearly legible on my dying day. Without that hope it isn't worth the trouble of going to work.

Berchem, Wednesday 2 April 1997

It's such a damn small world I live in and write about. But it is mine, inalienably. I have recorded that world, albeit only a fraction of a second of it, have signed with my own hand and passed on a square millimetre of it, and the circle of pain I drew round my personal chair with my personal voice was recognisable to some. *Actual* reality – that monster that journalists, critics and naïve philosophers are constantly talking about – remains for me an open question and a closed book. *Actual* reality is my reality, and if that's solipsism I can live with that. After fifty years in this anthill I've remained an ant without decorations and titles and functions, and with my ant's soul and ant's pen I crawl across the squared paper of my cheap exercise books and explore the immense world of a small room near Antwerp.

Missenburg, Friday 17 July 1998

Say we, us, everyone as little as possible. But in this case you're right: all of us, usually without realising it, are obsessed with the yearning to belong. Even those who supposedly distance themselves from the group, stridently or tacitly, are unconsciously joining the race of eccentrics and misanthropists, recluses and know-it-alls, tramps and lunatics, and perhaps half of young people paradoxically enough belong to the group of the marginalised. The desperate individual who does away with himself hasn't recognised himself in anything at all. He hasn't read a novel, heard music, not met anyone who could hold up a mirror for him to see himself in. But he too wanted to belong, namely to the society of the unseen, the insignificant, those not worthy of mention, the unrecognisable, the non-legitimated, the living dead, the dead. All of us are forced from and by virtue of our birth to belong, even if we want to annul that birth itself. Even when we refuse to say we, since even the words of that refusal are part of that we, belong to everyone.

Fifteen years in a ground-floor flat at Marc's place, seven years in Missenburg: twenty-two years in Edegem. For twenty-two years you came here from Antwerp almost every morning on the bus or by bike to find, or better, secure a place in the world. You didn't succeed. But you did intuit here the possibility of living a life that couldn't deceive itself by shaking the wrong hands, the parroting of smarmy polite phrases, the kissing of the wrong cheeks. Doubtless different, new lies were woven in this gap, but you don't know them. (Oh, that depressing rhetoric of interior monologue!) The books you wrote in those twenty-two years were actually nothing more than attempts to obey as often and as thoroughly as possible the demands of your true nature. What that comprises should be clear by now. If your poems and diaries constitute one big lie, so does your true nature. (No poet, no writer, no contemporary intellectual dares to utter the expression true nature… Your eternal naivety.)

Those twenty-two years, from twenty-nine to fifty-one, what else are they but your youth? The isolation of that long No to the mass, to the institutions of society, the isolation of that long Yes to the impossible dream and your personal destiny explain why you don't feel any age difference when you deal with twenty-year-olds. But they of course do feel it, except when they read your books and

realise that your instability has remained intact. Your only grown-up feature is that you have found a form for immaturity. No, you're still wet behind the ears, but you have deliberately chosen that wetness.

You've substantiated that weakness here year in year out.

The diary records the bank transactions, the poetry is the visibly covered cheque. The diary is the gold mine, the poem is the gold. The diary is the eternal I *in statu nascendi*, the poem is the actual birth certificate.

Berchem, Friday 6 September 2002

Making an inventory of your merits based on everything you've refused; you've straightened and strengthened your backbone by saying no aloud or under your breath. In the last thirty years never had a job, never worked for papers, never written reviews, never sat on juries, never spoken at book launches or private views, never operated in cliques or coteries, never accepted membership of political parties. Never indulged your ambition anywhere but in a small room, on a blank page. Never been born anywhere but in a note, never played the hero but in a poem. Never found the strength to say no anywhere but very close to a woman who gave you your head, the odd friend who's stayed loyal to you, two sons who haven't rejected your ways of living. In short: you've cultivated the stubborn myopia of your dream until it became visible and tangible to someone else. Or as Stefan wrote: you've made a profession of your soul. While here, next to your exercise book, four papers and a weekly hector your powerless gaze about the imminent commemoration of 9/11, the towers, the victims. What is the name of the proud brat who dares say I to the terror of a religious and nationalist, racist and fundamentalist *we*? I've forgotten who once wrote: *'Le fascisme est le lyrisme du troupeau.'*

Translated by Paul Vincent

From *A Poet's Diary 1979-2007*

(*Dagboek van een dichter 1979-2007*. Amsterdam-Antwerpen: Querido, 2009)

That Pumpin' Stuff

The Success of Rock Festivals in the Low Countries

[PIETER COUPÉ]

Do you remember the festival
We took those drugs I never thought
I'd get into that pumpin' stuff
A thousand eyes won't recognise us
'Cause I know you and you know me
That's all you need and all I think of
I know this ain't nothing very deep but it's good fun
So don't run into the crowd

dEUS, 'Memory of a Festival' (CD: *In a Bar, Under the Sea*, Island Records, 1996)

'Festival tickets selling like hot cakes' a Flemish newspaper reported in a headline at the start of the festival season in June 2009. Exactly one year later, just as the 2010 run of summer festivals was about to burst into life, the reporting in a competing newspaper was even more positive: *'Festival tickets selling faster than ever'*. Even after the summer of 2010, when the last plastic cup had been plucked from the grass and the smell of hamburgers had disappeared, the picture was a very positive one: Rock Werchter (queen of Low Countries festivals and a top player on the international stage) in the village of the same name: 320,000 visitors, sold out; Pukkelpop near Hasselt: just under 200,000 visitors, sold out; Tomorrowland in Boom: 100,000 visitors, sold out. And these are only three of the most successful festivals. Overall, in 2010, Flanders' festivals attracted 68,000 more visitors than in 2009. The trend in the Netherlands was the same: Lowlands in Biddinghuizen, for example, with 55,000 festival-goers, could also put up the 'sold out' notice. Want some more figures? Between 1999 and 2004, the number of festival days in Flanders increased by 500%, with a grand total of three hundred festivals. In the Netherlands you can even choose from two cultural festivals every day of the year, which has already tempted opinion-makers to use terms such as 'festival factory' and 'festivalisation'.

The quality of pop festivals in the Low Countries has also attracted international attention. In recent years, for example, Rock Werchter has been named 'Best Festival in the World' four times at the International Live Music Conference, and it also walked away with three trophies at the European Festival

Pukkelpop Festival, Hasselt.

Awards 2010. In the latter awards, the Netherlands and Flanders were successful across the board: the Cactus Festival (Bruges) and Pinkpop (Landgraaf) were also among the winners.

By now the figures are probably making your head spin, and you'll have got the picture, so we will try to pinpoint the cause of this continuing success. Why is it that visitor numbers continue to increase, even in the past two years when economic growth has slowed? One would expect, at such a time, that people would prefer to spend their money on more necessary things. But after the summer of 2009, the organisers were unanimous in their conclusion: people don't economise on festivals. So what makes the Low Countries such fertile ground for festivals, bringing about an annual pilgrimage of hundreds of thousands of 'pop pilgrims'?

'Cause I know you and you know me'

Festivals have been held in the Low Countries for some time. In fact, Flanders and the Netherlands lost no time in organising their own musical happenings. As far back as 1967 – two years before Woodstock, the international 'big bang' that heralded the beginning of rock festival culture – the Jazz Bilzen festival in the otherwise peaceful village of Haspengouw also began to feature rock groups on its posters. Events that paved the way in the Netherlands were the

Lowlands Festival, Biddinghuizen.

now defunct Holland Pop Festival – which in 1970 attracted 100,000 visitors to an area of woodland near Rotterdam and was a free state for three days – and Pinkpop, launched in the same year and now the longest-running annual festival in the world.

Not that Pinkpop 1970 bore much resemblance to Pinkpop 2010. The Pinkpop hippies of 1970 would be staggered at the expensive tickets, the rigid access control and the flawless organisation. During the past four decades, Flemish and Dutch festivals have been able to develop more and more and have consequently become more and more streamlined. Interviews given by organisers when festivals reach a milestone edition are full of heroic accounts of the chaotic early days, but the conclusion is almost always: 'It was fun, but accidents could have happened. It's a good thing everything is more professional these days.'

Professionalisation through years of practical experience, then. But the geography of the Low Countries has also forced the festivals to stand out from the rest: 'In a small country nothing is straightforward. That encourages you to be just that little bit more creative and organise everything just that little bit more efficiently so that you don't disappear from the festival map', explains Herman Schueremans, organiser of Rock Werchter. A colleague of his, Patrick Keersebilck of the Cactus Festival in Bruges, also praises the typical Belgian approach: 'We plan and organise our festivals down to the last detail. The artists and the public appreciate that.' A Dutch journalist made a similar comment about the events in his own country: 'Other countries can't believe their eyes when they see our summer festivals, and people are really keen to come to them (...) The programme runs perfectly. The site is set up, and taken down again afterwards in no time at all – the public are happy, and so are the artists. We do a professional job.'

According to Herman Schueremans, that professional job has a stimulating effect: 'It's like the story of the street with a good shoe shop. The shoe shop attracts other shops, and eventually you have a flourishing shopping street.' This appealing comment, from a man who is never short of a mercantile quote, straightaway explains the whole patchwork of festivals that exists in these

Pinkpop Festival, Landgraaf.

parts. Because in Flanders certainly, and also in the Netherlands, you see posters advertising local festivals displayed everywhere, even in the smallest villages. Most of them are initiatives by local associations, usually youth groups. One of those events could easily develop into the next Pinkpop or Rock Werchter: two mega-enterprises that both began as one of the many small, local festivals put on with the help of the Scouts or the local football club. That development can happen very quickly, as we can see from Crammerock (Stekene) and Feest in het Park (Oudenaarde), two Flemish summer festivals which, in the last two or three years, have suddenly moved up several ranks in the festival hierarchy. In the past they could have been dismissed as a garden fête that has got out of hand, but now they can flaunt big names and visitor figures in the tens of thousands.

Even Rock Werchter, a giant among festivals, still works together with a good many local organisations. If you park your car or put up your tent during the festival, it is very likely that you will pay the charge to a youngster who is working to raise money for their club. Pukkelpop is still organised by the *Humanistische Jongeren Leopoldsburg*, a humanist association for young people that launched a small-scale alternative festival twenty-five years ago because it was dissatisfied with what was on offer at the time.

Besides the historical link – rock festival audiences now span four generations – roots in the local community are also important. A festival, however large, is organised by people we (might) know, people like us, and that has an appeal. 'Cause I know you and you know me / That's all you need and all I think of', as the Belgian rock band dEUS sings in 'Memory of a Festival'.

Familiarity attracts, then, partly because it provides some common ground in the vast, anonymous mass of festival-goers. Although the size of the crowd is off-putting, it is at the same time an attraction: festivals are the quintessential social event, a moment of shared exhilaration.

Some people are slightly negative about this: one female journalist described festivals as 'secular church services for the zapping hedonist' and a blogger referred to mass gatherings as 'a ritual bordering on self-destruction'. Yet the fact remains: man is a social animal, and whereas in the past people would

Lowlands Festival, Biddinghuizen.

seek each other's company at fairs or football matches, today they do so at festivals, with music and friends. They meet like-minded people with whom they can share emotions. Incidentally, at Pukkelpop 2010 there was a genuine fair. The wheel has come full circle.

In the same way that many advertisers play on our emotions, festivals too make the most of the idea of shared emotions. Pukkelpop organiser Chokri Mahassine always responds with the same one-liner when asked why people keep coming to his festival: '*De wei, dat zijn wij.*' ('The field – that's *us*') Eric van Eerdenburg, the organiser of Lowlands, Pukkelpop's Dutch counterpart and an event that is famous for its unique atmosphere of togetherness, shares this view: 'The Lowlands feeling is about being with other people who have the same interests as you.'

dEUS sing 'A thousand eyes won't recognise us' in the song *'Memory of a Festival'*. Knowing that a thousand eyes are watching you may seem an uncomfortable idea, but festivals have different laws. Those eyes don't recognise us or judge us, precisely because they belong to people who are just like us, experiencing the same 'high' during the festival. For a little while the crowd is more important than the individual. The dEUS song quoted above was inspired by an old David Bowie single, *'Memory of a Free Festival'*, a beautiful musical interpretation by the British singer of the collective festival feeling and 'that pumpin' stuff' that dEUS sing about: 'Touch, we touched the very soul / Of holding each and every lie / We claimed the very source of joy ran through / It didn't, but it seemed that way / I kissed a lot of people that day.'

The role of the media is also conspicuous: in summer, radio stations suspend their normal schedules to make way for extensive festival coverage, and newspapers carry special supplements. The websites of both radio stations and newspapers publish photos and film clips depicting every aspect of festival life and focusing on visitors' experiences. This enormous exposure fuels the 'have to be there' feeling – after all, if the festivals are attracting so much media attention, they must be important. It is not surprising that young people in particular go along with this, receptive as they are to what life has to offer. For young people, therefore, festivals have almost become a modern rite of passage, a step on the road to adulthood; a couple more carefree summers with music and friends before they enter on working life. 'That's all you need and all I think of / I know this ain't nothing very deep but it's good fun', to quote dEUS again.

'Don't run into the crowd'

So long as there are young people, new visitors will continue to come to festivals. So the organisers don't need to worry about customer loyalty just yet. Festivals in Flanders and the Netherlands evidently have a 'strong brand image', but a few storm clouds are gathering above the otherwise sunny festival landscape of the Low Countries. We are not talking about the crisis (which, incidentally, has not impacted heavily on the festival sector, although a number of sponsors – mainly banks and small businesses – have withdrawn their support), but about the ever-tighter government rules and regulations that could so easily throw a spanner in the works.

In recent years the festivals have already invested heavily in health and safety measures in order to comply with statutory norms. No-one would dispute the need for this – although the organisers must have had to take a deep breath when the bills landed on the doormat – and since the tragic accident at the Danish Roskilde Festival (where nine people were crushed to death in 2000) nobody is taking risks, and rightly so. More alarming are the increasing complaints about the excessive controls on volunteer and holiday work undertaken by youth associations and students. 'If you force people to meet all sorts of requirements (...), you'll destroy part of the social fabric', remarks Pukkelpop organiser Chokri Mahassine. He may be over-dramatising the situation, but 'regulatitis' is certainly a problem. The more regulations you have to comply with, the less time there is for other – often more fundamental – tasks.

Even if you can put the above into perspective – after all, entrepreneurs always complain about too many rules and regulations – the investment necessary to comply with environmental standards is even more substantial. Festivals are finding themselves caught between a rock and a hard place: on

Rock Werchter.

the one hand they are under pressure from the public and the government to reduce their ecological footprint, but on the other as commercial enterprises they obviously want to continue growing. Organisers encounter all manner of obstacles, especially when growth involves expanding the festival site. In many cases, not only is there simply no room to do so, but local residents also protest about the pressure a festival puts on the surrounding area in terms of traffic chaos, excessive noise and tons of rubbish. The last thing the organisers want is to get on the wrong side of the neighbours – they are too important as a bastion of local support.

In addition, if a festival is to grow, the quality of the music must remain high – i.e. the programme should include the best bands. In the radically altered music landscape of the 21st century, that is anything but easy. Now that record sales have collapsed, bands have to go on the road to earn money. But what might appear to be a golden opportunity for festivals could well become a serious disadvantage because with more and more festivals emerging in Eastern Europe, the United States and Canada the competition for bands is becoming ever more intense and they can demand astronomical sums. Combine these costs with the limited opportunities for growth mentioned in the previous paragraph, and you begin to understand why festival organisers are worried. Incidentally, there are more and more grumbles about quality. Anyone reading the unprecedentedly critical comments by journalists, especially the ones about the latest edition of Rock Werchter (which included phrases such as 'identity problem', 'poorest programme ever' and 'few highlights'), can conclude that our rock events, or at any rate the largest of them, are approaching their 'best before' date.

Resilience

Our festival landscape has become quite crowded, in the last ten years particularly, and we should perhaps expect one or two of them to fall by the wayside. Nevertheless, it would be a shame to 'thin out' the festival landscape too much, now that the Low Countries have something to be proud of again. The governments of the Netherlands and Flanders – often regarded as meddlesome busybodies in this context – nevertheless recognise the uniqueness and importance of this festival culture: quite a few events have been receiving subsidies for many years. Moreover, there are two recent policy initiatives: since 2009, the PMV (*Participatiemaatschappij Vlaanderen*), an independent Flemish investment company, has provided loans through its investment fund CultuurInvest to the organisers of small and medium-sized festivals. There is a similar initiative in the Netherlands: the Dutch Pop Music Plan 2009-2010, whereby organisers are entitled to apply for a subsidy if they book bands from the Netherlands.We shall have to wait and see, however, whether these resources will remain available in the coming period of austerity.

But whatever happens, in the past Low Countries rock festivals have proved themselves so impressively resilient that Flemish and Dutch pop pilgrims need not worry yet: their 'sacred' fields and parks will still be here to welcome and allure them with 'that pumpin' stuff' for a good few summers to come. And anyway, there is always the music to turn to for comfort. ■

Translated by Yvette Mead

Versatile and Comprehensible

The Work of Soeters Van Eldonk

The work of the Soeters Van Eldonk firm of architects has many facets. Some of their designs can be recognised from miles away. There's the new Zaanstad city hall, for instance, an amplified take on the local tradition of building wooden houses and painting them green. Other works are barely noticeable, however, such as their treatment of the corner of Warmoesstraat and Sint Annenstraat in Amsterdam. If you don't pay very close attention, the fact that Warmoesstraat has acquired a new façade will pass you right by.

Architecture that is both exuberant and understated, elegant and serious, is typical of the firm's work, but Sjoerd Soeters and Jos van Eldonk and their co-workers are always on the lookout for something that suits the location, the residents and the client and that is tailor-made to fit the building's function. If circumstances demand a modest application, then the firm's solutions are as unobtrusive as possible – such as the apartment block on the Brouwersgracht in Amsterdam, which looks more like a warehouse than the ones that were there already.

No matter how diverse their oeuvre, it's clear that the work of Soeters Van Eldonk is far removed from mainstream Dutch architecture today, with its modernist inspiration.

Form follows function

The firm was founded in 1979 by Sjoerd Soeters, who took Jos van Eldonk as his partner in 1997, and it does produce distinctive architecture. But for Soeters Van Eldonk, the form of a building is less important than the contribution it can make to the way a city functions. Even though the firm designs such unusual buildings as a city hall composed of magnified Zaandam houses, a theatre in Heerhugowaard inspired by a red cabbage or apartment blocks with gigantic swans on the roof, their main purpose is not to enrich the world with such buildings. These structures are a - sometimes unconventional - means of forcing environments to make room for ordinary everyday life. How a city, a city centre, a residential district or a village is put together, how new buildings fit into the environment, how public space is organised, how routes run, how a diversity of

Castle Leliënhuyze, Haverleij Den Bosch. Courtesy of Aluphoto.

functions can be combined – in short, how the built environment can be made liveable – all that is more important to Soeters and Van Eldonk than architectural expression. Since a structure's exterior is not their top priority, where that's concerned they're quite happy to go a bit overboard on occasion.

Soeters and Van Eldonk want their architecture to be comprehensible. They don't make buildings that sit in autistic silence or deliver monologues; their architecture enters into a dialogue with the environment, it 'listens and responds'. In that respect, their work is not only *architecture parlante*, to quote an eighteenth-century French concept, but it's also *architecture entendante*. They want their architecture to relate well to the people who use the environment, and they do this by referring to it, expanding on it and responding to what is, or was, already there. They make their architecture comprehensible by having it speak an intelligible language, drawing on the traits and peculiarities of the context in which the project is located. The Austrian architect Adolf Loos once defined architects as bricklayers who have learned Latin. If we follow that definition, we might say that since almost no one speaks Latin any more, architecture is having to contend with being unintelligible. Soeters and Van Eldonk want to do their bricklaying in an ordinary language that everyone can understand.

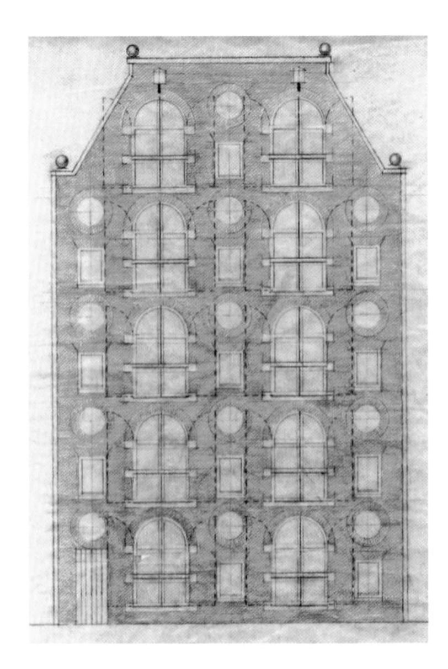

Brouwersgracht, Amsterdam.

Sketch, Brouwersgracht, Amsterdam.

This can be done by applying the adage 'form follows function' in its original sense, not as the hackneyed expression that is sometimes used to characterise functionalism in architecture. When the American architect Louis Sullivan coined this phrase at the end of the nineteenth century, he did not mean that buildings ought to show how they are engineered – that the weight of a floor is borne by columns or walls – but that buildings must express their nature and character. In line with the French *architecture parlante*, he argued that a tall building, say, should be designed so that everything, down to the smallest detail, emphasises the building's height.

When 'form follows function' is understood as Sullivan originally meant it, it becomes an argument for expressing the character of a building through its form, composition, size, location, ornamentation, symbolism and all the other means that the architect has at his disposal. You can take this very literally and build a hot-dog stand in the shape of a hot-dog, to cite a well-known postmodern example, but not every building lends itself to such a literal interpretation. Usually more subtle means are needed to articulate what a building is, and thus make it meaningful and recognisable rather than meaningless and interchangeable.

Cheerful environments

For Soeters and Van Eldonk, it is essential that architecture be comprehensible because architecture belongs to everyone. Architecture is there on the street, which means that everyone is affected by it. The fact that some people may be bothered by it, and it is the architect's responsibility to avoid this as far as possible, is sometimes forgotten. But not by Soeters and Van Eldonk. They do their best to ensure that their buildings don't have 'sides' and 'backs', where most of the time there's little going on. After all, the public domain means most where buildings look towards the street, thereby showing their public faces. So Soeters and Van Eldonk try to give their buildings as much frontage as possible.

Blaauwlakenblok, Amsterdam.
Corner Warmoesstraat.
Photo by Scagliola-Brakkee.

Shopping Centre Parada,
Nootdorp. Courtesy of ING.

They surround them with features that are oriented towards the street, while elements that have no relevance to the street, such as car parks, are incorporated within outwardly-oriented functions. Wherever possible front doors open onto the street as effective contributions to street life. So when it comes to creating a meaningful and well-functioning public space, the most important factor isn't the logic of the individual building but the logic of urban life. And of course the same goes for villages and neighbourhoods; no-one there wants to look at the backs of buildings, either.

With most architects there's no point talking about cheerfulness, but Soeters and Van Eldonk think otherwise. For them cheerfulness, homeliness, friendliness and familiarity are important. No-one in their right mind would argue that a cheerless world is a better world, yet few architects dare to admit that their aim is to produce cheerful environments.

According to Soeters and Van Eldonk, architecture has to be connected with the location so that people can feel at home. This can be done by seeking out

City Hall, Zaandam.
Photo by Scagliola-Brakkee.

the individual character of the place, which can be understood as a combination of what is there now, what used to be there, what is usual in that locality, the street scene and the landscape. Getting to the bottom of a place is not an exact science but a quest to discover how new architecture can link up with the environment. The method is always and everywhere applicable, and in that respect it is universal. For Van Eldonk and Soeters, however, the results are always different, say, because the sum of the characteristics of a place is different every time.

When their starting point is the context, their object is not to to use architecture to make a place unique. It's just the opposite: to bring out the uniqueness of the place in the architecture. When you connect with an area's individuality its character is strengthened. When you build on what is already there, what is new can appear to be only natural.

Bricoleurs

The means that Soeters and Van Eldonk use to make environments seem natural and matter-of-fact, to animate a town or city (if it's not a matter of all-out reanimation), often teeter on the border between conventional and unconventional. Ordinary means are sometimes used in an unusual way, unusual solutions are achieved by ordinary means. This is typical of the firm, and it gives Soeters and Van Eldonk a very specific position in the spectrum of contemporary architecture and urban design: tradition and history play such a major role in their work that its radically innovative quality is not immediately apparent; on the other hand, it is so obviously unconventional that it is difficult to fit it into a school such as contemporary traditionalism.

What further sets them apart is that the scale at which Van Eldonk and Soeters work often lies somewhere between architecture and urban design. For them the essence of the commission matters more than the individual building but less than the development plan. This is urban design that consists of buildings and architecture with an effect that extends beyond the boundaries

Sydhavn Sluseholmen, Copenhagen. Photo by Scagliola-Brakkee.

of the site. What Soeters and Van Eldonk do is achieve an interaction with the built environment and comes close to 'tinkering with the city', although in their case there are none of the negative connotations that messing about with the city might imply. Messing about with what is already there fits right in with Soeters' and Van Eldonk's preferred role as architects.

Soeters and Van Eldonk are engineers who have learned how to tinker, who have rediscovered an uninhibited inventiveness after completing their analytical training as architects. Both of them feel a greater affinity with the *bricoleur* than with the *ingénieur*, to quote a distinction made by Claude Lévi-Strauss. Lévi-Strauss distinguished between the engineer who works according to a set plan and the *bricoleur* or handyman who improvises. The handyman uses concrete, second-hand materials to make something that is needed at a specific moment. New forms emerge, even though innovation as such is not the goal. The engineer's design is based on one clear, basic idea, while that of the *bricoleur* elaborates on a variety of different ideas. The engineer works 'from the top down', starting with a system and adapting reality to suit it. The *bricoleur* starts from haphazard reality and adapts his plan accordingly.

The difference between the *bricoleur* and the *ingénieur* is reminiscent of another problem-solving classification described by Isaiah Berlin in *The Hedgehog and the Fox*, a book that Soeters often quotes. The hedgehog has one strategy, a total solution to every problem: as soon as danger approaches, the animal rolls himself up into a spiny ball. The fox, on the other hand, has no all-embracing solution; for every problem he encounters he comes up with a different idea. The aim of Soeters and Van Eldonk is to unite the characteristics of the fox and the *bricoleur* by devising an appropriate response for every problem instead of approaching every problem in the same way.

The 'tinkering' of Soeters and Van Eldonk is part of an architectural tradition that reached its high point in the nineteenth century, when this approach was used to devise suitable forms for all manner of new types of building. Historical styles and examples were used to develop buildings for completely new purposes such as railway stations, factory buildings or big apartment blocks.

The way Soeters and Van Eldonk work follows on from this and frequently shows a close relationship to it; for instance, in their use of the traditional idiom of the Zaan region's green wooden buildings for the unprecedented stacking of bus station and town hall, in the basilica-like covered car park at the heart of the Nootdorp shopping centre or the castle-like housing in Haverleij. Each and every one of these is an example of the kind of *bricolage* that was so popular in the nineteenth century.

Agreement by mutual promise

What goes for architecture also goes for Soeters's and Van Eldonk's approach to urban design: there, too, they manage to come up with unconventional solutions by playing around with everyday elements. An example of this is the canal that runs uphill in Zaandam, a city-centre canal that had been filled in and was to be excavated once again. This canal, which seems to break the laws of gravity, forms a natural escort for pedestrians as they walk from the city centre to the raised square where the entrance to the city hall is located.

Soeters's and Van Eldonk's pursuit of what is natural results in a preference for urban environments composed of clearly-defined streets and squares, surrounded by façades that are (or appear to be) a succession of separate buildings. In these environments the pedestrian has precedence. Motor traffic is relegated to second place. On-street parking is reduced as much as possible, with vehicles mainly restricted to underground car parks or buildings, supplies for shops are delivered to the back of the building and the intersection of motor and pedestrian traffic is kept to a minimum. In this respect Java Island, the centre of Nootdorp and the centre of Zaanstad all follow the same plan: they consist of spaces made for people, not for traffic.

Defining an urban space is made easier by the absence of the car. With no cars streets can be made narrower and squares smaller, which usually helps to demarcate a clearly defined shape and boundary in which opposing façades are not too far from each other. This makes for more pleasant surroundings. Most people are more comfortable in a clearly defined space than a boundless openness, just as they find variety more attractive than uniformity, and activity better than emptiness.

Another way to get in touch with the ordinary is by listening to the wishes of clients and users. Soeters and Van Eldonk are not the sort of architects who think that client input gets in the way of an uncompromising design. They don't see compromise as giving in. Rather, they adhere to the original Latin meaning of a *compromissum* as an agreement through mutual promises. These days almost no one still regards a compromise as an agreement from which both parties benefit, certainly not in architecture. Soeters and Van Eldonk do not see the design and building process as a battle with clients, future users and local residents as their opponents. Naturally, a new building is not just for the client or the people who live nearby, nor is it just for the user. There may be more important interests involved: the city, society, the arts – even eternity, if need be. These may all be reasons why the architect should listen to his own conscience. But architecture begins with a client who wants something and is willing to risk entrusting the realisation of this desire to a designer. Soeters and Van Eldonk see the *compromissum* as an incentive to create something that is more scintillating, more beautiful and better than the client, the neighbours and the users could ever have imagined.

The fact that the people who commission a building are rarely the ones who occupy it has created a gulf between the architect and the user. Because of this architects have of necessity more and more done their best for humanity as a whole while all too easily failing to consider the individual human being.

To escape this trap, Soeters and Van Eldonk make every effort to get to know the flesh-and-blood people behind the abstract notion of 'users' and to try to understand what moves people, what their priorities are and what they lack. This requires not only design talent but also good listening skills.

It also requires a grasp of the whole programme of demands and underlying ideas and assumptions, a willingness to be influenced by the situation and the environment, getting to know the users and their expectations and dreams, searching for the meanings that can be distilled from all this and exposing the secrets that lie hidden in the commission. What this leads to in the end is not *making* a form but *finding* a form, to quote the distinction made by Hugo Häring to which Soeters has so often referred.

As Soeters and Van Eldonk emphasise, finding that form is a matter not just of drawing but also of calculating. Costs and profits, direct and indirect returns, are crucial factors in the design process, especially when the designs are more complex. If something seems too expensive, cutting costs is always an option, but so is searching for ways of increasing the profits. That was one of the things that Soeters and Van Eldonk discovered in the plan for Mariënburg in Nijmegen: that it could be improved in two ways – by expanding the scheme and by reducing the public space. This not only resulted in more rentable square metres of floor area, it also made the streets and squares more compact, adding to the conviviality of downtown Nijmegen.

The ordinary within reach

A central theme in the work and thinking of Soeters and Van Eldonk is how to make architecture and urban design comprehensible and natural. That sounds simpler than it is. Naturalness is difficult to achieve in both architecture and urban design. There are few examples of this kind of naturalness, few traditions that have held up after two centuries of modernisation. The idea that something is good because that's the way it's always been done has been utterly demolished by a century of avant-garde iconoclasm. And even though the avant-garde has been pronounced dead, after that demolition it's no longer possible just to return to the naturalness of yesterday. That it's possible for something like a vernacular to exist, a way of approaching buildings that is the sum of the materials to hand, available techniques and skills, climate, habits and customs: this has perhaps become a romantic utopian dream after all the shocks of the New and a far-reaching globalisation. The paradoxical way in which Soeters and Van Eldonk use unconventional solutions to try to bring the ordinary within reach and attempt to graft architecture onto the environment clearly shows just how far today's architectural culture has moved from the ordinariness that was once so ordinary. ■

Translated by Nancy Forest-Flier

Leuven: a Badly Scarred City

Leuven is a deceptive city. That is not apparent from the monumental gables and gleaming pavements. You can count the tramps here on the fingers of one hand, and we have to import the beggars from Eastern Europe since we don't have any very noticeable poverty of our own. But we do dissemble. We lie about the basis of our being. The monumental gables have almost unanimously been rather conceitedly and extravagantly rebuilt after being set fire to by the Germans at the beginning of the First World War. The pavements have been cleared of chewing-gum, but beneath them the blood of many wars, disputes and executions clings everywhere. Everyone thinks this is a city of intellectuals, the seat of Western wisdom, but deep within them the people of Leuven are weary soldiers just waiting until they have to go yet another round with the Vikings, French, Dutch, Austrians and, inevitably, Germans.

From the moment you arrive at the station Leuven immediately shows the scars of one of those lost battles. In 1914 almost the entire city went up in flames. In my second book, *Flight* (Vlucht), I write about a German soldier and a Flemish woman. He murders her family during those savage August days in 1914. That can be done in a couple of pages, but in reality, too, it only took a couple of hours to slaughter the citizens of Leuven. They were jumpy, those lads who had been sent away far from their *Heimat*. Most of them drunk from the booze they had been able to plunder easily in this brewery town. And furious because they were convinced that the Flemings were not sticking to the military code of honour and were using *franc-tireurs* or snipers. Civilians taking pot-shots at soldiers, that was unheard of. '*Der Zivil hat geschossen...*', claimed the Germans. Even though none of those civilian had invited these soldiers to invade their city, and even though it turned out afterwards that there had been no snipers, but that in the confusion of advancing and retreating troops the Germans had been firing on their own men.

Today on Martelarenplein there is a monument commemorating that time. As so often happens with monuments in Leuven, it has long been an object of loathing. When it was unveiled in 1925 the people of Leuven whispered that it was a disgrace. They found that phallic symbol offensive and also too angular and too realistic in terms of the prevailing norms for sculpture. It stood there for many years, covered in grime and piss, until a few years ago it was listed and restored. Now it stands tall, white and golden, in front of the station, bearing the names of the citizens and soldiers who died then, while the traffic that once raced round the monument is diverted underground.

If we then walk along Bondegenotenlaan (formerly Statiestraat) and look up, we can see commemorative tiles set in each gable. 1914-1918. The modernist architects tore their hair out after the war when the affected citizens of Leuven opted to rebuild their houses in all kinds of grandiose neo- styles with the compensation they received for war damage. That is why the place has become such a hotchpotch. One advantage of the fire, though, is that it provided the opportunity for people to think more carefully about town-planning: they set a few things straight, got rid of what they no longer liked and built anew where necessary. One result of this was the building of a new city theatre that still offers the most important auditorium in the city.

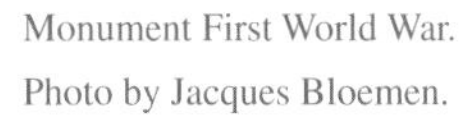

Monument First World War.
Photo by Jacques Bloemen.

University Library.
Photo by Jacques Bloemen.

Burning books

If we take one of the streets leading off Bondgenotenlaan to the left we come into Ladeuzeplein, now pedestrianised, which is almost entirely taken up with the University Library. It still looks impressive, even now, in September, when it is surrounded on all sides by fairground attractions. This library has done more for the First World War image of 'Gallant Little Belgium' than anyone dreamed at the time.

The first central University Library was established in 1636 in the University buildings in the Naamsestraat. In 1914 the building went up in flames when the German soldiers set fire to the city, as we mentioned earlier. There was enormous world-wide indignation at this. That war consumed people was normal, but anyone who set fire to books was a downright barbarian.

Committees of support were set up in twenty-five countries under the leadership of Herbert Hoover, later President of the USA, and they raised over half a million dollars towards the building of a new library and the acquisition of a collection of books and manuscripts. The American architect Whitney Warren took his inspiration from Renaissance and Baroque buildings in the Low Countries and the first stone was laid in 1921. Seven years later, on the 4th of June 1928, the library had its official opening. The arrangement of the stacks and the reading-room was very modern for the time and at the last minute a venomous anti-German slogan on the gable was scrapped, although the rest of the building is full of war symbolism and loving patriotic references. For instance, the English unicorn denotes the victory of the Allies. In accordance with article 247 of the Treaty of Versailles, Germany for its part had to contribute thirteen million Marks towards the cost of books. Thus there was a two-fold supply of books, so that in 1939 the library had some nine hundred thousand volumes. Because the Germans still clung to the myth of the snipers long after the end of the war and believed that they had justly punished Leuven for that cowardly attack by civilians at the start of the Second World War, in May 1940, they could not resist turning their fire on the library again. Once more it was almost entirely destroyed by the flames. Today the library contains around one million volumes, though I must not omit to mention a striking split in one part of the collection. After a long tussle in the 1960s the University of Leuven became 'Flemish' and decanted the francophone students and professors to Louvain-la-Neuve. But what to do with that unique collection of books and manuscripts? In the case of certain periodicals that I needed to consult during my Assyrian studies the best solution people could come up with was to store them in even-numbered years in Leuven and in odd-numbered years in ... Louvain-la-Neuve.

Beer and Beguines

To give our brains a bit of a rest we cross Herbert Hooverplein near the library and enter Sint-Donaas Park, where a remnant of the old city wall can still be seen. The tumble-down tower dates from the 12th century and is one of the few in Leuven to have survived the destruction and the wars, though it has had to be heavily buttressed. In summer and winter alike this is a favourite place for couples in love, walkers and students who want to get away from their '*koten*' ('hutches' - slang for student rooms).

By means of Vlamingenstraat and Parkstraat we reach Naamsestraat and cross it diagonally. Then we walk steeply downhill and come to the Groot Begijnhof. High heels are not recommended on the uneven cobblestones, but suddenly the Saturday rush and the din of the fair have disappeared without trace. In front of the beguinage, ironically enough, a huge wedding limousine is waiting, but apart from that all is peace and tranquillity. Here and there a tourist wanders around, gazing open-mouthed at the beautifully restored houses, while the Dijle ripples by and gives no inkling that it once brought the Vikings who tried, but failed, to break into Leuven in 891.

While it is true that the beguines dedicated themselves to their heavenly bridegroom and left the temptations of the flesh behind, unlike true nuns they did not have to relinquish their money and possessions. Because they did not take any lifelong vows they could abandon their religious life at any time if they wished to marry or had some other worldly prospect in view. The last beguine died in 1988.

Beguinage.
Photo by Jacques Bloemen.

The Beguinage was saved from further deterioration and neglect and painstakingly restored by the University in the 1960s and '70s. Now it is mainly students and (visiting) professors who live there. True citizens of Leuven will also grumble about this from time to time because for a native of the city one's chance of being able to live there is slim in the extreme. The Beguinage is on Unesco's World Heritage list and even after repeated visits it remains a delight to the eye, and also to ears tormented by the racket of the city.

Leuven has always had a somewhat unusual relationship with women. In my first novel, *Death of a Soldier* (Dood van een soldaat, 2005, Manteau), I introduce a female general practitioner, something that was still a real rarity in 1919. Although born in Hageland, she had to go to the University of Brussels to study. Women students were admitted there from the end of the 19th century, but Leuven kept its doors closed to *'porren'* ('pokes' - slang for female students) until 1920. At that time there was a widespread idea that all that intellectual effort was bad for the reproductive organs and delicate nerves of women. Nowadays there are more women than men studying at the Catholic University of Leuven, but it was only in 2010 that Katlijn Malfliet was appointed as the first female Dean in the Faculty of Social Sciences.

If we leave the Beguinage by Schapenstraat, to our right we see the Sint-Antoniuskerk towering above us. Here, at least according to the Flemings, is buried the Greatest Belgian: Father Damiaan, born Jozef De Veuster (1840-1889). He worked and died in the leper colony on Hawaii and in his time had to fight many battles with the Church in order to continue his work among the lepers. In that period it was still thought that leprosy was a result of syphilis, which meant that the unfortunate Damiaan, who eventually died of the disease, was regularly accused of unchastity. Since then he has been declared a saint, but, as befalls every saint, his body is no longer in one piece: his right hand was taken from his grave and is now buried on Molokai. He remains the only non-American to have a statue in the Capitol in Washington.

If we continue along Schapenstraat and turn into Parijsstraat, to right and left we can see all kinds of factory outlets, exotic restaurants and coffee bars.

As a student city, Leuven has never been averse to second-hand goods or food more adventurous than chips with mayonnaise. Anyone in need of a fresh pint can cut through one of the narrow streets on the right and end up in the Oude Markt, *De Langste Toog ter Wereld* (The World's Longest Bar) where according to rumour the locally brewed Stella is piped straight from the brewery to the multiplicity of taps.

If we stay on Parijsstraat, then where it crosses Brusselsestraat we only have to look right to come face-to-face with Leuven's best-known picture postcard: the Grote Markt with the Town Hall and the Sint-Pieterskerk. Here you can satisfy the thirsty, the believers and the argumentative in one go.

Leuven's Town Hall is one of the few monumental buildings that were not set fire to during the First World War, though only because the Germans had their headquarters in it. Aerial photographs from that time show a city in ruins with one single untouched building. Since then the Mayor of Leuven, Louis Tobback, has moved his office to the new City Offices at the station, but the City Council still meets here and a great many people still get married there on a Saturday. In the old days if there was a disagreement they would often toss an aristocrat or a butcher out of the window, but nowadays the arguments are limited to the

Town Hall.
Photo by Jacques Bloemen.

displays of verbal pyrotechnics for which Leuven's Mayor is renowned. Work on the building of the Town Hall began in 1439. The original plan for an L-shaped building with a bell-tower was changed while building was still in progress. The marshy ground persuaded the later architect to rein in his vanity and trade the 'higher-than-the highest' principle for sculptural tours de force at a lower level. Thus the three small towers on each short side rise straight up, giving the Gothic Town Hall something of the appearance of a shrine. When restoration work started in the 19th century, on the advice of the French writer Victor Hugo the empty niches were filled with sculptures of important figures from Leuven's history . Some of them have never been filled. It is doubtful whether the present Mayor will ever end up there, even though his party, the Social Democrat SP.a, continues to do well in every election.

Directly opposite the Town Hall, however, God is still on duty in the Sint-Pieterskerk. A church you can never get into a single picture and which has been tinkered with quite considerably over the years. An error in the construction and the swampy ground meant that it proved impossible to build the towers tall enough. During the First World War the roof was set alight by gunfire, and in the Second World War the church was bombed. Yet people still bravely keep repairing and maintaining it. And inside there is indeed something amazing to see, even though you have to pay for it: *The Last Supper*, a famous triptych by one of the most renowned of Flemish Primitives, the painter Dirk Bouts.

Erasmus.
Photo by Jacques Bloemen.

We walk up to the main entrance of the Sint-Pieterskerk and cross to the pedestrian part of Mechelsestraat. Here stands the statue of the humanist Erasmus, staring ahead with a somewhat irritated expression. The author of *In Praise of Folly* lived in the Low Countries from 1516 to 1521 as an advisor to Charles V, and during that time he also stayed in Leuven for a while.

If we walk along Mechelsestraat and on Vismarkt turn into Busleydengang, the first narrow alley on our right, we can see what remains of the Collegium Trilingue or Three-Language College that Erasmus founded in 1518 to fulfil the request of his late friend, the humanist Hieronymus Busleyden. It was the first college to teach the three sacred languages, Greek, Latin and Hebrew, and is one of the few surviving Renaissance buildings in Leuven. In those days there was no question of teaching my main languages, Akkadian and Sumerian, or the many other dead and living languages that people can now study at the University and speak with students and professors from every part of the world.

No writers, but photographers

In a city where the university and intellectual life play such an important part you might also expect the muses to be kept busy providing all the artists with inspiration, but that is another disappointment. Many writers have spent their wild youth here, but few have stayed. And unlike the trading city of Antwerp, Leuven has no official city author or poet. In a somewhat wayward manner, every two years the Leuven arts festival Kulturama appoints a 'creative ambassador' who can then set up all sorts of projects in his or her own field. In 2006 for the first time Leuven lashed out on a 'City DJ', Jimmy de Wit. Two years later we got our own 'City Chef', Jeroen Meus, and since 2010 the photographer Marco Mertens has been hard at work inviting the people of Leuven via his website to share their best photographs with him, and also putting on his own

Museum M.
Photo by Jacques Bloemen.

exhibitions. At present it is anybody's guess who will succeed him in 2012, but since the creative ambassadors have a voice in the selection of course there is already huge speculation.

Those who still have some interest in literature, though, can dive into Schrijnmakersstraat behind Erasmus and enjoy literature from all over the world, together with a cup of coffee, in the literary café De Dry Coppen.

If we leave the statue of Erasmus behind and walk through Jodenstraatje to Fochplein , we reach our final stop in Vanderkelenstraat. Literary life in Leuven may be on the back burner, but with the 'M' (for Museum) the city has now well and truly blown the dust off its run-down art collections and locales. In September 2009, on the site of the former public library and the municipal museum, the fabulous M opened its doors, bringing together ancient and modern art. It was designed by architect Stéphane Beel, who has spread six storeys over two existing and two new buildings.

Jan Fabre, *Totem*.
Photo by Jacques Bloemen.

For once the people of Leuven, who are not known for their broad-minded approach to architecture, kept their mouths shut – even when faced with this striking cubist design. The first temporary exhibition, on Rogier van der Weyden, immediately attracted huge numbers of visitors, making it very difficult to make a reservation, and the opening hours had to be extended. But the M's permanent collection of mediaeval to 19th-century art is also worth a look. These days, of course, a measure of cross-fertilisation is essential: so the museum promises to delve into the university cellars regularly or to play host to local young artists.

And so, via M we find ourselves back on Ladeuzeplein, where the Ferris wheel suddenly no longer looks out of place beside Jan Fabre's impaled iridescent beetle. This artwork is a gift from the university to the city on the occasion of its 575th anniversary. Needless to say, not a single citizen of Leuven knows that the work is called '*Totem*'. It is simply 'That Beetle' or 'That Insect'. And there is no doubting that, underground, the muttering about phallic symbols will rumble on until the whole city is aware of it. ■

With a Poet's Eye

A Few Dutch Poems on Dutch Paintings

No painting is safe from Dutch Poets. In fact, the writing of poems based on paintings seems to have become a national sport.

From a reader's perspective, picture-poems distinguish themselves from all other poems in one very important way: the poem's source of inspiration, whether it be sculpture, painting or photography, can always be traced back to its original state. Everything changes or disappears, but a work of art remains as it is. This means that you can look at a work of art through the eyes of the poet and it is still as he saw it, at least if it hasn't suffered some calamity. You can even visit the Tate Gallery with an accompanying anthology under your arm filled with poems that were all inspired by artworks in that museum: namely Pat Adams' *With a Poet's Eye: A Tate Gallery Anthology*. And in Brussels' Museum for the Fine Arts one can not only view Brueghel's *Landscape with the Fall of Icarus* through the eyes of Auden and nine Dutch poets, but also through thirty other pairs of poetic eyes. For the *Mona Lisa* you can consult more than one hundred poets. But whoever expects that poets, by means of their picture-poems, intend to make paintings more accessible or visual to their readers, will come away feeling cheated. Most poets would agree with Rutger Kopland that a picture-poem must stand on its own two feet without the help of the painting. Indeed, it is only very rarely that poets provide illustrations of the works to which their poems owe their existence. Nevertheless, the fact remains that the combination of painting and poetry can richly contribute to our experience of the artwork as well as to our understanding of the poem it inspired.

In what follows, I would like to consider six different relationships between poet and painting: the poet P.C. Boutens' reflections on a painting of the Flemish School; Rutger Kopland's and Anna Enquist's contrasting perceptions of Pieter Brueghel's *Hunters in the Snow*; Jan Eijkelboom's self-recognition in a painting of Aelbert Cuyp; Vermeer's *View of Delft* as seen by Willem van Toorn; Ed Leeflang with his, and Rembrandt's *Self-Portrait as the Apostle Paul*, and finally Ida Gerhardt, who appropriates Jan Asselijn's *The Threatened Swan.*

We will begin with *Little Girl with a Small Dead Bird*, painted by an unknown Flemish master around the year 1520. For P.C. Boutens (1870-1943) this relatively unknown panel possessed 'eternal value' and he dedicated a poem to it in his last published volume. The painting depicts a girl of about eight years old, whose gaze is nearly mask-like. One could say that she looks disappointed, but then you allow the bird in her hands – which could perhaps symbolize the vulnerable soul or the brevity of life – to play too great a role. Or the entire painting might be explained as a symbol for the Pietà. In any case, the painting raises the question of the relationship between the girl and the little bird. Has it fallen out of its nest, was this the deliberate murder of a beloved pet, or was it the work of the cat? And, most importantly, is this the child's first confrontation with death? The verse that the old Zeeland poet wrote about his favourite painting is surprisingly simple, considering the style of most of his work; but the voice and style used here are quite appropriate as the entire poem is addressed to a child:

Anonymous, *Little Girl with a Small Dead Bird*, ca. 1520. Oil on wood, 37.7 x 29.8 cm. Royal Museum of Fine Arts, Brussels. Detail.

Little Girl with a Dead Bird *Musée des Beaux-Arts, Brussels*

Do you remember that other time,
The pain that then still was unknown,
How deeply the first hurt could sting
When you were not yet used to pain.

Now suddenly a strange cold
Pierced your body through the heart,
Froze the bird you tried to console
In your small trembling fingers.

We *did our best in word and deed,*
Yet suffered just as you, poor thing:
His own advice no man should heed
From his first step to his wedding ring.

We *were warned repeatedly*
About the sorrows that cause our tears.
We only learned through our own pain
The things that matter in the end.

For to live, my child, is to survive,
Emerge from sleep, sorrow, pain of death.
And only experience does benefit
By life's flickering signals.

Just act as if you did not hear
And live by the light of your own wit.
On the long road that brings greyness near,
No crime worse than to kill a child's spirit.

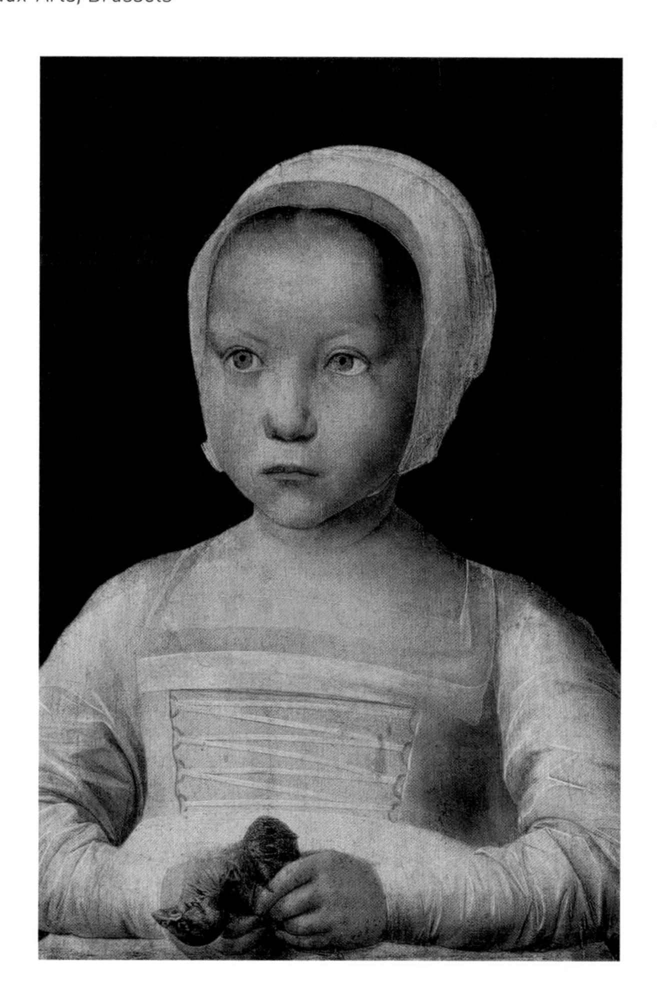

(Translated by André Lefevere and Valerie Robillard)

The conversation in the poem –which is in fact a monologue – begins in the middle of events. In the first line, there is already mention of 'the other time'. We also find that there is something concealed that directly followed the pain, which the poet refers to as 'the first hurt', but what this 'hurt' is or what caused it remains undisclosed to the reader. In the second stanza, it is apparently not the unwanted death of the bird that is caused by the child, but rather the freezing of it. In the third stanza, the speaker emphasizes that these things happen to us adults as well, especially when we try to offer council or help, and this is due to our own inability to know ourselves. It is particularly interesting that the poet here suggests that wilfulness is a character flaw that will pass with marriage ('the wedding ring'). In the fourth stanza, the speaker paraphrases a good Dutch expression: one only becomes wiser by making mistakes and not by listening to wise men. It is clear that the poet (speaker?) himself is undergoing some of the same lessons, even though he minimalises their importance in the final lines. Considering the pedantic nature of the preceding stanzas, these lines take a totally unexpected and engaging turn: the speaker says, in essence: 'Don't listen to all this moralising of mine. Just do what your heart tells you. It's a pity to spoil your innocence with the chatter of an old man.'

In the meantime, we have left the second-to-last-stanza for what it is. Here, in my opinion, lies the essence of the poem. The child is taught that life means being confronted by tragedy and that these 'emergency signals' of life can only be interpreted by one who has had experience. This would mean, then, that the girl because of her young age had not been able to understand the death of a bird.

If you look at the relationship between the painting and the poem, you see that the second part of the second stanza contains the only pictorial lines in the entire poem. You might, then, ask yourself if you could have derived the pictorial source from the poem, if the poet hadn't added *Musée des Beaux Arts, Brussels* to his title. For without this title, it might just as well have been inspired by the poet's memory of a similar lesson of life from his own father. As you have seen, Boutens has done nearly nothing with the pictorial elements in the poem; it appears that for him, the painting is merely an occasion for extracting an important lesson.

The return to the life below – but what life?

Brueghel's *Hunters in the Snow* (1565), one of the highlights of the Kunsthistorisches Museum in Vienna, belongs to a series of paintings that depict the months of the year. Art historians claim that each painting represents two months and *Hunters in the Snow* would then represent December and January, or possibly January and February. Among poets, this poem is nearly as popular as *Landscape with the Fall of Icarus*: the American poets William Carlos Williams and John Berryman, for example, each dedicated a poem to it, as did at least eight of their Dutch colleagues. Among these are Rutger Kopland (1934), still one of our most popular poets, who, under his real name – R.H. van den Hoofdakker – was a professor in Biological Psychiatry in Groningen, and Anna Enquist (1945), also a psychiatrist. Let me begin with Kopland's poem:

Brueghel, *Hunters in the Snow*, 1565. Oil on wood, 117 x 162 cm. Kunsthistorisches Museum, Vienna. Detail.

Winter by Brueghel, the hill with hunters
and dogs, at their feet the valley with the village.
Almost home, but their dead-tired attitudes, their steps
in the snow – a return, but almost as

slow as arrest. At their feet the depths
grow and grow, become wider and further,
until the landscape vanishes into a landscape
that must be there, is there, but only

as a longing is there.

Ahead of them a jet-black bird dives down. Is it mockery
of this laboured attempt to return to the life
down there: the children skating on the pond,
the farms with women waiting and cattle?

An arrow underway, and it laughs at its target.

(Translated by James Brockway)

Kopland accentuates, as Tom van Deel notes in *Looking at Poems: an Anthology of Picture Poems* (Gedichten kijken, een bloemlezing beeldgedichten, 1987), the contrast between the tiring, earth-bound return 'of the hunters to the valley where they live and the free, unrestricted flight of the bird in the air, slightly above the middle'. The hunters want to get home but it seems as though they will never reach it. Their goal seems more distant with every step they take: 'the depths / grow and grow, become wider and further', and home exists in the end as an image imprinted in the spirit, 'as a longing is there'. For the 'jet-black bird', the 'return to the life / down there' is simple; in contrast to the hunters, the bird 'laughs at its target', because reaching it is so simple to him.

Return of the Hunter

The afternoon was a paradise of light. The high
snowfield absorbed him. There was no time, no
hunger and the valley where his tired house should be
was no longer there. No guilt, no regret.

When the sun relentlessly leaves him the hunter
finds himself again, numb and angry. As for a child,
time to him becomes place, becomes distance that he
kicks away. Around his shoulders heavily nestles,

like the denied years, the killed animal. Strangling.
Thus opens the ashen valley, where people
that he knows toil with fire and wood. He hears
the quiet scraping of skates on the pond. Hates

the house where he lives and is safe. Humiliated
he bows to season and hour. The hunter flings
the treasures he brought into the dirty snow:
a bag full of death, frozen blood, cold fire.

(Translated by Tiny Hobma and Anne-Marie Petter)

Anna Enquist entitles her poem *Return of the Hunter* (in the singular), which is a subtle deviation from the title under which Brueghel's painting is also known: *The Return of the Hunters* (in the plural). Her poem seems to be more of an answer to Kopland's poem than an independent reaction to the painting. In contrast to Kopland's hunters, her hunter doesn't want to return home, although he must. After sharing in the euphoric and mystical experiences far from home depicted in the first stanza, he must return from his sought-after solitude to the valley of duties and unwanted relationships.

In the second stanza, as evening falls, he comes to his senses: 'When the sun relentlessly leaves him.' The moment of return becomes very concrete for him and is translated into the steps he still must take. It is only at the end of the second and third stanzas that the painting itself comes into view – the point at which the hunter (probably the man standing exactly between the first and second tree) struggles home with 'the killed animal'. The hunter is apparently someone who wants to forget a past that is bound up with the valley, a past that he could only forget for too short a time in that timeless 'paradise of light' – a past that has something to do with 'denied years'. He doesn't want to return to the confinement of 'the house where he lives and is safe', but he must; it is cold outside. The innocent, mystical experience in 'the high snowfield' from the first stanza can never last.

Kopland's 'dead-tired' hunters long to reach home but are unable to; Enquist's hunter doesn't want to return 'to his tired house' but he must. What is longed for in Kopland's poem, 'the return to the life below', is rejected by Enquist: 'the ashen valley, where people / that he knows toil with fire and wood'.

It is tempting to go further and to find in the last poem an answer to the first. Enquist tells Kopland that we do not want to take the familiar road, but seek the sublime moment outside the marked footpaths. That we must always return disillusioned is another matter. One psychiatrist answers another? It seems so.

Master and Servant

From Vienna to the Mauritshuis in The Hague, to the Aelbert Cuyp *Portrait of Pieter de Roovere, Lord of the Manor of Hardinxveld*, which was painted before 1652, and to Jan Eijkelboom's (1926-2008) portrait of that portrait:

Pieter de Roovere as Lord of the Manor of Hardinxveld *(Aelbert Cuyp)*

Sculptured against the sky
the man on his horse looks straight ahead
while pointing at the salmon
held below him by the servant
who stands there and looks up
at him. He lifts the gill
of the freshly caught fish
so his master, if he looks,
will see bright red, just like
the cap on the boy's head.
The master himself wears a plumed hat
of a more refined, dusky red.
The connoisseur admires the velvet
of his elegant coat. My eye
will not rest, it moves
between the horseman and the boy,
from the worn-out, still haughty
but dead-tired look
to that wide-open way of looking
timid but infinitely free.

Against a strip of scanty light
under the judgement of the clouds
the realization finally comes:
I am like both of them.

(Translated by Johanna H. Prins and Johanna W. Prins)

Aelbert Cuyp, *Portrait of Pieter de Roovere, Lord of the Manor of Hardinxveld,* before 1652. Oil on canvas, 123.5 x 154 cm. Mauritshuis, The Hague.

The Dordrecht poet, Jan Eijkelboom, begins with a description of a painting, whose creator was also from Dordrecht. In an earlier version of this poem, he emphasized the art-historical focus of his first stanza by using the words 'Sculptured against the sky', which came from a 1904 study on Cuyp done by still another citizen of Dordrecht, the art historian Jan Veth. Up to the central line of the poem, 'My eye / will not rest', the poem does indeed take on the nature of an art-historical observation. Here, the poet displays a good eye for one particular pictorial element: the red colour of the fish's gill, the hat and the plume. In the second stanza, the poem becomes more personal: the eye shifts between the master and the boy, between the weary man who has seen it all and the boy for whom everything is just beginning, and the viewer recognizes himself in both. The painting which was originally a portrait of the Lord of the Manor of Hardinxveld has, in the hands of the poet, become a double portrait of master and servant.

A woman to be slept with

We are going to stay in the Mauritshuis and spend some time on Johannes Vermeer's *View of Delft* as interpreted by Willem van Toorn (1935). Van Toorn, together with C.O. Jellema, Ed Leeflang and J. Bernlef, is one of those poets who are regularly inspired by the visual arts, just as Albert Verwey was around the turn of the nineteenth century, and Simon Vestdijk after him.

Vermeer: View of Delft

I make you appear in this.
Your shadow announces you
round a corner. Had done some shopping
in invisible alleys. Quivering

painted sunlight touches you
when you turn up on the quay.
Hatted governors are waiting
for dead vessels.

Their eyes follow you. Young miss. For certain
I'll let one of them sleep with you
tonight, if I keep you alive,
three hundred years from here.

(Translated by Ria Leigh-Loohuizen)

In this poem, Van Toorn focuses primarily on one of the two women in the left foreground of the painting, the one with the shopping basket. Tom van Deel, compiler of a collection of poems about the visual arts called *I Love the Red of the Jewish Bride (*Ik heb het Rood van 't Joodse Bruidje lief, 1988), has written a very illuminating essay about Willem van Toorn's picture-poem in *If I could paint* (Als ik tekenen kon, 1992). In this essay, he of course devotes some attention to *Vermeer: View of Delft*. Nevertheless, I am not sure whether Van Deel is right when he states that Van Toorn in his Vermeer poem 'simply creates a damsel by talking about her (...) both in the poem as well as on the canvas – whom he causes to move over Vermeer's painting for the duration of the poem'. In my opinion the damsel is already present in the painting and she is therefore not created by the poet. After she has done her shopping 'in invisible alleys', she falls into conversation with a friend 'on the quay'. This is what Vermeer shows. In the third stanza she moves off again, watched by the men. If the poet has anything to do with it, one of them will sleep with her that night. In the second stanza, the painting as a frozen moment of time, a motionless picture, is part of a simple story in which a woman is doing her shopping, is being watched and (who knows?) will be slept with. According to the poet, the city-scape must become a love story, if at all possible. The reality of the painting is changed into the poet's pipe dream.

Johannes Vermeer, *View of Delft*, ca.1660-1661. Oil on canvas. 96.5 x 115.7 cm. Mauritshuis, The Hague. Detail.

Some years ago, when I was busy compiling *An Angel Singing behind a Pillar* (Een engel zingend achter een pilaar), a collection of poems in Dutch inspired by the paintings of the Flemish and Dutch masters from the fifteenth to the eighteenth centuries, I came across the poem *Like St. Paul* in the relatively unknown volume *The Ferries* (De veren) by Ed Leeflang (1929-2008):

Like St. Paul

We stare out without hope in anyone,
our chin moves even closer to our chest.
The reference book that's in our hands
distracts, they almost let it rest.

Our forehead furrows in the mocking light,
our eyebrow, after all the peering,
in its highest arc now stands.

In our face our cheek has frozen,
and our eyes have opened wide
refusing to show scorn,
revulsion or self-reproach,
and resist the impulse so to do.

Outside, the seasons are changing:
meaningful for neighbours, but
we are alone and our gaze has taken off,
turning away from walking,
towards the mirror.

(Translated by Paul Vincent)

Is this a picture-poem or not? Being relatively well-versed in the Scriptures as I am, I had not interpreted it as a poem inspired by a painting, but rather by Paul's first epistle to the Corinthians; to be more precise, by First Corinthians 13, verse 12: 'For now we see in a glass, darkly, (...)', mainly because of the title and the first and last lines. Th elderly 'poetic I' identifies himself with the apostle Paul, onto whom he projects his feelings of loneliness, disillusionment and resignation. The 'we' which is constantly used – not the *pluralis majestatis*, but used to denote Paul as well as the 'poetic I' – draws attention to the fact that both see themselves as old and full of days. They are no longer the slightest bit interested in the outside world. They are only interested in themselves. In short: the 'poetic I' permits itself to concide with the aged, disillusioned apostle, who is pondering the past with no regrets, and who is only roused by his own reflection. The poem can be read in this way with no problem at all. However, information from the poet himself, when I confronted him with this reading and he told me that the poem refers to Rembrandt's famous *Self-portrait as the Apostle Paul* in the Rijksmuseum, Amsterdam, changes the matter.

Rembrandt, *Self-portrait as the Apostle Paul,* 1661. Oil on canvas. 91 x 77 cm. Rijksmuseum, Amsterdam.

It turns out that there is a layer between 'the poetic I' and Paul; 'we', in a complicated way, are three: Paul, Rembrandt, 'I'. At the root of this poem is not a confrontation between the poet and his reflection, but rather a self-portrait of Rembrandt. This is not something you can surmise from the poem, not even from the title *Like St. Paul*, which is the clearest indication of a possible reference to a painting. After all, you could imagine '*Self-portrait*' in front of the title *Like St. Paul* and then end up with Rembrandt (or another painter). If only the poet had made use of the attributes peculiar to Paul, as Rembrandt has, such as the sword in the fold of his cloak – symbolizing Paul's beheading in Rome – or the rolls of paper covered in Hebrew script in his hand, which probably represent Paul's epistles to the Christian communities in Asia Minor, then we could have linked the poem with a portrait of Paul, or with a painted self-portrait as Paul, and we could have come up with Rembrandt. Now we have to rely on the poet and the question is, of course, if we can trust him. If we believe him and view the poem with him as an interpretation of Rembrandt's *Self-portrait as the Apostle Paul*, then we must reconsider our idea that the first person plural used throughout the poem refers to Paul and the 'poetic I'. 'We' refers, then, to the double entity Rembrandt and the apostle. The poem, which can be read as a self-portrait of the 'poetic I' as Paul, turns out to be the poetical interpretation of one of Rembrandt's last self-portraits.

'What have you done to your children?'

We are going to stay in the Rijksmuseum and move on from Rembrandt's *Self-portrait as the Apostle Paul* (1661) to *The Threatened Swan* by Jan Asselijn, one of the most important of the so-called Italianizing Dutch painters, who painted landscapes which looked Italian, often peopled by picturesque figures such as herdsmen, merchants and tramps. *The Threatened Swan* is unique in Asselijn's oeuvre, which otherwise consists only of landscapes. After his death in 1652, the painting was changed by the adding of captions from a realistic natural tab-

Jan Asselijn,
The Threatened Swan,
before 1652.
Oil on canvas. 144 x 171 cm.
Rijksmuseum, Amsterdam.

leau – a swan defending her nest against the attack of a dog – into an allegory on the politics of Grand Pensionary Johan de Witt. In this, De Witt (the white swan) is defending the nest of eggs (the Netherlands) against an attack by the dog (England). The allegory refers to De Witt's role in the second Anglo-Dutch war (1665-1667), which ended in triumph for the Dutch. The captions which were later added to the painting are clearly legible: above the head of the dog is 'the enemy of the state', next to the swan's right foot is 'the Grand Pensionary', and on the left egg is 'Holland'.

Ida Gerhardt (1905-1997), however, in her poem *Confrontation* from *The Bracken* (De adelaarsvarens), based on Asselijn's swan, notes: 'Allegorical depiction of a terrifying swan whose nest is threatened *by people*.' Thus she is falsifying the picture to a certain extent in order to give it a different interpretation: not a historical-political one, but an ethical one. She is not concerned with the responsibility of the statesman, who ought to defend his country, but with that of parents, of whom a considerate and fit parenthood is asked. Perhaps the difficult relationship which the poet had with her mother, and which she expresses in various poems, has something to do with this attitude, and so the poem could be read as a reproach to her mother, with Asselijn's swan being held up as an example.

Confrontation
Rijksmuseum Amsterdam

The Swan of Asselijn, large as life,
spreads its wings diagonally
across the canvas and expels by force
whoever dares approach its aerie.

An archetypal swan guarding its nest,
where something barely feathered restlessly
seeks daylight and taps against the shell.

Soon it will risk the water, fearlessly.

And whoever casually passes by
or shops short in his steps
will be summoned to a brief trial.
The hearing, long delayed, begins:
'What have you done to your children?

(Translated by Johanna H. Prins and Johanna W. Prins)

Anything goes

This brief excursion has shown that a poet can do to a painting exactly what he does to anything else that inspires a poem: just about anything he wants. He can, for example, like Boutens, use it to extract a lesson about life and virtually ignore the depiction as such; he can use it to enter into a discussion with a colleague, as Anna Enquist has; he can see a self-portrait in it, as did Eijkelboom, or transform the painting into a banal love story, as Van Toorn does in his *Vermeer: View of Delft*; he can also set us off on the wrong track by telling us nothing about the source of the inspiration for the poem, as Leeflang does with his poem about Paul; and he can, as Ida Gerhardt does, falsify the reality of the painting as it suits him ...or her. In short, the poet subsumes the painting, and any other thing which actually inspires him, into his own themes and conceptual world, and, in the final analysis, he subsumes it to his own immutable personality as an artist. The main characteristic of a picture-poem for the reader is that he can return to the source of inspiration for the poem, and thus can occupy the same starting point as the poet. He can look 'With a Poet's Eye' at what the poet saw, and that's not something he can usually do. ■

Translated by Valerie Robillard

Herman Gorter (1864-1927): Poet, Lover and Revolutionary

[PAUL VINCENT]

If Herman Gorter's name (1864-1927) is still familiar to anyone outside the Low Countries, it is more likely to be as a revolutionary propagandist and an opponent of Lenin's strategy at the Third International in 1920 [1] than as the most gifted Dutch poet of his age. At home he tends to be pigeonholed as the author of the poem *May* (Mei, 1889), the anthem of the Generation of 1880, while his other, and particularly his Socialist, verse is largely neglected.

Roots

A Mennonite upbringing left its mark on Gorter's social commitment and independence of mind, while in his teenage years he was greatly influenced by the rebellious genius Multatuli (pseudonym of Eduard Douwes Dekker, 1820-1887), author of the great colonial novel *Max Havelaar* (1860). Both Gorter's emotional dependence on his mother and his attachment to, and subsequent detachment from, a succession of mentor/father figures, from the composer Diepenbrock to the German Marxist Karl Kautsky, can perhaps be attributed in part to the loss of his father, also a writer, at the age of sixteen.

The young Herman was the beneficiary of a major reform in Dutch secondary education introduced in 1864, attending a new-style high school, the Higher Civic School (HBS). Ironically, though the syllabus at these institutions was largely science and modern language-based, Gorter's great love was Classical studies, which he went on to study at Amsterdam University, where in 1889 he received his doctorate for a thesis on Aeschylus' use of metaphor (after having a more daring project on poetic inspiration rejected). Shortly afterwards he was appointed to his first post as a Classics teacher and the following year married his fiancée Wies Cnoop Koopmans, despite expressing some last-minute doubts. Those doubts were not unfounded. Though the couple remained together until his wife's death in 1916, it was an 'open' marriage, at least on Gorter's side, and a childless one. The poet's powerful erotic drive sought an outlet in two intense long-term relationships, with Ada Prins and later with Jenne Clinge Doorenbos, of which he made no secret. Jenne, herself a writer, became his editor and collaborator as well as muse ('the Spirit of Music' as the poet dubbed her in Nietzschean style).

Young Herman Gorter in 1884. Collection Letterkundig Museum, Den Haag.

Poetic début

In 1889 he also published his first Dutch poetry in the influential magazine *De Nieuwe Gids*, or New Guide, which in this period was dominated by the poet Willem Kloos (1859-1938), a radical aesthete who advocated a literature both non-sectarian and non-utilitarian. Poetry, for Kloos, was 'the supremely individual expression of the supremely individual emotion'. Kloos was deeply impressed by Gorter's 1889 début, *May* , an epic poem of some 4,000 lines, mostly in rhyming five-foot iambics (not coincidentally the metre of Keats' 'Endymion'), which soon became an iconic work of the so-called Movement of 1880. (Only fragments of this seminal poem have so far been translated into English.) Generations of Dutch secondary schoolchildren have been able to quote its opening lines:

A newborn springtime and a newborn sound:
I want this song like piping to resound
that oft I heard at summer eventide
in an old town, along the waterside –
the house was dark, but down the silent road
dusk gathered and above the sky still glowed,
and a late golden, incandescent flame
shone over gables through my window-frame.
A boy blew music like an organ pipe,
the sounds all trembled in the air as ripe
as new-grown cherries, when a springtime breeze
arises and then journeys through the trees.

This short extract immediately exhibits some of the poem's key features: vivid sensory images, a celebration of the Dutch landscape, extended Homeric similes, and the onward impulse of the lines with their frequent enjambements. In all senses the poem came as a breath of fresh air in a literary culture dominated by plodding moralistic verse, often churned out by clergymen-poets. *May*, however, is not all joyful celebration: an underlying melancholy increasingly asserts itself. Its heroine embodies the month of May and her burgeoning prime is destined to be short-lived. Her encounter with the blind Norse god Balder (for whom 'music is the soul's life') poignantly dramatises the unbridgeable dichotomy between mind and body. Whole libraries have been written on the interpretation of the poem's symbolism, debating whether the poem should be read as a variation on Nietzsche's *Birth of Tragedy from the Spirit of Music*, whether it conceals Gorter's incipient disaffection from the values of 1880, whether it portrays the incompatibility of the material and the spiritual or on the contrary presents a synthesis between them, etc. The poet himself made light of the ambiguities, declaring that:

> *I wanted to make something full of light and beautiful sound, that's all. There's a story running through it, and a bit of philosophy, but that's by accident, so to speak.* [2]

Nevertheless it is hard not to see the poem at least in part as an exercise in 'lyrical autobiography', while others have pointed to the presence of two opposing impulses throughout his work: lyrical compression and epic expansion. One of his earliest efforts was the ambitious 'Lucifer', partly inspired by his reading of Milton. There was some resistance in literary circles to Gorter's expansive mode, as found in his later larger-scale Socialist verse, *A Little Epic* (1906) and *Pan* (1916). At the other extreme is the almost *haiku*-like compression of the late love poems, *Songs* (Liedjes), most of them published posthumously, which form a private lyrical counterpoint to his public political statements:

> *All things fade quite*
> *When you dance into sight.*

Perhaps the distinction should not be seen as an absolute one: 'lyrical expansiveness' in fact characterises some of the poet's best work. As even his sternest critics conceded, Gorter was 'great in jubilation'.

Icon of a generation

Given the warm reception of *May* by most of his peers and by younger, progressive readers, Gorter might have been expected to continue in this epic vein. Instead, under the influence of the critic and novelist Lodewijk van Deyssel (1864-1952), whose response to *May* was lukewarm, the *Poems of 1890* mark a radical new departure, not only in a Dutch but in a European context. Van Deyssel had called for uncompromising artistic individualism, or 'sensitivism', which was to record fleeting, fragmentary moments of experience with an almost mystical intensity. Gorter's collection, in which there are parallels with Rimbaud's late work, is in part an attempt to realise Van Deyssel's vision.

International Meeting of the SDAP (Social Democratic Workers Party, founded in 1894) at Watergraafsmeer (14/8/1904). Gorter (in the centre) was one of the speakers, along with Troelstra and Wijnkoop.

The result is a series of eighty-seven poems, some of only two lines (for example, 'You're a dusky white lily girl, /You're a butterfly velvet swirl.') and none longer than a few pages, still retaining a thread of rhyme, mostly in full rhyming couplets. (It needs to be stressed in this context that unlike elsewhere, and specifically in the Anglo-Saxon world, poetic modernism in the Low Countries is not synonymous with blank or free verse like that of Eliot or Yeats. Attachment to rhyme persists in such interwar poets as Martinus Nijhoff and after the Second World War in the remarkable work of Gerrit Achterberg.) Set against this are irregular line lengths and syntax, a radical use of neologism, synaesthesia, surging eroticism, a haunting fragmentary musicality and occasional astonishingly simple and direct love poems. Gorter's explosive and sometimes tortured expressionism recalls that of his contemporary Van Gogh. This linguistic extremism is one of the main challenges for the translator.[3] Gone is the vaguely Classical and Norse framework of *May*, possible the legacy of Gorter's close friend, the composer Alphons Diepenbrock (1862-1921), a keen Wagnerian. This is a celebration of life in a different key but, as in *May*, beneath the energy and assertiveness there lurks a sense of alienation and even despair.

The contrast with the work of his first mentor Kloos is striking. While Kloos' solipsism ('Deep in my inmost thoughts a god I tower') is expressed in conventional forms like the sonnet and is autumnal and elegiac in mood, while Gorter's energy is life-affirming – he was a keen sportsman and outdoor enthusiast – and 'his' season is unquestionably spring. The following poem evokes the parallel approach of spring and of the beloved:

The spring comes from afar, I hear it come hither
and the trees hear too, the tall trees that shiver,
and the tall skies, the heavenly skies,
the tingle-light skies, the blue-and-white skies,
shiver skies.

Oh I hear her come,
oh I feel her come
and I'm filled with fright
at trembling desires, all bright,
just about to break...

However, exaltation alternates with a perplexed alienation that can assume almost surreal form:

... Across the world's face
things were probably alike,
the world and the human race
are scarcely alive.

I walked and watched the scene
scared and content,
below, ever loyal and keen,
my footsteps bent.

Changing course

The sense of a disintegrating world and an increasingly isolated self became so strong in Gorter that after 1890 he began, like a number of his contemporaries, to look inwards in search of a unifying philosophical framework. He found this briefly in Spinozan thought, which stressed the oneness of all being, but still felt disconnected from the huge social and political struggles then convulsing Europe that were to culminate in the First World War and the Russian Revolution. A collection of 1895 (*School of Poetry II, 2*) ends with a cry of anguish:

Oh God! The side I'm standing on is wrong.
I'm going under.
My love has come to naught.

In 1897 he resolved to act and joined the fledgling Social Democratic Workers' party (SDAP), and his poetry now extolled the triumph of the revolution, sometimes in a naïve mode that provoked mockery from his former literary allies:

The working class dances a great round
along the shore of the world's Ocean...

His inspiration was henceforth the glorious future rather than the elusive, vanishing present; whereas the bourgeois individual was isolated, the Socialist individual will be one with his fellow men. Formally, Gorter's verse becomes noticeably more regular, often reverting to the sonnet form, and his imagery more conventional.

Gorter sailing with Jeanne Clinge Doorenbos (Loosdrecht/Kaag, 1919).

In 1909, tiring of the SDAP's constitutional gradualism, he left to form the splinter SDP (the nucleus of the later Dutch Communist Party). In 1920, having travelled secretly to Moscow for the Third International, after an epic six-week journey, partly hidden in the hold of a ship repatriating Russian prisoners-of-war, he addressed a critical Open Letter to Lenin – in response to Lenin's earlier scathing attack on 'Leftists' in his *Teething Troubles of Communism* (1920). Gorter argued for a different revolutionary strategy in Western Europe from that adopted in Russia (where, for example, the status of the peasantry was very different), an end to the opportunistic use of parliamentary and union structures, and an intelligentsia-led campaign of direct action. Gorter's 'bottom-up' proposals were laughed out of court, especially by Trotsky.

Gorter's propaganda skills had been acknowledged by Lenin before their clash [4] and a steady stream of articles, pamphlets and books continued to flow from his pen, appearing at home and abroad in such publications as Sylvia

Gorter, standing on the left, with his Cricket Club, ca. 1880.

Pankhurst's *The Workers' Dreadnought*, where he proposed a Fourth Workers' International to oppose the centralism of Moscow (1921). Most influential was undoubtedly his widely translated *Historical Materialism Explained for Workers* (1908). While conceding that truths are historically determined, this work reveals Gorter's belief in a core of dynamic individualism that was anathema to the Bolshevik leadership but inspired free spirits in the Marxist movement. 'We do not make history of our own free will. But... we do make it... not through blind fate, but through living society.'

Interestingly, the book's greatest and most lasting impact may have been in China, where his committed translator, Li Da, used the German and Japanese translations to produce his version and wrote extensively to promote Gorter's reservations about economic determinism. One possible convert, direct or indirect, to the cause may have been the young Mao Zedong. [5]

Distantiation from the Movement of 1880

In literature, Gorter disowned the individualism of his former allies in the *New Guide* group in his 'Critique of 1880' (1897-1900) and in a series of critical essays in *The Great Poets* (collected posthumously in 1935), he extolled figures like Aeschylus, Shakespeare and especially Shelley, who combined sensibility with revolutionary fervour. It is in this work that he gives his striking, if simplified, definition of the unconscious – he had dismissed Freud's explorations as a bourgeois distraction:

> *The unconscious is not, as bourgeois writers believe, an unknowable, mysterious power. It is perfectly knowable, and consists of three forces: the urge to self-preservation or love of self, the sexual urge or love for woman, and the social urge or love for the community.*

Are poetry and politics compatible?

Gorter's principal poetic work after his conversion to Marxism is the epic *Pan* (1912, rev. ed. 1916). In it Gorter unfolds a Utopian vision of a post-revolutionary world, generally playing down the necessary intervening violence and bloodshed, though the second expanded edition of 1916 does allude to the pointless slaughter of the international working class on the battlefields of the First World War:

> *... Choked in the gases, slaughtered by*
> *Bullets, torn asunder by mines*
> *The Workers lay strewn on the earth.*
> *Sacrificed by their rulers and omnipotent*
> *Capital, to bring them Possession*
> *Of the Earth the Workers lay*
> *Dead and dismembered all across the Earth*
> *The earth was full in the glorious light of May*
> *And the glittering sea was full of their floating*
> *Corpses, millions and millions,*
> *Such as the world had never seen...*

The sincerity of Gorter's compassion, anger and sense of waste is patent, but compared to, say, the raw immediacy of a Wilfred Owen, these lines seem distant and generalised – as a Socialist in the neutral Netherlands Gorter saw the war as a capitalist-orchestrated distraction from the rising tide of revolution.

Gorter was accused by some of having quit literature for the simplifications of dialectical materialism, but he himself saw his work as a continuum. In his socialist poems we hear the voice of a benign revolutionary anxious to share his joy in the world with all classes. His epic *Pan* ends with a moving renewed commitment to the art of poetry:

With my heart's blood I've lived for you,
Dear poetry, and, now death comes closer by,
Now I want to tell you one last time.
From childhood on I felt you, poetry,
I can remember nothing of which you weren't
Part. The reflection of my thoughts,
That I sensed in all things, was you.
The sweet murmur of the sea, my Mother's voice,
The gait of my comrades, the light
Of the world. People walking. The night.
They all mattered only for your sake. –
It was for your sake too that I loved. –
Love itself meant nothing but for your sake.
The body's deepest joy meant nothing to me.
Women's dark womb meant nothing to me.
The oblivious self-giving meant nothing,
Except that I found deep in their womb,
Deep in the infinite obscurity
Nothing but you – you, you, dear poetry.

Gorter was a formative influence on his contemporary Jan Hendrik Leopold (1865-1925), and on the post-Second World War generation of 1950s poets, especially Lucebert (pseudonym of Lubertus Jacobus Swaanswijk, 1924-1994), who defiantly borrows the name of one of Gorter's collections, 'School of Poetry', for his own didactic 'little revolution' in literature. Gorter remains one of the greatest love poets in Dutch; it is no accident that in both his very first preserved poem and in the one he finished just before he died, love is central. Indeed, '*Liefde*/love' is the very last word he wrote as a poet, recalling the final line of the masterpiece of his beloved Dante: *'l'amor che move il sole e l'altre stelle'*. ■

NOTES

1. H. Gorter, 'Offener Brief an den Genossen Lenin', *Kommunistische Arbeiter-Zeitung* (Berlin, August-September 1920).

2. To his uncle K. Gorter, 23 March 1889.

3. The English critic Edmund Gosse, whose background essay 'The Dutch Sensitivists' prefaced both the English translation of Louis Couperus' novel *Noodlot (Footsteps of Fate*, 1891) and the US edition of Couperus' *Eline Vere* (1892), derived most of his information from the young writer Frederik van Eeden (1860-1932), very much a literary insider. However, Gosse made one spectacularly erroneous claim: '... the Dutch seem ... to leave their mother-tongue unassailed, and to be as intelligible as their inspiration allows them to be.' Even the most cursory reading of *Poems of 1890* would have corrected that misapprehension.

4. Letter of 5 May, 1915, Lenin, *Collected Works* 43, Moscow, 1977, pp. 453-454a.

5. N. Knight, 'Herman Gorter and the Origins of Marxism in China', *China Information* 2005, 19, 381-412.

Frozen Emptiness

The Work of Koen van den Broek

[ANNE-MARIE POELS]

In 2008 the Flemish artist Koen van den Broek (b. 1973, Bree) won first prize for the best one-man show at Art Brussels, Belgium's contemporary art fair, with his presentation *Who will lead us?* Paradoxically, the show was put on not by a Belgian gallery but by his gallery in Cologne, Figge von Rosen. This is typical of Koen van den Broek's career which, initially at least, seemed to be developing at two speeds: while the artist immediately reached great heights abroad, in Belgium the attitude was a hesitant 'wait and see'. By 2006 his work was already to be found in a number of foreign collections, while of the Belgian museums of contemporary art only the one in Ostend then possessed work by him.

International

Perhaps Koen van den Broek is himself responsible for this situation. After all, it was he who in 1998 chose to exchange Belgium temporarily for the United States to seek inspiration there. At that time he had come to a dead end in his work. From highly expressive paintings produced under the influence of Jean-Michel Basquiat in the mid-'90s, he had started to simplify, ending up with minimalist works, made after drawings, with a single little house, the shape of a tree, or some lines on a white canvas – literally point zero.

He had by then already been enrolled at various institutions: first spending two years studying engineering and architecture at Leuven and then – resolutely opting for painting – two years at the Royal Academy of Fine Arts in Antwerp and another two at the Sint-Joost Academy of Visual Arts in Breda. Neither in Antwerp – where he had to repeat his first year and was sent away at the end of it – nor in Breda was he appreciated by his teachers.

Disappointed by his academy experience, but convinced of his own ability, he boldly took the entrance exam for the Higher Institute of Fine Arts (then still in Antwerp), where he was immediately accepted and had a studio between 1997 and 2000. "The Institute was a very good experience. That's where I met people like Jan Debbaut, who later went to work for the Tate in London. We were a good class: Wim Catrysse was there during the same period, and Charif Benhelima." He also decided, fresh from the Institute, to acccept the invitation

Koen van den Broek, *Wing*, 1999. Oil on canvas, 200 x 300 cm. © The artist and Galerie Figge von Rosen, Cologne.

of Jay Jopling of the White Cube in London to exhibit there. This exhibition, *Borders* (2001), ended up as part of an international selection, *Art to See*. In other words, Koen van den Broek simply skips the step which is the normal route for most artists - gaining acceptance abroad via a Belgian gallery: he is catapulted directly into the international art scene.

The photograph as source material

In 2007 Koen van den Broek wrote of the time when he left for the United States: "I was inspired by the great figures from art history and looking for a new challenge. I thought the art scene at the time was too predictable and I was convinced that somewhere on this planet there had to be a painter who had a different approach, someone who really dared to put the medium of painting up for discussion." He was looking for a new way of painting, something different from the European way. "Everyone was painting very much in the same manner. Either from photos, the way Richter painted, or from maps and their keys, which led to a schematic way of painting." In America he hoped to find a measure of freshness.

Although Van den Broek had to conclude that on the other side of the ocean they paint in exactly the same way, albeit with rather more colour, his stay there still provided him with the inspiration he sought, and in more than one

Koen van den Broek, *Viaduct*, 2002. Oil on canvas, 280 x 420 cm. © The artist and White Cube, London.

way. For instance, he discovered a method that gave him something to go by in his painting. While up till then he had avoided the use of photography, as being 'too obvious, since everyone was doing it', he now bought a camera and began taking photos that would provide source material for his paintings. Being taken through the lens of his camera, which creates a distance between him and the outside world, the photos provide their own frame.

'When I look through a camera, I have the feeling that the world becomes frozen, even though I may be standing in the middle of a busy city like New York. Aided by that sense of distance, I start looking for images.' Van den Broek thinks it is important to take the photographs himself and thus put forward his vision of reality. His background in architecture is clear to see when he photographs the urban landscape with its buildings, streets, sidewalks, viaducts – but he also photographs details, like the shadow on the ground, the wing of an aircraft, the bend in a road, a lonely cabin in a deserted landscape ... roll after roll of film, from which he later makes a selection.

The artist may base himself on reality, yet he never literally shows it. That is due to the translation process, from reality to photograph to painting, in which all superfluous details are jettisoned. And especially because of the odd way of framing he chooses for his photographs. That is particularly noticeable in the *Borders* that meander like a constant thread through his oeuvre. This series is made up of paintings with ground-level details in which one can observe sidewalk kerbs and drains and the edges of fields - narrow bands of red, yellow or blue that guide your eye down the canvas and separate the different blocks of colour.

There are never any people on these canvases, only elements that imply their existence: the buildings they erect, the roads they build, the urban landscapes they create. Figures, to Van den Broek, are disturbing elements that break up his emptiness. Absence, he has already made clear, is more important in his work than presence. *Ghost Truck* (1999), a painting of an abandoned truck in a desolate landscape, is a good example of this.

Building up the space around us with a few lines within the space of his canvas and working from photographs that depict reality, Van den Broek creates paintings that straddle the borderline between the figurative and the abstract – sometimes it is only the title that brings them back to reality. *Eighth Avenue* (1999), for example, consists roughly of one black and one white block, representing a pavement and a building. Except for the title, nothing in this image refers to the long avenue that connects North and South in New York City.

Sabbatical

The year 2006 brought a period of doubt. With his constant fear of falling into the trap of merely continuing to produce, he again found himself in a dead end ('I thought that my way of working might become predictable'), so he decided to stop painting altogether. He also moved, from a studio with white walls throughout to one with hardly any white wall surface. "I suddenly had to buy an easel." The situation made him think about the purpose of his work and to go back to its foundation, his first paintings. On the basis of these old works he made a series of new paintings, *Angle*, which are completely disconnected from their photographic source material and do not refer to any geographical location. Because of this the details in the paintings, unlike, for example, the kerbs in the *Borders* series, are totally detached from their background and seem almost to float in a vacuum. For Van den Broek it was a way to find out whether a painting, even when disconnected from reality, could still hold up.

Although after *Angle* the artist again reverted to photographs as source material, the influence of the series can also be detected in his most recent work. The objects he paints now are treated more independently of their surroundings than before. Stripped of all superfluous detail, they create a sense of space. More than ever, Koen van den Broek is balancing on the borderline between abstract image and representation of reality.

Collaboration

During his stay in the United States in the late '90s, Koen van den Broek also found inspiration in the dynamic art scene of Los Angeles. Compared to New York, when it came to contemporary art the city was then still the underdog - until then art had been very badly served there, certainly when compared with film and

Koen van den Broek, *Hillstreet*, 2008. Oil on canvas, 200 x 300 cm. © The artist and Galerie Figge von Rosen, Cologne.

music. But as a result of this the people he met there were a lot freer: they operated quite independently of the official art world and were not afraid to take risks.

Van den Broek got to know some interesting artists there, among them Mike Kelley, Ed Ruscha, Charles Ray and John Baldessari. And he encountered a mentality that was much more generous than he had been accustomed to in his own country: he was invited to studios, attended dinners and was taken to museums and galleries where he was introduced. Through Jan Debbaut he made the acquaintance of John Baldessari – a contact that developed into a friendship and years later, in 2008, would lead to a collaboration. Together the two artists created a series of works, *This an Example of That,* with Baldessari sending Van den Broek a number of enlarged black-and-white stills from old B-films to which Van den Broek then takes his brush. He didn't paint over the images but added stripes, blocks of colour and various accents, which prompt one to read the images in a different way. The works remain recognisable as photos, but at the same time become part of the pictorial abstraction that is so typical of Koen van den Broek's output.

Baldessari also inspired the artist to accept the invitation of director Bart De Baere of Antwerp's Museum of Contemporary Art to organise a show from the Museum's collection. In the spirit of the exhibition *Magritte and Contemporary Art: The Treachery of Images* compiled by Baldessari for the Los Angeles County Museum of Art in 2007, Van den Broek in *Fantasy* looked for links and similarities between different works, oeuvres and artistic practices and made connections as only an artist can.

Koen van den Broek, *Museum*, 2008. Oil on canvas, 89 x 115 cm. © The artist and Galerie Figge von Rosen, Cologne.

Nor does Van den Broek shrink from less obvious collaborations. With Fred Bervoets, the one-time teacher at the Antwerp Academy – who never taught Van den Broek but did visit him in his studio and constantly encouraged him to continue painting during his years at the Academy – he creates a number of paintings in 2007. It may seem an odd combination, the expressive work of Bervoets and the near-minimalist details of Van den Broek, but in Van den Broek's view they have a similar outlook. 'Art is about making decisions. It's not *how* you paint, but *what,* that's important. Every painting needs a reason to exist. If you have nothing to say, you shouldn't create anything.'

And even less likely is the scenery he designed in 2008 for Pol Heyvaert's stage play *René* about his uncle René Heyvaert. An artist, who like Van den Broek has a background in architecture and with whom, for that if no other reason, he feels a great affinity.

Making up for lost time

The collaboration with Antwerp Museum in the form of an exhibition put together by Van den Broek and the invitation to design the scenery for a play: these are just two indications that Koen van den Broek has been making up for lost time in his own country and is being received there as an artist with enthusiasm. His paintings are now also to be found in the collections of the various museums of contemporary art in Belgium. 'I think that at first my work

Koen van den Broek, *The Edge #3*, 2009. Oil on canvas, 120 x 180 cm. © The artist and Galerie Figge von Rosen, Cologne.

was regarded as too easy. I have never worked with political or sociological propositions. My work looks very straightforward, but it has a different kind of layering, one that is harder to take in; that's why my paintings were regarded with suspicion. But they couldn't go on ignoring me. Artist friends would talk about me and I was being exhibited in leading galleries - it's no small thing of course when at the age of twenty-seven you are asked to come up with the closing piece for an exhibition at MOMA in San Francisco on the influence of Matisse on art history.'

In Spring 2010 the Municipal Museum of Contemporary Art in Ghent presented the first major exhibition of Koen van den Broek in Belgium, with new paintings and work from the previous decade: not only paintings from collections in Belgium and London, but also canvases that had to be flown in from, for example, San Francisco and Sydney. *Curbs & Cracks* was built around some well-defined clusters of works that are related by their form, theme or content. Van den Broek was assisted by curator Andrew Renton, who is attached to the prestigious Goldsmith's College in London and specialises in contemporary painting, in providing a fresh outlook on his work.

The Royal Museum of Fine Arts in Antwerp also scored a first, again in early 2010: here, in a small project called *Preview*, works on paper by the artist were shown for the first time. These are works Van den Broek created a year earlier in a studio in a Case Study house in Los Angeles, not only to find out if he could really create new work there (an earlier experience of working in a studio in Los Angeles had not gone well since he had been quite unable to work there) but also to find out whether working on paper was something for him. He wanted to achieve a certain spontaneity in this way and surprise himself once again.

Since the exhibitions at the museums in Antwerp and Ghent, paintings by Koen van den Broek have also been shown at two big group exhibitions: the *14th Vilnius Painting Triennial: False Recognition*, at the Contemporary Art Centre in Vilnius, Lithuania, and the *Biennale of Painting: Beyond Sublime*, in both the Dhondt-Daemens Museum and the Roger Raveel Museum.

In September 2010 Koen van den Broek again had - for the first time since the results of his collaboration with John Baldessari were shown there - an exhibition of new paintings at his Belgian Gallery Greta Meert. The works were based on photographs taken in the immediate vicinity of The Geffen Contemporary at MOCA (Museum of Contemporary Art) in Los Angeles, and once again presented highly abstracted images of its surroundings: a viaduct over a freeway, the shadows cast by a number of buildings, the kerb of a sidewalk. ■

Translated by Pleuke Boyce

FURTHER READING

Crack: Koen van den Broek Painting (Wouter Davids ed.)
Lannoo, Tielt/Valiz, Amsterdam, 2010

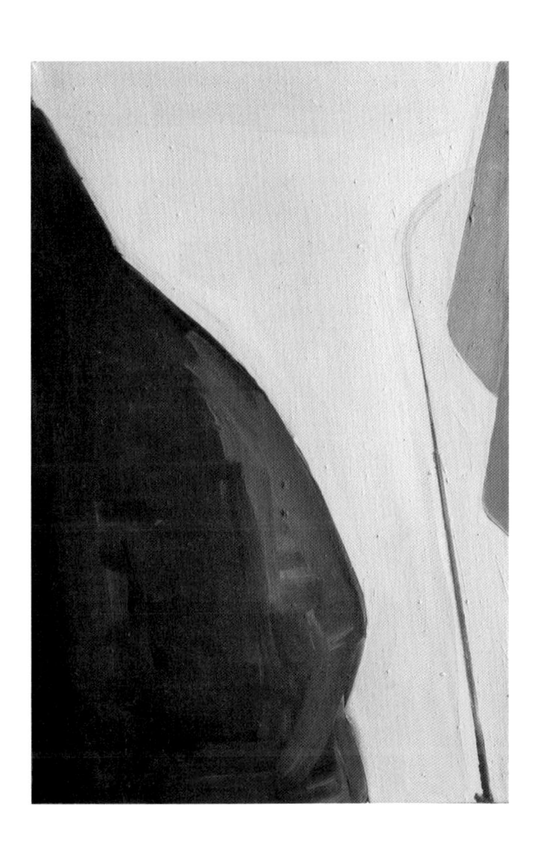

Koen van den Broek, *Pitstop*, 2009. Oil on canvas, 75 x 50 cm. © The artist and Galerie Figge von Rosen, Cologne.

A Handful of Maeterlinck from Wales

Maurice Maeterlinck is the answer to a quiz question: who is the only Belgian ever to have won the Nobel Prize for Literature? Yes, it was Maeterlinck, a century ago, in 1911. Half a century ago, when I was on a European Literature course at the university in Ghent, the city where he was born, the name Maeterlinck (1862-1949) was never mentioned. He was Flemish and wrote in French, in 1914 found himself on the Catholic index of forbidden books and at the start of his career as a writer moved to France for good. Education and the cultural life of Flanders had been 'Dutchified' in the first half of the twentieth century. All those Flemings who wrote in French, and Maeterlinck in particular, were sidelined: they were still the object of academic study (often outside Flanders), but were no longer read by the general public. Not even by the more limited group of professional readers, among whom I must count myself. But chance played a part in changing this.

Twenty-five years ago I visited the book village of Hay-on-Wye in South Wales. In an old cinema that had been converted into a secondhand bookshop I picked up my handful of Maeterlinck. A small pile of five books. They were fine little books with hard cloth covers and one was even bound in leather. They gave off the delicious aroma of mature dust and all five volumes suffered from brown age marks, which in any English book catalogue would have earned them the damning description of 'slightly foxed'. Without much thought I got out the round sum of five pounds and took possession of this pile of Maeterlincks. Translated into English. Why does one do such things? A vague sense of guilt, perhaps, as occasionally arises when one sees books by well-known writers one has not yet read. And after all, this was a writer from my home town *and* a Nobel Prizewinner. A typical encounter with a compatriot abroad? People with whom you would otherwise never exchange a word are greeted as old acquaintances. It must have been something like that: I clasped Maurice to my bosom.

On arriving home I took the package from my luggage and subjected the books (octavo: 11 by 17 cm) to a thorough examination. None of the titles was familiar. There was a short biography of the writer and all the books had been published shortly before or during the First World War. In one of them I even found an *Ex Libris* decorated with military paraphernalia: a revolver, sabre and medal, plus a rudimentary WWI landscape with a ruin and the skeletons of trees. The name was Gordon Furze, and written in pencil above it was 'from A.H. Dickinson 1/8/1916'. Had these books once lain in a British officer's knapsack? Had they picked up their damp stains in the trenches? Books should have a black box that records their history. What was I going to do with these impulse purchases? I picked them up in one hand and looked at the shades of colour in their spines: grey, rust-brown and greenish, with gold lettering. A fine set. I couldn't find the right place for them in the bookcase so for the time being I put this quintet amongst the porcelain in a small English glass case. They lay there exuding their scent for twenty-five years. They survived a house-move and were then returned to the same place.

And then these dormant little books were brought back to life. First of all there was a play entitled *Maeterlinck* at Ghent's civic theatre that irritated me immensely. Maeterlinck wrote a couple of dozen plays, hardly any performances of which are ever given in his own city or country, and then they had the nerve to make a collage on his life and work which at no time referred to the

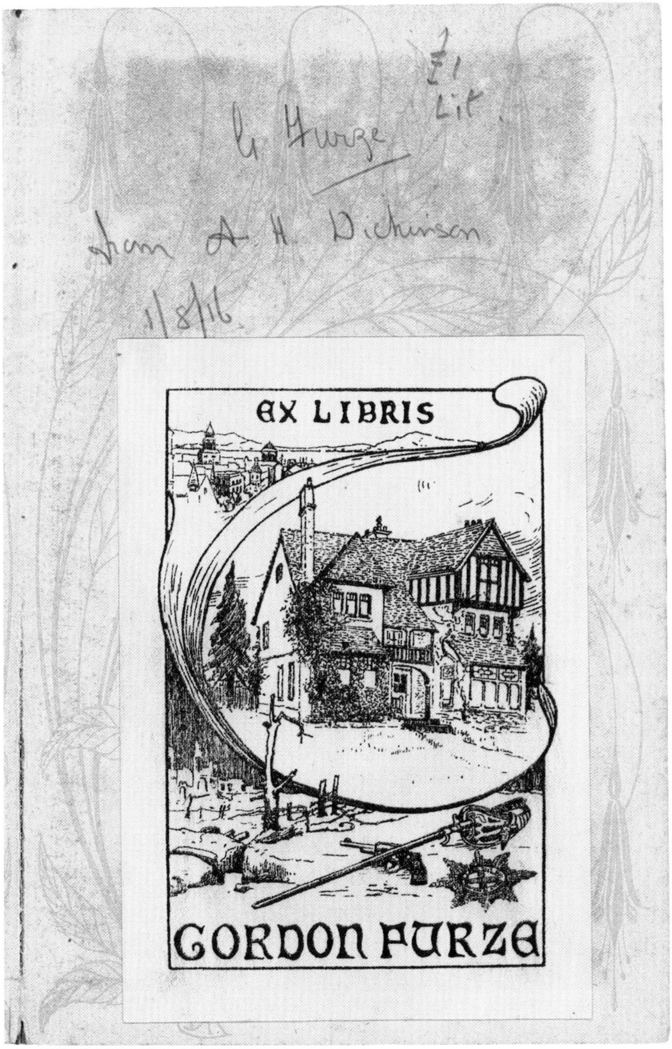

Ex Libris in *The Treasure of the Humble*, translated by Alfred Sutro, Pocket Edition, December, 1915.

Saint-Barbara College, Ghent, run by the Jesuits. Photo of the "Rhetoric" class, i.e. the final year of secondary school. Maeterlinck is seated first on the right. The symbolist poet Charles Van Lerberghe is the second from the left in the second row. Grégoire le Roy, also a writer, is the second from the right in the same row.

essence of his message or dramatic work. Maeterlinck was the first and most important representative of symbolism in the theatre and is seen as an inspiration for such theatrical innovators as Beckett and Ionesco. Why couldn't the repertory theatre in the city of his birth present some authentic Maeterlinck rather than this odd cocktail of words and images for which the writer really only provided an excuse? Fortunately, the theatre-goers of Ghent were compensated a month later by two French-language productions brought in from abroad: *Pelléas et Mélisande* by the Comédie de Reims and *Les Aveugles* by the UBU company from Montreal. The former was an unadventurous, fairly traditional performance. The elements that continue to resound are its repetitions and echoes, techniques to which Beckett and Pinter have accustomed us. It was the latter play that was the big surprise. The Canadian company had made it into a fascinating multimedia production. It is a one-act play set on an island. A group of blind people led by an old priest has lost its way in a wood. While they are resting the priest dies. The blind people aren't aware of it, and bombard the audience and each other with existential questions.

> *Quelqu'un sait-il où nous sommes?*
> *D'où venez-vous?*
> *Pourquoi êtes-vous venus ici?*
> *Qu'allons-nous faire? Où irons-nous?*

This Litany of Lost Souls was delivered by the projected faces of twelve actors who, with increasing urgency, confronted the audience with their metaphysical fears. Anyone looking for the origins of *Waiting for Godot* and *le drame d'attente* was offered it on a plate here.

A few weeks later, when friends were visiting, I told them about these Maeterlinck plays and one way or another the five English Maeterlincks found themselves being used as evidence. They were out of the case now, and they stayed out. At first I started just browsing through them, but that changed into reading. Systematic reading. But before I say any more about that, I'll give you a brief introduction to the 'Wales Five'.

Gérard Harry, *Maeterlinck: A Biographical Study*, George Allen & Sons, London 1910.

This 'biographical study' is the first edition of the English translation and is recognised as the first biography of this writer. Gérard Harry was born in Paris of English parents and established himself in Brussels as a journalist, where he made friends with Maeterlinck. In 1890 he translated *Princesse Maleine* into English. This was very topical, because *Princesse Maleine* was the first play by Maeterlinck to be reviewed by the authoritative French critic Octave Mirbeau, who praised it extravagantly on the front page of *Le Figaro* on 24th August 1890: '*... supérieure en beauté à ce qu'il a de plus beau dans Shakespeare*.' And Mirbeau didn't write this after seeing a performance, but after only reading the play.

Maurice Maeterlinck, *The Treasure of the Humble*, George Allen & Unwin, London 1915.

The English translation of *Le Trésor des Humbles* (1896), a collection of essays, was first published in 1897. By 1915 it had already been reprinted fourteen times: Maeterlinck was a bestselling author. The collection was dedicated to the French actress and opera singer Georgette Leblanc, who was Maeterlinck's partner from 1895 to 1918. The most important piece is 'The Tragical in Everyday Life', a sort of manifesto for his early plays ('*le premier Maeterlinck*').

Maurice Maeterlinck, *Wisdom and Destiny*, George Allen, London, 1911.

A translation of *La Sagesse et la Destinée*. The French edition appeared in 1898 and the first edition of the translation came out in the same year, which once again proves how popular Maeterlinck was in England. By 1911 the translation had been reprinted nine times. Unlike *The Treasure of the Humble*, this collection does not consist of separate essays, but of 112 short chapters in which the author unfolds his philosophy of life.

Maurice Maeterlinck, *Life and Flowers*, George Allen, London, 1914.

A translation of *L'Intelligence des Fleurs*. The French edition came out in 1907 and the first edition of the English translation appeared in the same year. A fairly heterogeneous collection which includes essays on boxing (surprisingly one of the writer's hobbies) and making perfume (Maeterlinck lived for a while in the perfume town of Grasse). The *pièce de résistance* is 'The Intelligence of Flowers', the title piece in the French collection.

Maurice Maeterlinck, *Death*, Methuen, London, 1911.

The fifth book is the thinnest and the most intriguing. It appeared in 1911 and is a first edition. In that year there was as yet no French edition available. It was only in 1913 that a full French version of this essay, *La Mort*, came out. Shortly afterwards, in January 1914, Maeterlinck was put on the Catholic Index. Celebrated in Sweden in 1911, denounced by Rome in 1914. The year of publication is notable: a year prior to the outbreak of the First World War. Death is omnipresent in his early playwriting, so it comes as no surprise that the essayist also focused on the subject. Shortly before the greatest slaughter in history would begin. Once again the question arises: had this book ever lain in a soldier's knapsack?

Théo Van Rysselberghe, *La Lecture*, 1903-1904, detail. The man in red, reading, is Emile Verhaeren. Maeterlinck is sitting on the right. Left of him is the French writer André Gide.

Wounded to death, but radiant and free

A thousand pages of Maeterlinck in English and three stage performances. I was ready for Maeterlinck in the original. An excellent way to approach this was through the quite recent anthology (1999) by Paul Gorceix published by Complexe in Brussels, two volumes of which are devoted to the plays and one to poetry and the essays. I also got hold of the biography by W.D. Halls: *Maurice Maeterlinck. A Study of his Life and Thought*. An outstanding biography, but with two shortcomings: it dates from 1960 and is quite concise, comprising only 200 pages. There is still no 'standard' biography.

As a newly-graduated jurist, Maeterlinck stayed in Paris for several months in 1885, ostensibly to study the pleas of the French lawyers in court. However, he spent most of his time in literary cafes and one of the people he met there was the poet Villiers de l'Isle Adam, under whose influence he turned radically against realism. The theatre that Maeterlinck advocated was intended to restore wonder and mystery. To achieve this he recommended two techniques: 'dialogue of the second degree' and 'the third character'.

Dialogue of the second degree is any dialogue that doesn't contribute directly to the unfolding of the plot. These dialogues are an unconscious exchange of intuitions between congenial characters. As chance would have it, the Flemish director Ivo Van Hove, in connection with his production of *Cries and Whispers*, a scenario by Ingmar Bergman he had adapted for the stage, gave a perfect explanation of what a dialogue of the second degree is: 'Bergman talks about something that no one wants to experience, but which everyone is faced with: death. Not in grand contemplation, but in short, simple sentences such as 'Come here for a moment' and 'Shall I wash you?'. Behind this lies a world of silence, full of fear, frustration and yearning.' (*De Standaard*, 20th March 2009). And the third character? This is precisely the mystery that is evoked by one of these dialogues of the second degree. The magic of theatre works when the ordinary words – with all their hesitations, repetitions and silences – are able to evoke the mystery of existence. When seemingly trivial dialogue is able to give presence to this third character, which is mystery, fate, death or some such. In many cases you also sense the characters' inability to express their deepest thoughts and feelings. In 'Silence', the opening essay in *The Treasure of the Humble*, Maeterlinck suggests that the highest form of communication between two people – especially two lovers – consists of silence: 'Speech is of Time, Silence is of Eternity'.

One of the most inspired pieces in this Welsh assortment is the long essay 'The Intelligence of Flowers'. Here, Maeterlinck repeatedly and convincingly commits the sin of the 'pathetic fallacy' (attributing human qualities to natural phenomena). He writes for example of the problem of the *Vallisneria*, a small water plant that lives at the bottom of ponds until it wants to reproduce. The female flower then slowly uncoils its stem until it reaches the surface of the water, where it subsequently blossoms. The male flowers in the surrounding water try to imitate this, but their stems are too short and they get stuck half-way. How do they solve this?

Maeterlinck as motorcyclist, 1909.

Did the males foresee the disillusion to which they would be subjected? One thing is certain, that they have locked up in their hearts a bubble of air, even as we lock up in our souls a thought of desperate deliverance. It is as though they hesitated for a moment; then, with a magnificent effort, the finest, the most supernatural that I know of in the annals of the insects and the flowers, in order to rise to happiness they deliberately break the bond that attaches them to life. They tear themselves from their peduncle and, with an incomparable flight, amid pearly beads of gladness, their petals dart up and break the surface of the water. Wounded to death, but radiant and free, they float for a moment beside their heedless brides and the union is accomplished.

Has anyone ever attributed human feelings more empathically to an insignificant water plant? Maeterlinck does not consider this a 'fallacy', but the central idea in his world-view. Man and nature are inspired by the same forces. It is above all in *Wisdom and Destiny* that he gives shape to this philosophy. Reason is not, in his view, the supreme human faculty. There are many situations and problems that reason is unable to grasp. He writes of intuitions that emerge from the unconscious and form the basis for many moral choices. When we do good it sometimes goes against all reason, and in everything related to love our decisions are also rarely informed by reasonable considerations. And yet we do not drift through our lives. These intuitions enable us to reconcile ourselves with our destiny in life. We are able to draw on our soul, our unconscious, for the necessary strength. Maeterlinck saw the soul and the unconscious as synonymous. The unconscious is no Pandora's Box, as Freud thought, packed with repressed sexual desires, but a source of wisdom, the most profound basis of our being, which connects us to the rest of the universe. At certain God-given moments, the soul even becomes accessible.

The heritage of unconsciousness is for all men the same; but it is situated partly within and partly without the confines of normal consciousness. The bulk of mankind will rarely pass over the border; but true lovers of wisdom press on till they open new routes that cross over the frontier. If I love, and my love has procured me the fullest consciousness man may attain, then will an unconsciousness light up this love that shall be quite other than the one whereby commonplace love is obscured.

The enchantment restored

Maeterlinck's place in world literature is unique. After his debut, the poetry collection *Les Serres Chaudes*, saturated with symbolism and surrealism, he introduced symbolism into the theatre. It is above all in *le premier Maeterlinck* (published between 1890 and 1894), which includes *Les Aveugles*, *L'Intruse* and *Intérieur*, that the mystery is restored to its rightful place. The enchantment of the world having been so thoroughly eradicated by the Enlightenment and in literature by realism and naturalism, was now returned to the half-darkness of mediaeval castles, enchanted forests and deathbeds dimly illuminated by candlelight. Maeterlinck's symbolism is constructed around suggestions that the sensory world is an illusion behind which lies mystery. In the nineteenth-century *fin de siècle* and in the years prior to the First World War, Maeterlinck briefly restored enchantment. In the first place via the avant-garde theatre of the time, but through his essays also in the world at large. ■

Translated by Gregory Ball

Renée Dahon, Maeterlinck's wife, at Villa Orlamonde, Nice.

Villa Orlamonde, Nice. Last residence of Maeterlinck. He died here in 1949. Photo by Nicolas Maeterlinck.

'Let Us No Longer Express Ourselves in a Local Patois'

Gerard Reve and England

Looking back, we cannot imagine Dutch literature of the second half of the twentieth century without great writers such as Willem Frederik Hermans and Gerard Reve. However, when these writers were at the beginning of their careers in around 1950, they found themselves confronted with a literary atmosphere in which they felt anything but comfortable. Reve saw that most novels at the time had some social or ethical purpose and that this was a literature dominated by Christianity. Around the end of 1951, he wrote: '99.8 % of Dutch writers are Christian writers, which is all the more tragic since they do not know that Christianity stinks, that the God of the Christians has been dead for centuries [...]. They are not even remotely aware that churches should be burnt to the ground and the places where they stood rinsed with carbolic acid.' According to Reve, who then had no idea that in 1966 he would be baptised into the Catholic Church, Dutch writers needed to become more heathen, but the problem was that such authors would not find a publisher and would sell few books to a readership that consisted of notaries' wives and elderly nurses.

Reve could speak from personal experience. In 1947, his novel *The Evenings* (De avonden) had caused a scandal among a large section of the literary world. However, another and equally significant group of readers had welcomed the novel with delight. *The Evenings* gave a voice to the cynical, disillusioned young people of the post-World War II period. The book sold well, but in a small language area even this success did not produce sufficient income for a decent living. And Reve wanted to make his living as a prose author, not as a supplier of short articles, reviews and page-fillers for newspapers. He looked with envy at countries with fully developed literatures, such as France, England and America. And it was in this direction that he sought a solution:

'Let us no longer express ourselves in a local patois, but instead publish our writings in, for example, English. The 863 Dutch people who usually buy our work will continue to do so. Perhaps then we can escape from the nurses and, more importantly, people will be able to get to know our work in Paris and New York.

'If we really have something to say, the work will find its own way and not be forever buried in Sunday afternoon social clubs and book groups, as it is here.'

Reve was the only writer to heed his own call. His decision to write solely in English was reinforced by an incident that occurred in Spring 1951. Every year

Gerard Reve in 1954.
Photo by Cas Oorthuys.

the Dutch government provided a number of travel grants to enable writers to expand their mental horizons. Authors competed for these grants by submitting a story anonymously. Reve had sent in an excerpt from *Melancholia*, a novel in progress, about a young man during World War II. During a raid his protagonist hides on top of a wardrobe, where the tension becomes so great that he masturbates. The jury awarded a grant for the excerpt, but the Culture Minister decided to revoke the award, because he believed the government should not reward such immoral literature. A commotion ensued, with a small group of right-minded people supporting Reve, but, significantly, the collection to compensate Reve for his loss of income met with little success.

King James and parliamentary proceedings

Reve had only studied English at grammar school for a couple of years, and he had had to leave that school early because he had failed a re-sit exam in – of all things - English. He sought help from John Vandenbergh, a literary translator from English into Dutch. Vandenbergh recommended a number of grammar books for Reve to study and worked with him on translations of some excerpts from his work. That summer Reve met the American poet and translator James S. Holmes, with whom he fell violently in love. Holmes, who with his partner Hans van Marle was already working on the translation of Reve's story *The Downfall of the Boslowits Family* (De ondergang van de familie Boslowits), was much more in tune with Reve's work than Vandenbergh. Over the next year and a half, Reve and Holmes spent every Friday working on the English translation of *Melancholia*, with Holmes doing his best to limit the sessions to literary work, while Reve was inclined to interrupt them with amorous interludes. James Holmes, who translated works by many Dutch authors into English, sought to maximise his options for placing translations by steering a course midway between British English and American English, in a style that he referred to as 'mid-Atlantic English'.

Reve also tried other approaches during this time. He attempted unsuccessfully to gain admittance to English lectures and examinations at the university. Then he entered into correspondence with American universities that offered courses in creative writing. He even considered emigrating to America. However, these plans foundered on a lack of finance, so he was more or less forced to resort to private study. In his prose he employed a rather formal style of Dutch, including official phraseology and allusions to the classic seventeenth-century Dutch Bible translation. In order to master this same register in English, Reve diligently studied the King James Bible and read the proceedings of the English Parliament. After the failure of his attempts to travel to America, he turned to England for his future. From November 1950 to August 1957 he would no longer be part of Dutch literature, but instead endeavour to transform himself into an English-language author.

It soon became clear to Reve that to achieve a decent grasp of the language he would have to live in England. After a humiliating and demoralising period of going cap-in-hand to shipping companies and the Ministry of Culture, he finally made it to London in 1953 on a grant from the British Council. He was however required to take a course with the British Drama League, intended for directors of amateur theatre companies. Reve took a serious approach both to the course and to his immersion in English. He refused to speak his mother tongue with Dutch participants in the course; even with his then wife, the poet Hanny Michaelis, he spoke and corresponded only in English.

'Sir, I am a Dutchman'

Once in London, he tried to establish contacts with writers, magazine editors and publishers. In a letter to his wife Reve described his first meeting with Angus Wilson, which was the start of a long friendship. He had read Wilson's collection *The Wrong Set* and decided to visit the author. Reve wrote: 'I got to know his address and it was my courageous day.' In the gigantic block of flats where Wilson lived no one opened the door when Reve rang. An average-looking man came down the corridor and Reve asked him if he was '0-2', the number of the flat. When he said yes, Reve asked if he was Angus Wilson. This too was confirmed. To which Reve responded: 'Sir, I am a Dutchman who started writing English two years ago. I read some of your work. I just came to see you and I don't come for any money, food, or assistance whatsoever.' Wilson was briefly taken aback, but then burst out laughing and invited Reve in. Reve wrote:

'He is 39, but looks 50, is completely grey and washed up. He is the caricatural representant of queerdom, with a ridiculous, very high-pitched voice. Immediately, in spite of my protests, he took me to a restaurant with a married couple that had just arrived. I thought I would have to go to bed with him for my career, but after the couple had gone and we were back in his flat we had very fine and frank talks. The first time, really, I met a queer without that horrible religion about it. At first, especially in the restaurant, he casted glances upon me which I took for proofs of desire. He showed me the luxurious swimming-pool of the flat and asked me if I would like to come and swim there some day. I answered, 'Like the little fish of that great Roman emperor?' He almost choked in laughter and said, "Don't be afraid. I am not going to talk with you about Michelangelo and boys' statues." There was, I must say, an immediate and deep understanding. Everything was like in a dream. I had never thought it possible that people existed with such an enormous, swift wit and deep sarcasm. Meeting him was a revelation. For the first time I felt completely freed out of that horrible circle of queerism. He said he had, for years and years, been running after boys, but now he had got a friend he didn't do it any more. I told him that I was only very slightly and occasionally interested in queerism.'

The next day Wilson was going on holiday for nine days; without hesitation, he offerred Reve the use of his flat while he was away. He also promised to read Reve's stories.

Wilson was one of the many friends and acquaintances who would look at Reve's English stories in the years that followed. The problem was that some of these readers were English, and some were American, and they all had their own ideas about what constituted good writing. Reve received lots of advice, much of it contradictory, but he did not lose heart. He submitted the stories to magazines, but there were two problems apart from the language issue. Firstly, his stories usually took place in a typically Dutch setting (memories of his Communist youth in Amsterdam and of his family in Enschede), with which British editors did not feel a great deal of affinity. Secondly, there was the length of the stories. Most literary journals were not looking for stories forty to fifty pages long. His salvation came from another country. By a roundabout route which started with Angus Wilson, Reve came into contact with the American writer Eugene Walter, who was involved with *The Paris Review*. This magazine was founded in 1953; it was based in Paris, but addresses in New York, London and Geneva also adorned its stationery. It featured mainly creative work: English-language stories and poems and also in-depth interviews with authors. Over the years *The Paris Review* published many authors who were later to become world famous, from Philip Roth, William Styron and Jack Kerouac to Italo Calvino and V.S. Naipaul. Walter was enthusiastic about Reve's work and showed his story 'The Acrobat' to the editors. Editor-in-chief and financier George Plimpton liked it. 'The Acrobat', inspired by a short stay in Vienna, was published as the opening story in the fifth issue of *The Paris Review*, in Spring 1954. Plimpton announced that its thirty pages made it the longest story they had ever published and that he found it a remarkable achievement for a first attempt in English. The same issue of *The Paris Review* included a contribution from Samuel Beckett and an interview with William Styron. Ten years later one of the magazine's editors stated that Reve's stories had come at the right moment for the editorial team; these stories were exactly what they were looking for at the time.

Three stories by Reve appeared in *The Paris Review* in the space of three years, which was a success, but his efforts to find an English publisher for a collected version of them was unsuccessful. Eventually the Dutch publisher G.A. van Oorschot decided to publish *The Acrobat and Other Stories* in English, initially in the hope of finding an English co-publisher. This too was unsuccessful. The book, published in 1956, attracted hardly any attention in England. Out of desperation, a year later Reve decided to start writing in Dutch once again. The novel *In God We Trust* (Dutch title: *De drie soldaten*), which he wrote simultaneously in a Dutch and an English version, was never completed.

Gerard Reve in his secret country house in France, Drôme, 18 May 1998. Photo by Klaas Koppe.

From the early 1960s Reve's star rose rapidly in the Dutch literary firmament, but this did not result in greater fame abroad. He continued to look longingly at the English-speaking world and the massive sales that could be achieved there. He reacted with growing mistrust and anger to experts from universities and embassies, who were often of the opinion that his work was in fact untranslatable. All told, over the years only one novel by Reve has appeared in English translation: *Parents Worry* in 1990. In 1993, Richard Huijing, who translated this work, also edited the *Daedalus Book of Dutch Fantasy* and included Reve's 1949 novella *Werther Nieland* in this collection.

Reve retained his affection for England and its inhabitants. He visited the country almost every year and had a number of good friends there, including the Renaissance specialist Perkin Walker. In 1980 he even bought a house in Harwich. Inspired by his stay there, he revived his plan to write a new book in English. The working title of the book was *Guilty But Insane*. The main character was the young policeman Andy Moonley, who under the influence of the Moon Goddess would commit all manner of perversions. The action was set in Reve's house in Harwich and on the beach there. At the end of 1981, however, with over one hundred pages in manuscript , he abandoned the project. Reve realised that his English was not 'rich' enough. He felt that the English language was incomparable in its richness, precision and tension, but he himself had not been granted the ability to express his vision satisfactorily in it.

From the mid-1970s on Reve lived mostly outside the Netherlands , in France and Belgium. He never felt completely at ease anywhere and on reflection he could find fault with every country. However, the English still came out ahead of other nationalities: 'The French bourgeoisie is in general the worst kind of scum on God's earth. The Frenchman is moreover entirely a herd animal, one of the masses, with no ideas or world view of his own. Among the English you can find many people who have something human and warm-hearted about them.

Translated by Laura Watkinson

FURTHER READING

Further details about Gerard Reve's relationship with England can be found in NOP MAAS, *Gerard Reve. Kroniek van een schuldig leven*. Amsterdam, Uitgeverij G.A. van Oorschot. Part 1, 'De vroege jaren 1923–1962', published in 2009; part 2, 'De "rampjaren" 1962–1975' published in 2010. Part 3, 'De late jaren 1975–2006' will probably be published at the end of 2011.

Erasmus' *The Praise of Folly* Printed Five Centuries Ago

[HANS TRAPMAN]

Quinten Massys, *Erasmus*, 1517. Oil on panel, 50 x 45 cm. Galleria Nazionale d'Arte Antica, Palazzo Barberini, Rome.

'In absolutely every activity of life, the pious man flees from whatever is related to the body and is carried away in the pursuit of the eternal and invisible things of the spirit.' We could employ a term that is often misused and call this an expression of 'spirituality'. Is it a quote from a mystical work? No, it comes from the conclusion of *The Praise of Folly*, the first edition of which was published in Paris in 1511. The words may sound surprising and appear difficult to place in a book that is generally seen as witty and ironic, sometimes cutting and most certainly irreverent. A few years ago, a brochure from the Wissenschaftliche Buchgesellschaft (not just any old publisher) described the *Folly* as a 'cheerfully ironic settling of scores with the Church and morality, and at the same time a personal plea for liberation from dependence'. These words sound as though they might come from a declaration of principles during the Enlightenment. And *The Praise of Folly* is usually still understood in this enlightened spirit, although there has been a change of opinion since 1980, mainly as a result of Michael Screech's book *Ecstasy and The Praise of Folly*. Since then, more attention has been devoted to the religious conclusion of the *Folly*; sometimes this long-neglected section of the book seemed to become the main issue, even the climax of the book. But this shift in opinion was limited to the world of Erasmus scholars, one of whom went so far as to call the *Folly* a 'religious pamphlet'. However, for the general public, the book is still first and foremost an entertaining satire that denounces wrongs within society and particularly in the Church. The conclusion of the *Folly* still receives the least attention. Have countless readers got it wrong for centuries? Or was Erasmus simply asking for trouble and was the conclusion not in fact meant as seriously as many Erasmus experts believe? Is it the climax or simply an added extra?

Whatever the case, the *Folly* is famous throughout the world; new translations are published all the time in many different places. In the Dutch-speaking countries, no fewer than three modern translations are in circulation and sales figures are good. In addition, three older translations are widely available from antiquarian book dealers. The book is on many people's shelves and it is reasonable to assume that they also pick it up and read it once in a while. In 1930, the now-forgotten Dutch author Jan Walch published his book *Boeken die men niet meer leest* (Books We No Longer Read), one of the chapters of which was

Monk and woman. Pen drawing by Hans Holbein in a copy of *Moriae Encomium*, Basle, 1515.

Copper engraving by Caspar Merian after Hans Holbein, in *Moriae Encomium*, Basle, 1676 (first edition with Holbein's illustrations).

The monk refuses to touch the money but does touch the woman.

Once the woman is gone the monk touches the money.

Copper engraving by Jan van Vianen in *Moriae Encomium* (Desiderii Erasmi Opera Omnia, part 4, 1703, Leiden. Expurgated engraving).

devoted to *The Praise of Folly*. Times have changed. This is thanks in part to the revival of interest in Erasmus since 1936, the year when Europe commemorated the 400th anniversary of his death, when he had once again become relevant for many people as an example of tolerance and moderation, in contrast to the totalitarian powers of fascism and communism. Interest in Erasmus has only increased since then. Exhibitions, international conferences and a rapidly growing number of publications are evidence of this change.

Conceived on horseback

The Praise of Folly occupies a very modest position within Erasmus' oeuvre, which consists of around one hundred writings. Most of these are related to the Bible, faith, the Church and theology. Nowadays the *Folly* is seen as Erasmus' most notable work; he is judged on the basis of this book. He would himself have regretted this situation, as he attached much more importance to his text editions of classical writers and Church Fathers, his *Adagia* (over 4000 classical adages with commentary) and his edition of the New Testament (the Greek text with a Latin translation and notes). Erasmus wrote the *Folly* simply for relaxation. He gave the following explanation of how he came to write the book. He was riding a horse on his way from Italy to England and thinking about the English friends he hoped to see again, particularly Sir Thomas More, a man with a great sense of humour. A few years previously, they had worked together on a translation of the satirical and derisive Lucian (2nd century) from Greek into Latin. The association of the name 'More' and the Greek '*moria*' (foolishness, idiocy) gave Erasmus the idea of writing a eulogy to folly. He would choose the form of a 'paradoxical encomium', based on classical examples, which praised things that did not actually deserve praise. There was, for example, an encomium in praise of baldness, of the three-day fever and the fly. Once he arrived at the home of the hospitable Thomas More, he got down to writing, which helped him to forget the pain of his kidney stones for a while. He finished the book in just over a week.

Erasmus is believed to have written his *Praise of Folly* (in Greek *Morias Egkomion*, written in the 'Latin style' as *Moriae Encomium*, while the Latin title was *Stultitiae Laus*) in 1509. The text of the *Moria*, as Erasmus preferred to

Moriæ encomium. Erasmi. Roterodami declamatio.

σὺν ταῖς μούσαις

σὺν ἀθηνᾷ καὶ χεῖρα κίνει

καὶ τύχη τέχνην

Gilles de gourmont.

τέχνη τύχην ἔστερξε

Moriae Encomium, first edition, 1511, Paris (title page).

call it – and we will follow his example from this point on – initially circulated amongst his friends. As previously mentioned, the first printed edition did not come out until 1511. It is not known whether Erasmus made any alterations to the text in the intervening period. Even in his own lifetime, thirty-six editions of the Latin text were published, two of them in the Low Countries: in Antwerp (as early as 1512) and in Deventer (1520). By the middle of the sixteenth century, French, German, English and Italian translations were available and the first Dutch translation came out in 1560.

The number of editions demonstrates that the *Moria* was well received. Contrary to prevailing opinion, its popularity was not a result of Holbein's famous illustrations. The sixteenth-century editions look fairly unappealing by modern standards: the *Moria* takes the form of a continuous text without paragraphs and without the familiar division into 68 chapters, which in fact dates from the 18th century. The 82 illustrations that Holbein created for one copy of the *Moria* (which is still preserved in Basle) were known only to a few enthusiasts. It was not until 1676 that they appeared as engravings in a printed edition. This example was widely imitated and since then everyone has associated Erasmus' text with Holbein's illustrations. Many later artists drew inspiration from Erasmus' words, particularly in bibliophilic editions. Some continued in Holbein's footsteps, while others, such as the Belgian artist Frans Masereel, who died in 1972, struck out on their own.

L'Eloge de la Folie, translated by Pierre de Nolhac, illustrated by René de Pauw, 1945, Brussels (cover).

Erasmus was more a man of letters, an essayist, even a journalist, than a philosopher or theologian in the traditional sense. His writings are deliberately not constructed in a systematic way and this is certainly true of the *Moria*. For this reason, A.E. Douglas found the *Moria* a 'brilliant but artless and uneven improvisation', but such expressions of negativity are rare. Other scholars have continued to attempt to find a particular scheme in the text, but without a great deal of success.

The title *The Praise of Folly* is intentionally ambiguous, because it refers to praise both *of* and *by* Folly: it is Folly who is speaking and she is therefore praising herself. With a little effort, we can distinguish roughly three parts in the work.

In the first part, where Dame Folly introduces herself and her companions, who include Self-love and Flattery, she declares herself to be a source of life, festivity and mirth. Without her, everything becomes bleak and colourless. Without her, friendship and love cannot exist, for if one becomes too wise and critical, all human relationships soon run aground. A certain kind of flattery is benevolent and innocent and 'the honey and spice of all human intercourse'; it is in any case preferable to dullness and a wagging finger.

In the middle section of the *Moria*, Folly's mockery is aimed at targets including elderly people who behave like lovelorn fools, hunters, architects, alchemists, dice players, schoolmasters, poets, orators, lawyers, philosophers, theologians, monks, sovereigns, courtiers, popes, cardinals and bishops. Theologians and monks have the most criticism vented upon them, particularly in Erasmus' extended edition of 1514. In these passages, Folly's tone is often sharp. She frequently slips out of the role she is playing and then we hear Erasmus himself, the critical voice that we know from the rest of his work. Is this a weak point in the composition? Quite the contrary. Erasmus knew exactly what he was doing. If we automatically had to assume the opposite of everything that Folly praises, the *Moria* would become rather monotonous.

Moriae Encomium or *The Praise of Folly*, translated by Harry Carter, illustrated by Frans Masereel, 1954, Haarlem (frontispiece).

The final part concerns the Christian faith, which is presented as a form of elevated and divine folly. This was in response to Biblical texts such as 'Because the foolishness of God is wiser than men' (1 Corinthians, 1:25).

Offended Theologians

Not all readers were enthusiastic. However, no criticism was forthcoming from Rome. Erasmus was pleased to report that the art-loving Pope Leo X (Giovanni de' Medici) had appreciated the *Moria*, even though it dealt harshly with the papacy in particular. But there were serious objections to the book among the professional theologians attached to the universities of Paris, Cologne and Louvain, bastions of conservatism and orthodoxy.

The first theologian to enter into discussion with Erasmus was Maarten van Dorp from the University of Louvain, generally known as Dorpius. This Dutchman, born in Naaldwijk and twenty years younger than Erasmus, had a humanist education and was an admirer of Erasmus. However, he found his criticism of theologians too harsh and felt that the last part of the *Moria* in particular mocked religion. He gave Erasmus the well-meaning advice that he should now write a Praise of Wisdom, to avoid any possible misunderstanding.

Dorpius' criticism, which he set down in a long letter in 1514, actually suited Erasmus rather well, because it gave him an opportunity to compose a comprehensive response. This apologia was such a success that it was soon published together with the *Moria*, for the first time in the 1516 Basle edition. He draws attention to the striking fact that only the theologians had openly taken offence; the other groups examined in the *Moria* had not protested, because they understood that the satire applied only to those among their number who were no good. Erasmus responded to Dorpius' reproach that some passages at the end of the *Moria* sounded 'godless' by saying that the folly in this context was obviously no ordinary foolishness, just like the 'foolishness of the cross' mentioned by the Apostle Paul. He therefore deliberately employed formulations such as 'a kind of folly' or 'a certain foolishness' in the *Moria*. Erasmus did not intend to write a Praise of Wisdom. If he had to take all sorts of stupid theologians into account, he'd never put pen to paper again. Let those gentlemen first learn Greek properly, said Erasmus, so that they could read the New Testament in the original language. This theme also played an important part in the discussion between Dorpius and Erasmus.

Dorpius was convinced by Erasmus – and also by a detailed letter from Thomas More – and their relationship remained good. However, Dorpius' reaction was followed by attacks from theologians who were distinctly hostile; the Sorbonne held a particularly strong grudge against the *Moria*. In 1559, the book finally ended up in the Index, the Church's list of banned books. As recently as 1913, the then authoritative *Catholic Encyclopedia* assessed the *Moria* as follows: 'It is a cold-blooded, deliberate attempt to discredit the Church, and its satire and stinging comment on ecclesiastical conditions are not intended as a healing medicine but a deadly poison.'

However, in the *Moria*, as in his other works, Erasmus only ever speaks out against wrongs, superstition and hypocrisy, never against the Church, let alone

Bespectacled fool amongst his books, in *De la declamation des louenges de folie*, 1520, Paris (illustrations in this edition are borrowed from Sebastiaan Brant's *Ship of Fools*).

the faith itself. He feels compelled to point this out repeatedly to his conservative Catholic opponents. However, what he ridiculed as superstition was for many people sacred. University theologians viewed him as a threat, particularly after Luther's actions in 1517, when Erasmus' criticism appeared to support the cause of the Reformation. This fear was not unfounded, because supporters of the Reformation were able to put certain statements by Erasmus to good use in their pamphlets and polemics, both during his lifetime and after his death. In the fiercely anti-Catholic *Byencorf der Heilige Roomsche Kercke* (Beehive of the Romish Church), written by the Calvinist Marnix van St. Aldegonde and published in 1569, the *Moria* is quoted to demonstrate the absurdity of Roman-Catholic theology. Erasmus was well aware that, with the rise of Luther and his followers, his satire had become potentially dangerous. If he had seen it coming, he might not have published his book, he stated in January 1518. But we shouldn't take this assertion too seriously, because Erasmus actively continued to work on new editions of his *Moria* up until 1532. He had been living in Catholic Freiburg for a few years by that point, because Basle had chosen to follow the Reformation.

The *Moria* also proved useful to the anti-ecclesiastical polemic of the Enlightenment. The book was attractive to scholars like Nicolas Gueudeville, a former French Benedictine monk who had taken refuge in the Netherlands. In 1713 he published a French translation of the *Moria* in Leiden, with Holbein's illustrations. This free translation saw many reprints and was intended not only for export, but also for the Dutch elite who could read French, the language that was starting to replace Latin as the international medium of communication. Gueudeville also published translations of Erasmus' *Colloquia* and Thomas More's *Utopia* in Leiden.

Witty and erudite

The impression may have arisen that the *Moria* was employed only as a weapon in the fight against everything that was wrong in the Church, state and society. But for most readers the book was first and foremost a source of relaxation and pleasure. That was indeed Erasmus's aim in writing the book. The Greek words that he had sprinkled throughout the text and the many references to classical authors, sayings and mythological figures were no barrier to his friends; on the contrary, if hidden allusions were involved, so much the better. They were able to appreciate the value of this erudite game. Contemporary readers have greater difficulty, but they need not feel ashamed - an edition with a commentary was already deemed necessary in 1515. This edition is attributed to Dutch doctor and scholar of Latin, Greek and Hebrew Gerard Lister (Listrius), but an unknown percentage of the commentary was written by Erasmus himself; the many apologetic remarks are certainly his work. This commentary was used by various scholars, including the first Dutch translator in 1560 and Gueudeville for his *Eloge de la Folie*, and it forms the basis of all modern commentaries. 'Nothing requires greater talent than being witty in an erudite way,' Listrius remarked. However, not all readers are as erudite as Erasmus and his friends and they could do with some help. Sometimes, however, we feel that the commentator is too helpful. When Folly remarks that priests like to leave the practice of devotion to the people and that they do so 'in their modesty', the note reads: 'this is ironic' – but we already knew that much.

When Folly ridicules the cloistered quibbling and pretentious jargon of the medieval scholastic theologians, she appears most dated, but the opposite is in fact the case. Their successors are amongst us: philosophers, theologians and literature experts whose prose may be erudite, but is mainly depressing and maybe even unreadable. At such times, it is good to be able to escape for a moment to Erasmus and his *Moria*. Because as soon as Dame Folly appears on stage with her fool's cap and begins her speech, everything changes. 'Hence it is that as soon as I came out to speak to this numerous gathering, the faces of all of you immediately brightened up with a strange, new expression of joy.' ■

Translated by Laura Watkinson

NOTE

The quotes from the *Moria* are taken from Clarence H. Miller's translation: *The Praise of Folly*, New Haven/London, 1979.

The Graphic Novel in Flanders

Why Comic Strip Artists of the Older Generation are Gnashing Their Teeth

Men who let their beards grow, horny hares that make whole African villages pregnant, limbless kids set in some ancient Little Nemo decor, a Flemish farmer from the polders who willy-nilly becomes Hitler's doppelganger, a surrealistic story about a real-life suicide, and so on - for a while now something remarkable, joyful even, has been happening in the world of Flemish comic strips. More and more artists of the younger generation are managing to get themselves published by foreign publishing houses – and not just any publishers either. Twenty-four-year-old Brecht Evens, for example, has recently seen his third graphic novel *The Wrong Place* (Ergens waar je niet wilt zijn) published in translation (by Drawn & Quarterly, a Canadian publishing house that has the world's greatest graphic novelists in its catalogues. Many an author would kill to be published by them. By the way, *The Wrong Place* won the Prix d'Audace at the prestigious Angoulême Festival in January 2011. And this is far from being a one-off event. Something similar happened to Randall C. and his *Sleepy Heads* (Slaapkoppen), a dreamy/poetic book that was snapped up straightaway by

the French company Casterman, another internationally renowned publisher. The list doesn't end there: both Glénat France and Le Figaro came knocking at Pieter De Poortere's door for his wordless stories about the pessimistic little farmer – known simply as *Boerke* (Dickie in English)- who doesn't shrink from committing suicide at the end of the page. And then there was the quiet Jeroen Janssen, who once worked in Rwanda and had a minor hit in Flanders with his stories, based on his life there, about the adventures of a cunning hare, Bakamé - he managed to have his 300-page collection published simultaneously by his own publishing house Oogachtend and the French company La boite aux bulles.

These are just a few examples, but they do illustrate the international interest in the new generation of Flemish authors. And this is new. But where has this major sea-change come from all of a sudden? Probably it is largely due to the way the new generation thinks of today's comics, and their resolute break with earlier generations.

Randall C., *Sleepy Heads.*

Successes in France

In its heyday, Belgium used to be called the Mecca of the comic strip. But its success was due to its Walloon authors rather than those from Flanders: Peyo, Jijé, Franquin, E.P Jacobs, Hergé, and many more. With *The Smurfs*, *Jerry Spring*, *Blake and Mortimer*, the *Marsupilami* and *Tintin* they showed what their small country had to offer. Their approach, talent and enthusiasm gave rise to some of the most successful comics ever published in Europe: *Robbedoes/Spirou* en *Kuifje/Tintin*, which sold so many copies they would make the editors of today's top magazines blush with shame. The comics not only attracted European authors to this little country, they also generated space for local talent to develop. But once again these authors were mainly French-speaking, with the majority of Flemish comic strip artists remaining stuck far too long in the Flemish clay. Even now, a great many of the older authors are still stuck fast in the same clay.

Jeroen Janssen,
The Revenge of Bakamé.

The facts speak for themselves; a survey of the five best-selling comic series in Flanders comes up with the following: *Jommeke*, *Kiekeboe*, *Suske en Wiske*, *F.C. De Kampioenen* and *Urbanus* – in short, purely Flemish comics. And even though each of them sells 100,000 copies on average, with the one exception of *Suske en Wiske,* the Walloons, the Dutch and the rest of the world ignore them completely. Critics, too, often turn up their noses at them. During the 1980s a second generation tried to get a foot in the door with such major Walloon comic publishers as Lombard, Dupuis and Dargaud. But that was no easy task. They purged their stories of any trace of Flemish identity so as to reach a larger (read: more international) readership. William Vance achieved unprecedented success with his *Bob Morane* and *XIII*, as did Griffo, Ersel, Ferry, Marvano and, more recently, Steven Dupré. But this was often at the cost of a lot of blood, sweat and tears, and some of these authors were ignored for a long time by the typical 'Flemish' comic artists, who may have sold a lot of copies but were seldom talented.

Earning a place on the world map

During the last decade a new generation – the third – has dared to take things one step further. Their sources of inspiration are not the great comic strip giants of yore but rather those international authors who dare to experiment with storyline, colour and style, those who dare to evolve from being merely one who draws comic strips to a comic strip author to a comic strip artist, those who are no longer willing to comply with the demands and norms of the traditional publisher. They also looked at the work of film makers and visual artists, at TV series and animated film series, the Flemish Primitives and legendary American comic strip artists. Heroes and series or stories 48 pages long were no longer an end in themselves. This new generation seemed to look for inspiration mainly in longer stories, many of them (semi-) autobiographical. Their characters are almost without exception real flesh-and-blood people. Their stories became more literary and were more quickly, though sometimes wrongly, termed *graphic novels*. The result was a completely different, more refreshing approach, and one which, probably to their own surprise, caught the attention of an international audience. Their Graphic Novels put Flemish comics on the world map. But something needs to be said here: for some years now they have had the unconditional support of the Flemish Literary Fund (Vlaams Fonds voor de Letteren, VFL), an organisation that subsidises literature at some remove from the government but uses government money to do so. For the last few years the VFL has promoted this new generation abroad, which has resulted in a considerable number of foreign contracts. To their great delight, the one-man publishing houses Bries and Oogachtend, the true discoverers of this new generation of Flemish comic strip authors, found that an agent in the form of the VFL was working for them: new translation grants were awarded, and a major exhibition about these young authors organised by the VFL during the Angoulême comic strip festival did the rest. Again thanks to the VFL, these authors had plenty of time to work on their books. Grants were made available for work, production and travel.

Judith Vanistendael,
The Virgin and the Nigger.

In the meantime, criticism from members of the second, in-between, generation whom strangely enough the Fund refuses to subsidise, is becoming increasingly loud. And their criticism is to some extent justified, for some of these young authors seem now to be subsidised for life, while the Fund persistently refuses to offer grants to authors from the second generation (Marvano, Ersel, Bosschaert, Ken Broeders, Bosschaert, Tom Bouden, and others), despite the fact that their comics are of equally high quality.

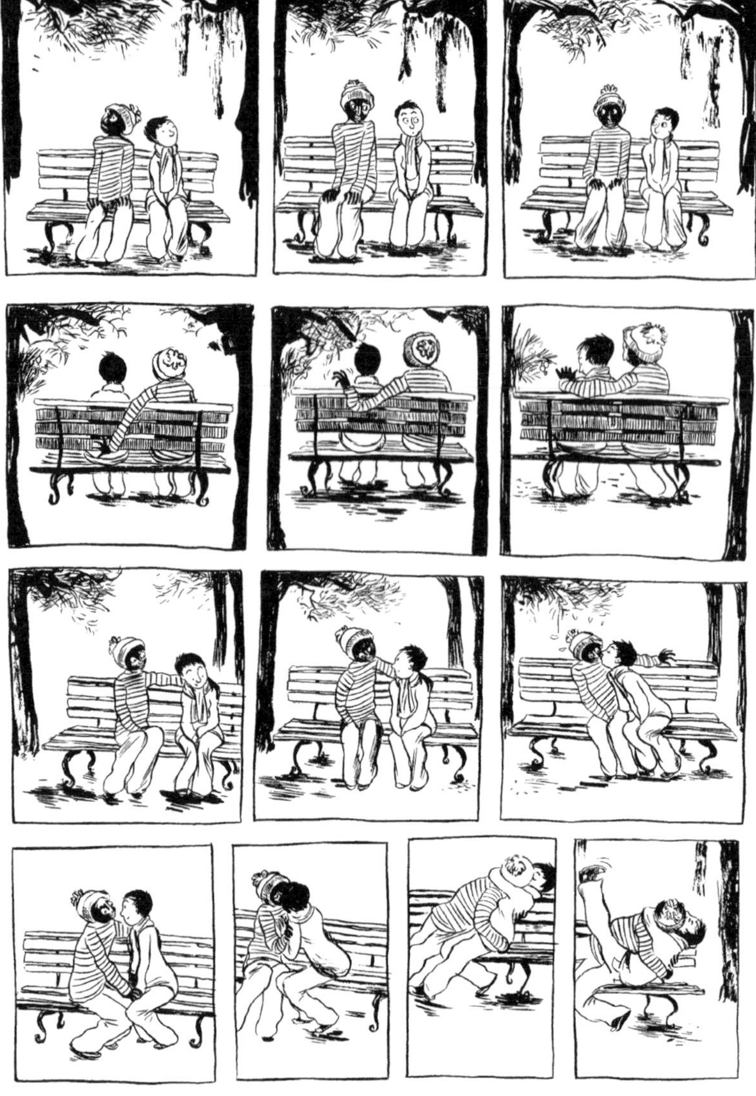

Judith Vanistendael,
The Virgin and the Nigger.

Be that as it may, the new generation is flourishing as never before. And compared with the preceding generation, you come upon more idiosyncratic worlds when you look at the work of each of this new generation of Flemish graphic novelists. One of them has attempted an autobiography of Louis Armstrong (Philip Paquet), another has produced a pure soap in which three sluts – these are his own words –set out to drain the glamour and glitter of Paris to the dregs (Maarten Van de Wiele), while yet another places a limbless young boy in a setting undeniably inspired by the American master, Winsor McCay's *Little Nemo*. Others again – bearing in mind the international trend in the graphic novel – have taken the autobiographical track. In *No Stories*, Serge Baeken worked out of his system an old incident in which a man was murdered right in front of his house. Judith Vanistendael drew on her love for an asylum seeker from Togo to tell us a heart-rending story about lack of understanding, love, cultural differences and a defective Belgian asylum policy. Success doesn't seem to stop for Vanistendael. After a French translation, there is now one in English too. And they are not the only ones.

More than Flemish

Nowadays, though, open-minded first- and second-generation Flemish comic strip artists are also looking further than ever before. For example, following his popular humorous Biebel series Marc Legendre turned to producing graphic novels which were outstanding for their dark themes and artistic graphic styles. He was even nominated for the Libris Prize, which till then had seemed to be reserved exclusively for 'real' literature.

But perhaps the most striking among them is Willy Linthout, the creator, please note, of the arch Flemish folk comic strip *Urbanus* – a comic that is in the top five best-selling comic strips in Flanders. The surrealistic approach he used in that resurfaces in his heavily symbolic graphic novel *Years of the Elephant* (Jaren van de olifant) in which he tried to come to terms with his son's suicide. The work has been published in translation by many foreign companies but in 2010 the U.S. provided the cherry on the cake with its nomination in not one but two categories: Best U.S. Edition of International Material en Best Writer/Artist Non Fiction. He won neither of them. A few years earlier Judith Vanistendael's *The Virgin and the Nigger* (De maagd en de neger) just missed out on the top prizes at Angoulême. It was a pity for them, but the very fact that they were nominated for these Oscars of the comic world was a feather in the cap for Flemish comic strips in general, comic strips which at last are no longer purely Flemish. As a result Flemish graphic novels will only continue to grow in importance. They are centre stage now in Belgium. ■

Translated by Peter Flynn

Proud Guardians of Civic Liberty

Belfries in the Low Countries

[LUC DEVOLDERE]

All photos by Michiel Hendryckx.

In the Middle Ages trade and the cloth industry were thriving mightily in North-West Europe. As a result, the middle classes in the towns of the Southern Netherlands became rich and increasingly influential. Belfries or hall towers were a symbol of this urban and middle class freedom and power. For before this only the rulers and the church had had the money to finance such large buildings.

As the safest place in town, the belfry often housed the town's archives, its strong-rooms and sometimes the prison as well. Bells were hung in these towers. Because of their height they were also used as watchtowers to warn of approaching enemies in time and to spot fires in the town quickly. The town bell was then rung. From the 16th century on carillons came into vogue as well.

A group of 56 belfries in Belgium and France has been included in the UNESCO World Heritage list.

Nearly all the belfries still in existence are in Belgium (26 in Flanders and 7 in Wallonia) and in Northern France (23). The only Dutch belfry, the one in Sluis, is in Zeeland Flanders, on the Belgian border.

Here we shall show you eight belfries from the Southern Netherlands. Those of Aalst, Arras (Atrecht), Douai, Ghent, Ypres, Kortrijk, Sluis and Tournai.

All eight of them have a tale to tell.

NEC SPE 1900 NEC METU

Nec spe nec metu

Nothing is what it seems. Inscribed on the belfry in Aalst is the Roman-Stoic motto NEC SPE NEC METU - without hope or fear - and beneath it the year 1200.

The motto and the year were added in 1555, on the occasion of the joyous entry of the Spanish King Philip II of Spain, who was also Count of Aalst. Philip had succeeded his father, Charles V, following the latter's abdication in Brussels that same year.

It was the monarch's personal motto. And 1200 was a round-figure date for the construction of the original Aldermen's House, which dates from 1225, making it the oldest in the Netherlands. In 1380 the Aldermen's House burned down when the men of Ghent laid waste to the town. Part of the house burned down again in 1879, after fireworks set fire to it during the fair. The bell-tower itself and the carillon only date from 1460.

In the spring of 1576 Spanish troops, who had not been paid for a very long time, started plundering the Southern Netherlands. Without hope and without fear. Because of its central location, the mutinous troops chose Aalst as the base for their merciless raids. In November 1576 this Spanish fury reached Antwerp. Thousands were put to the sword. These events sent an enormous shock-wave through the Low Countries and led to the Pacification of Ghent on 8 November.

The treaty stipulated that the Spanish armies should leave the Low Countries and that there should be freedom of religion. Nothing could be less true. But when there is no hope any more, one may very well learn to fear nothing too.

The one-time financial centre of the Low Countries

Atrecht, or Arras, is now part of France, but in the twelfth century it was the most important producer of cloth in the Low Countries and the most dynamic town commercially. In the thirteenth century it was also the Low Countries biggest financial centre. Back then Atrecht had 25,000 inhabitants. But in 1212 the French King Philip II Augustus managed to filch the town and the Artois region from the County of Flanders.

Atrecht's role as a financial centre was taken over by Bruges in the fourteenth and fifteenth centuries, by Antwerp in the sixteenth century and by Amsterdam in the seventeenth.

Nonetheless, Atrecht maintained its major role in the revived textile industry, especially in tapestry weaving.

In 1579 the Union of Atrecht was concluded, reconciling a number of Walloon regions with the Spanish Governor-General, Alexander Farnese. As a reaction to this, in the same year the Northern regions came together in the Union of Utrecht. A difference of just one letter, but the Low Countries were now split in two.

From that time on Atrecht was part of the Spanish Netherlands, until the city fell permanently into French hands in 1659 and became Arras.

And the belfry? The belfry of Atrecht/Arras is the clock-tower of the town hall. The town hall and the 75 metre high belfry date from the 16th century. '*Prodigieux beffroi mince, dentelé de mille caprices, qui dresse jusqu' aux nuages ( ) sa masse énorme et légère* ', as Paul Verlaine said of it in 1889: incredible slim belfry, indented with a thousand caprices, that raises its huge, light structure to the clouds.

The belfry suffered badly in the First World War, but was meticulously rebuilt after hostilities ended. It still dominates one of the two *grandes places* and is surrounded by 155 houses in Flemish baroque style.

The belfry is adorned with the imperial crown of Charles V, ruler of the Low Countries,

It was inspired by that of Oudenaarde and reminds us that the County of Artois once formed part of the German nation's Holy Roman Empire. *Honi soit qui mal y pense.*

France's carillon capital

Along with Lille and Orchies, Douai was a part of the County of Flanders which has been French-speaking since the twelfth century. In the thirteenth and fourteenth centuries the town was a plaything in the struggle between the French kings and Flanders.

King Philip II of Spain founded a university there in 1562, the second in the Low Countries after Leuven. The university became a bulwark of the Catholic Counter-Reformation, but at the end of the nineteenth century it was lost to Lille.

In 1837, long after Douai had fallen into decline, Victor Hugo passed through Douai and wrote to his daughter Adèle:

'There is there the most beautiful belfry I have ever seen. Imagine a Gothic tower, topped with a slate roof, consisting of a multitude of little cone-shaped windows one on top of the other; on tip of each window a weather vane, on each of the four corners a turret; and on the top of the belfry, a lion turning with a flag between its paws; and out of this highly amusing, crazy, lively ensemble comes a carillon. In every little opening you can see a bell working away madly like a tongue in a mouth. I drew the tower, and when I look at my drawing, I seem to hear again that joyful carillon escaping like natural vapour from this mass of pinnacles.'

The carillon was installed as early as 1391 and Jehan Lourdel was appointed by the aldermen to set the rhythm of the town's life with his playing of the bells. He was the first of a series of, to date, 35 carilloneurs.

The bells were melted down by the Germans in 1917. By 1954, though, the tower once again housed 47 of them, in addition to the two heavy bells dating from 1471 that, though damaged, had survived the war and been restored: 'Joyeuse', a 5500 kg (108 cwt) A pitch and 'La disnée', a C of 2400 kg (47 cwt).

Today there are 62 bells in the tower, spanning five octaves. Douai is the only town in France that still has a paid carilloneur and can therefore rightly be called France's carillon capital.

Go and have a listen.

The Ghent dragon

For the last six centuries there has been a dragon on the Ghent belfry. It is 3.55 m (11.65 feet) long, 1.50 m (4.9 feet) wide, 1.80 m (5.9 feet) high and weighs 398 kg (7.83 cwt). It has an iron body and is covered with sheets of gilded copper.

This is its story.

During his crusade against the Seljuks between 1107 and 1111, the Norse King Sigurd Magnussen was given a dazzling reception in Constantinople by the Emperor Alexius Comnemus. On his departure for the North the monarch is supposed to have given the gilded dragon from the prow of his ship to his imperial host by way of thanks. The Emperor in his turn is said to have had the showpiece installed on Hagia Sophia or on the Boukoleon Palace. Less than a hundred years later the Flemish Count Baldwin IX took part in the Fourth Crusade and in 1204, after the recapture of Constantinople from the Turks, he was crowned Emperor of the Byzantine Empire in Hagia Sophia. Supposedly he had the Norse dragon brought from Constantinople to our part of the world and gave it to the town of Biervliet in Zeeland Flanders, whose warriors had fought so courageously against the Turks. The impressive trophy – so the story continues – did not stay in the possession of Biervliet very long, because shortly afterwards it fell into the hands of the people of Bruges. Following the battle of Beverhoutsveld in 1382, the people of Ghent in their turn took the dragon from Saint Donat's Tower and carried it off triumphantly along the River Lieve to Ghent as plunder of war. There it was placed on top of the belfry. *Se non è vero, è ben trovato*: if it's not true, it's a good story. The dragon has always been very popular with the people of Ghent. It was even made to breathe fire during festivities. This was first done on 17 March 1500 on the occasion of the baptism of the future Emperor Charles V. The last time that the dragon breathed fire was in 1819 when the Prince of Orange was visiting Ghent.

Risen from its ashes

The belfry in Ypres stands high above the Cloth Halls, one of Europe's greatest medieval civic buildings. In October 1914 the advancing Germans briefly occupied the city, only to leave it again, probably on 12 October.

On 13 October 1914 British troops marched into Ypres. They would hold the town for the whole of the war. Surrounded by the enemy on three sides, Ypres would be blown to smithereens over four long years. On Sunday 22 November 1914 the Cloth Halls and the belfry caught fire for the first time.

Eye witnesses wrote: 'On Sunday 22 November the Cloth Hall was bombarded, a grandiose monument highly praised in art history, the renown of Ypres. (...) First a breach on either side of the tower, then the clock came down and the Carillon collapsed; around 11.30 the tower caught fire and soon the monument was nothing but one huge inferno.' 'Around 9 o'clock on Sunday 22 November many bombs fell; they hit our building with uncommon accuracy (...). The clock, and the two carillons as well, fell right through the tower and finally, around 11 o'clock, the incendiaries hit their target and started the fire that cries out for vengeance. (...) And contemplating your skeleton, O suffering treasure of art, we hum silently: "Ypres, Ypres, Your greatness built up once again and industry and trade and work brought forth! Then shall the carillon play from all your tower battlements."'

In 1915 the last civilians left the town. By 1918 there was not a wall left standing in Ypres and a man on horseback could see clear across the town. Not until 1967 was the total restoration of the Cloth Hall and the belfry completed.

The perfect marriage

In Kortrijk, or Courtrai, the belfry now stands abandoned, stripped of the old cloth halls that had surrounded it and which were only demolished at the end of the nineteenth century. At the time they were even thinking of pulling down the whole building.

Enthroned on the top of the tower is a gilded statue of the Roman god Mercury, the god of trade who rightly rules this industrious town. It is not him we are interested in, though, but the town's oldest citizens: Manten and Kalle, who ring the bells in the belfry.

In the fourteenth century a bell on the Hall Tower was linked to a clock, operated by a metal automaton called Manten who struck the hour. When the Burgundian Duke Philip the Bold plundered Kortrijk after the battle of Westrozebeke in 1382, his engineers very carefully took the famous mechanism away with them. They put it on the Church of Our Lady in Dijon, where it can still be seen. In 1651 the inhabitants of Dijon gave their mannikin, or jacquemart, a wife called Jacqueline and two children because: 'It's not good for a person to be alone'.

Kortrijk quickly acquired a new Manten to strike the hour, and in 1424 this was granted the company of 'a Mantine to strike the bells'.

She would soon go down in history as 'Kalle'.

Manten and Kalle became an inseparable couple and today they still take it in turns to strike the bell every half-hour. 'They get on like Manten and Kalle' is an expression used to denote couples who living together in harmony. And Flanders would not be Flanders if no local beers had been devised to bear the names of the inseparable pair that marks the hours on Kortrijk's main square.

Arranged marriages

Philip III, the Good, Duke of Burgundy (1396-1467), married three times, had thirty known mistresses and eighteen acknowledged bastards.

In October 1428 Philip of Burgundy sent a delegation to Lisbon to negotiate a third marriage. The delegation included the artist Jan van Eyck. Two copies of the portrait he painted of Princess Isabella were sent by courier to the Duke. On 25 July 1429, a day after the signing of the marriage contract, 'la infanta Isabel' married the Burgundian Duke in Portugal by proxy or, as the Dutch expression goes, 'with the glove'. The religious marriage was solemnised on 7 January 1430 in the belfry in Sluis and followed by a week of celebrations with jousting tournaments and banquets in Bruges.

Three sons were born of this marriage, two of whom died young.

In 1468 the only surviving son, Charles the Bold, was betrothed to Margaret of York, the sister of the English King, in the same belfry. The truth is that Margaret arrived in Sluis by ship on 25 June and Charles, who was also on his third marriage, came to check out the looks of his future bride. Whom he first set eyes on in the belfry.

The marriage was solemnised in the church in Damme and then they proceeded in a stately procession to Bruges, where the Papal Nuncio, six bishops and innumerable nobles indulged themselves in a whole week of extravagant banquets and tournaments.

And incidentally, you can hire the belfry in Sluis, the only one in the Netherlands, for your own wedding.

A dragon, an eagle and a Phrygian cap

The oldest belfry in Belgium is in Tournai, now Wallonia, the French-speaking part of the country. In 1188 the French King Philip II Augustus conferred the bell right on the town, which automatically implied the right to build a belfry.

Clovis, the founder of the Frankish kingdom that would eventually become France, was born in Tournai in 465. The town would remain French from the time of Philip Augustus, who strengthened his power in the north at the expense of the Count of Flanders, till 1513.

Tournai then became English for five years under Henry VII (the only Belgian town ever to suffer this fate!), French for three years under Francis I, and eventually came under Hapsburg rule from 1521 with Charles V.

Louis XIV deeply regretted the fact that "this old French town" became Austrian after the Treaty of Utrecht in 1713. But he could not have everything.

The Austrian Emperor Joseph II had the dragon on the belfry replaced by a globe with the eagle on top. The French troops who took the town in 1792 then replaced the eagle with the Phrygian cap, a symbol of freedom, but in 1794 this was again removed by the Austrians and replaced by a triangular banner.

The belfry has survived it all – fire, restorations and structural alterations. In 1294 the town decided to increase the height of the bell-tower. The tower look-out needed to be able to see farther over the growing town and the construction of the cathedral choir impeded the view to the north. The secular power had to be brought into balance with the spiritual power. *Honi soit qui mal y pense.*

Translated by Lindsay Edwards

An Explosive Spirit

The Romantic Poetry of a Neo-Dadaist: Hans Verhagen

'To err is human. In time you learn to appreciate the quality. And if you can't see it you're a dickhead'. This pronouncement by the poet Lucebert (1924-1994) gives the briefest possible summary of the history of the critical appreciation of Hans Verhagen (1939) – from disparagement to praise, both in the most absolute possible terms.

Lucebert was the principal poet of the 'Fifties Generation, the movement based on Dada and expressionism that was often caricatured and dismissed as romantic-surrealist verbal mush, resulting in incomprehensible poems.

In the 1960s Lucebert – and he was not alone – was alarmed at the new avant-garde that was emerging, most notably in the magazines *Gard Sivik* and *De Nieuwe Stijl*. These journals were inspired by the tabula-rasa version of Dadaism and the conceptual art of the 1960s that had been influenced by it. In 1964 Lucebert talked of the 'commercial exploitation of the avant-garde concept' and was irritated by the noise and brashness with which Verhagen and his colleagues presented themselves.

The contrast appeared absolute: Lucebert was above all an artist, while Verhagen's interests and activities go in all directions. He has worked for newspapers, magazines and television. In the 1970s and '80s he made documentaries and talk shows and as the producer of the Zeeland band *Dragonfly* he had a

Hans Verhagen.
Photo by Klaas Koppe.

brief spell in the pop music business. In short, Verhagen was much more than just a poet, and poetry for him sometimes seemed to be a side issue rather than a vocation.

But that is only one side of the picture. Verhagen was young, fast and modern, but he was also a poet who wanted to savour language in a way that sometimes resembled the 'Fifties Generation's use of imagery more than critics at the time seemed to realise. This dualism was already implicit in the title of his début collection from 1963: *Roses and Engines* (Rozen en motoren).

It is not free of roses
nor is the use of engines
alien to my body

Beneath my weary hair crows
a nightingale and sings gnashing
of dying; the process
of silence, truly, is not
complete in me

The traditional images (roses, nightingales) fight for precedence with the 'engines' which represent the fashion of the age. Verhagen's poetic side was certainly seen and appreciated by reviewers, but their comments often reveal a negative attitude as regards the poets and magazines he was associated with. This review of his first collection is typical: it 'groans under the burden of group deficiencies, but here and there personal angularity and dry humour are visible.' In brief, Verhagen is a good poet; but he should distance himself from the nonsense of his fellow group members.

In 1968 *Stars Circles Bells* (Sterren Cirkels Bellen) was published, and here Verhagen was even more extreme in his seemingly deadpan passion for the experimental. The technique of the ready-made is used regularly, for example in the trilingual series 'Kanker/Cancer/Krebs': poems put together from separate sentences about cancer found in both medical and popular publications about the disease. There is a section dealing with television and there are ready-mades on housekeeping and lighting. The collection was glamorously designed by Wim T. Schippers, with whom Verhagen worked at the progressive TV station VPRO. Yet here too appearances are deceptive, and a romantic vision does definitely surface in various poems:

Let me take you
where the dreams lead
that stay longest in the memory.

The poet vanishes

With hindsight it is easy to see that the objective style of *Gard Sivik* and *Nieuwe Stijl* did not really suit Verhagen. Hans Verhagen 'never really thought about it much and was the first to move on,' is how Martin Bril sums up his attitude in an essay which was published in the survey *De Nieuwe Stijl 1959-1966* (1989).

After 1968 we hear very little from Verhagen, – especially when he retreats to the island of Walcheren for a while. His stay was recorded in the TV feature *Where is Hans Verhagen?* The programme depicts him as a man with Messianic tendencies and the collection he is working on at that moment seems to represent a major shift in his work. The 'engines' have largely disappeared from *Thousands of Sunsets* (Duizenden zonsondergangen) and romanticism takes the lead:

Long dissipated morning red
pursues me behind my eyes,
deep raspberry red reflects deep
in the plundered cages of
neon.

The rift with his fellow group members was not lost on the critics: 'the poems from *Thousands of Sunsets* [seem to be] by a different poet than the one who wrote *Stars, Circles, Bells*'. That is an exaggeration for two reasons – firstly, there is still room in *Thousands of Sunsets* for the deadpan humour which is definitely part of Verhagen's work:

I understand perfectly young man,
I'm a total arsehole myself.

In addition, the romantic tendency was already a strong presence in Verhagen's poetry in the 1960s. In *Stars Circles Bells* there is a cycle called 'The Poet's Dream' ('De droom van de dichter'), which according to the blurb is the account of a 'psychedelic experience' and the distance from this to the romanticism of *Thousands of Sunsets* is not that great.

A dust particle, dancing
in the sunlight, gleaming golden,
silvery glistening thing

Nor does Verhagen himself see the contrast in such rigid terms. In an interview in 1971 he spoke about his development: 'anti-romanticism is after all itself a form of romanticism. That is an issue in my poetry: that affirmation of the opposite.'

But although Verhagen's early poetry also tended towards ambiguity, in these poems he seems to have found his own voice. It is not always easy to make out, but it does gain Verhagen his most enthusiastic responses so far - including that of Lucebert, who is so important to him.

But hand-in-hand with finding a voice goes a stagnation in his development, and so with this collection Verhagen disappears from literary history. Verhagen ceases to be cutting-edge, after *Thousands of Sunsets* his poetry no longer fits in anywhere, and for a while he withdraws from poetry in order to resume his TV career. It was a period full of drug-taking and miserable personal circumstances, the low-point of which was the suicide of his wife and muse Connie.

The fact that from 1976 he had, tentatively and at long intervals, started writing poems again, emerged only when the collection *Cold Feet. Poems 1976-1983* (Kouwe voeten. Gedichten 1976-1983) appeared. In it his darkness had found expression. Whereas *Thousands of Sunsets* had contained a cycle entitled 'Higher' ('Hoger'), Verhagen now writes a series called 'Lower' ('Lager'), in which he struggles with his personal demons:

Everything fell under grief's spell,
butterflies in the rubble sat quiet as mice,
even the children were silent as the grave

The collection had a strikingly unenthusiastic reception – so dark, so negative, and poetically far from innovative. From 1983 Verhagen would again preserve a long silence as a poet: he discovered painting.

Authority of Emotion (*Autoriteit van de emotie*) appeared almost ten years later: a collection that moves between the two concepts contained in the title: authority, control, domination versus emotion and spontaneity. Verhagen begins with a self-portrait 'I am not the maker of the poem / but as receptive as possible', in which he defines himself as someone who is attuned to the 'chords' transmitted to him by the strings of 'this moment in time'. He is an intermediary, a medium for emotion. Being in love is a 'professional activity' – love is the material of poetry, but if the poem is to succeed the poet must stay in control of his emotions.

In the following collection, *Echoing Well and Castle in the Air* (Echoput & Luchtkasteel, 1995), there is again a struggle with a comparable opposition. The poems are more personal than ever – and in addition Verhagen now clearly makes a choice, spirit rather than body, dream rather than death: 'I may live in a castle in the air, / it does me more justice than living in a /coffin.' With this choice he returns to the exuberant spontaneity of the early 1970s – he distantiates himself even more emphatically from his 1960s work. Emotion is allowed to win out over authority and although that sometimes results in poems in which the associations are so personal that the reader may feel excluded, it also produces wonderful works, especially those in which madness is observed from a distance.

But the more personal Verhagen's themes become, the more marginal his literary-historical role as a poet. There is a poem in *Triumphant Walks* (Triomfantelijke wandelingen, 2000) that can be read as a concise description of this development, 'Step'('Stap)':

And they grow
not from small to large,
but from large to small.

And hence they discover
that a faux pas,
however catastrophic,
nonetheless notwithstanding
proves to be a step forward.

Here Verhagen has captured his role as a poet moving from large to small in a striking image. And if with his choice, his step, he has made a catastrophic faux pas, he accepts that. It is also a step forward because the poet Verhagen has been liberated.

In *Quasi-kamikaze* (2002), he goes even more unmistakably in search of his past. In this collection he also reflects on the reception of his work, in grandiose, if not overblown terms: 'Over all heads cast onto a solitary height / Trodden into the ground by the million.' It is no coincidence that Verhagen 'defends' himself with a reference to Lucebert's collection *From the Abyss and the Sky Man* ('Van de afgrond en de luchtmens'): 'Descending from sky man to foot soldier/ I experienced not as humiliation/ but as a completion of my profundity.'

One must live

This collection marks the turning point in the history of the appreciation of Verhagen's work. Two important Dutch poets review it in the two major Dutch dailies: Ilja Leonard Pfeijffer in *NRC Handelsblad* and Piet Gerbrandy in *de Volkskrant*. With the appearance some time later of his collected poems (*Eternal Flame* / Eeuwige vlam, 2003) Verhagen's reputation as an important poet is re-established – and secured. In the first regular collection to appear after the collected poems (*Mother is a Robber* / Moeder is een rover, 2004) Verhagen is often amusing, but never without a sharp edge: 'Who of all people wants to reproduce a human'. On other occasions he proclaims striking truths: 'When you're dead you can still renounce survival'. Images can be 'beautiful' in an old-fashioned way: 'Pearl-like the rain strings itself along a gossamer line' and then again extremely down to earth: 'Listen to how space slides down kitchen sinks into the wide world of the sewage system'.

Both roses and engines can still be found in his poetry – but where Verhagen opts for romanticism the emphasis is beginning to shift. Because in the meantime his involvement with the world has become more and more explicit – no longer does he write mainly about coming to terms with events in his own life, but society comes increasingly to the fore. In *Dragon* (Draak, 2006) Verhagen paints a pitch-black vision of a world full of 'rich businessmen / and revolving-door criminals (both thieves)', of a railway worker whom he suspects of dreaming 'of, in the absence of the ss, being authorised /to castrate the homeless by the railway police'. This is a world in which

Cutely glazed babies are fattened
and then, heavily armed,
are deployed for a noble and criminal universal end

In a word: a 'cancerous society'. These poems give the impression that Verhagen was 'angry' with the world, but he denies this vehemently in an interview: 'In every review of my most recent collections I am called angry, but I'm not angry at all. When you see the kinds of misery that are possible, and what is made of it, things aren't too bad.'

And it's true that Verhagen also has an eye for beauty, for love, and invariably writes out of great involvement: 'I don't get this place at all / We live here to our heart's content / while misfortune nevertheless lies in wait in the eye of the calm on the corner / for a blind spot.'

Verhagen goes on looking for that other world, inspired by beauty, animation and higher things. In the cycle 'Walhalla' he describes how artists go in search of a world situated between sleep and waking, intellect and instinct, art and nature.

Opposites continue to play a part. There has always been the world of love, romance and freedom – and always the reality which frustrates ideals.

Verhagen's most recent collection is *Black Holes* (Zwarte gaten, 2008). Here too the vision of the world is a dark one. Here too existence is a life-and-death struggle that in the nature of things is doomed to fail. Dreams, plans, solutions, liberation: all are possible. But we must not forget what life consists of, it all takes place 'as we die'. But until it gets to that point, we have to live, there must be amazement at every level, from the cosmic ('Snatches of clouds steeped in vision travel round in cyclones', reads the first line) down to the mundane – with the emphasis on politics: 'Once more we let the route be set / by anxious hypocrites and arch-betrayers': in the context of contemporary Dutch affairs it sounds almost like editorial comment.

The central opposition in this collection is between the black holes of the title, the infinite mass from which there is no escape, and the lightness of an approach to life. The airiness is in the language, in the age-old procedure that creates space for imagination, movement, and humour: 'a supersonic football-girl in an eleven-man foldaway bed' or 'Let's all go to Japan / where after all the earth moves by itself / for those who can't dance.'

Roses and engines

Verhagen is versatile – his poems range from unadorned ready-mades to exuberant psychedelic fantasies, and embrace all modes in between. He laid the foundation for this in his very first poems, in the image of roses and engines. In the forty years since then his works have oscillated between these two poles. At one moment the objectivity of the modern world seemed to have the upper hand, at others Verhagen opted for the standard, not to say clichéed, image of poetry.

In the narrative of literary history those poems feature most prominently in which Verhagen, with the objective poets of his generation, seemed to take a stand against the poetry of the 'Fifties Generation. However, the poet himself seemed more at home in poems that were personal, associative and full of imagery – which had more in common with the work of the 'Fifties poets, and especially with Lucebert, than you might expect.

When Verhagen looks back in 2003, it emerges that he found a form that enabled him to relate to Lucebert. In 2003 he says in an interview that he regards the 'liberating poems' of Lucebert as 'the true source of inspiration' for his work. And the following exchange from another interview speaks volumes:

'What poet influenced you most? "Lucebert."

What poet were you most opposed to? "Lucebert."'

Both attitudes can exist alongside each other and so Verhagen has found his niche in Dutch literary history. The reappraisal that began at the start of this century and culminated in the award of the P.C. Hooft Prize in 2009 has clearly done him good. He is more productive than ever, and the struggle between romanticism and reality is no longer the problem but has become the thematic starting point of his poems. Verhagen has discovered that reality is so absurd that the romantic vision imposes itself almost automatically. He no longer needs to choose. The madness is channelled, what is ordinary is made special, the roses have reconciled themselves with the engines and the poet has found his true form. ■

Translated by Paul Vincent

Lucas van Leyden

Painter of Civic Life

[ILJA VELDMAN]

Last summer, visitors to Museum De Lakenhal in Leiden were asked to name their favourite work of art in the museum. One in ten answered without hesitation that they had lost their hearts to the triptych featuring Lucas van Leyden's *Last Judgement*. It is easy to see why this work from almost 500 years ago came out on top. Lucas was greatly admired even in his own lifetime and his fame has not diminished over the course of the centuries, mainly because of his engravings and woodcuts. Lucas's prints, which made their way all over Europe, quickly gained him a great reputation, similar to that of Albrecht Dürer. Lucas demonstrates astounding creativity and originality in all of his work though, not only coming up with unusual themes, but also presenting traditional subjects from new perspectives. His works place particular emphasis on the human aspect, often exhibiting striking psychological insight. It is no surprise therefore that his prints and paintings were very popular among the ordinary middle classes. Most of Lucas's work was not destined for churches and monasteries, but for the homes of art-loving citizens. This was a new phenomenon. It also explains why the themes of Lucas's work often reflect this early urban or civic culture.

Prodigy

In his *Schilder-boeck* (Book of Painters, published in 1604), Karel van Mander emphasises how Lucas excelled at painting and engraving from his earliest youth. Van Mander states that Lucas was born in 1494 and that the boy preferred a pen, brushes and engraving tools to his toys. Lucas supposedly engraved images on copper at the age of nine and when he was twelve he is said to have painted a Saint Hubert for a member of the town council. Van Mander obtained this information from one of Lucas's grandsons, who was born while Lucas was on his deathbed. However, other details in the book are not entirely correct, so it is not certain that the date of 1494 is reliable. Artists' biographers often had the tendency to exaggerate in order to emphasise an artist's prodigious skills. What is certain is that Lucas's first dated engravings are from 1508. However, he had already produced a large number of prints in the preceding years. For this reason, it has been suggested that the year of his birth was earlier than 1494. Even if Lucas was born in 1489, that means he was producing signed engravings for sale from the age of seventeen, which is still unusually young. It was also extraordinary that Lucas engraved on copper, as there was no tradition of copper engraving in Leiden. At an early stage in his career, Lucas must have had access to prints by other artists, which he then used as models for his own work. His father, the painter Huyg Jacobsz, taught him the rudiments of painting, after which the boy is believed to have worked as an apprentice to Leiden painter Cornelis Engebrechtsz.

Nature and eroticism in Lucas's early prints

Lucas started working as a printmaker at a time when painters had little interest in making prints. One of the reasons for this decision was most probably that making prints did not tie him to a particular client, as prints could be sold from the studio, through booksellers and at fairs, and also that printmakers were not required to join a guild. Moreover, this medium allowed Lucas to experiment with new and unusual subjects for sale on the open market. His early prints, for example, reveal a great interest in nature and innocent eroticism. This period produced a number of small, idyllic scenes, such as *Naked Boy with Trumpet and Dancing Children*, *Pilgrims Resting in Nature*, *Naked Woman with Hind*, *Naked Girl Removing Fleas from a Dog* and *Milkmaid with Farmer and Cows*. Karel van Mander greatly admired the latter two prints, both dated 1510. *Resting Pilgrims* appealed so much to the Italian engraver Marcantonio Raimondi that he copied the print himself.

Lucas van Leyden,
Naked Girl removing Fleas from a Dog, 1510.
Print, 10.4 x 7.2 cm.

Lucas van Leyden,
Milkmaid with Farmer and Cow, 1510.
Print, 11.5 x 15.7 cm.

None of these works belong to the traditional religious repertoire, so it is easy to see why critics have attempted to find hidden meanings in them. The naked girl with her dog, for example, was seen both as a prostitute and as the symbol of idleness. However, the most important challenge for the young Lucas appears to have been the accurate reproduction of the female nude. While in earlier prints his nudes sometimes appeared rather clumsy, the engraver succeeds here in reproducing the soft, smooth female body in a more natural way, contrasting it with the rough hair of the dog's coat. Other contemporary works demonstrate that a naked woman with her lapdog had erotic connotations. His *Milkmaid* also features erotic elements. The man's reaction to the milkmaid is underlined by the tree trunk he rests his hand upon, with its angled protuberances. The theme of a girl milking a cow is traditionally a motif for the month of April, as erotic innuendo is commonly associated with that spring month. Lucas probably took his inspiration for the motif of a cow occupying the length of the picture from Dürer's print *The Little Horse* (1505). However, rather than a horse, Lucas chose a typical Dutch dairy cow and he replaced the armour-clad halberdier with two Dutch peasants. It is only a small step from full udders to full breasts and other sexual metaphors are obvious.

A virtuoso engraver

Lucas's engraving technique reached its peak in terms of skill and sophistication in around 1517. His focus was now on more traditional subjects involving lots of figures and complicated compositions in a large format. According to Van Mander, Lucas made a great deal of money with this art. He met Dürer, his great role model, in Antwerp in 1521. This encounter, at which the two artists exchanged prints, was described by Dürer in his diary. It was the start of a new period for Lucas, in which Dürer's work was once again a major source of inspiration. In the late 1520s, however, Lucas became increasingly interest-

Lucas van Leyden,
Venus and Mars, 1530.
Print, 18.8 x 24.3 cm.

ed in Italian art, particularly the portrayal of the idealised nude. He modelled his work on Marcantonio Raimondi's engravings of nudes in various postures, which in turn were largely based on designs by Raphael.

Lucas's *Venus and Mars* (created in 1530) is one of these later prints featuring monumental figures, which were strongly influenced by Italian art. The postures of the two figures are taken from seated portraits of emperors in prints by Raimondi. This work is one of the few pieces in Lucas's oeuvre presenting a classical theme. The engraver treats the popular mythological story of the affair between Venus and Mars in a highly original and witty manner. While the discovery of the adulterous couple by Venus's husband Vulcan is usually depicted as a risqué bed scene, the lovers in Lucas's print have no physical contact. Venus gazes at her lover, looking rather tired and resting her melancholy head on one arm, while her son Cupid provocatively reaches out to tweak her nipple and stir her passion. Mars, the virile god of war, has removed his armour and is ready for action. His sword not only functions as a phallic symbol, but also as a barrier between the two lovers. The partially visible sphere in the foreground, the symbol of inconstancy, appears to be an allusion to the unstable nature of physical desire.

Lucas van Leyden,
Aristotle ridden by Phyllis.
Woodcut, 40.7 x 29.3 cm.

Human folly and competition between the sexes

Other prints by Lucas devote a surprising amount of attention to relationships between men and women. This is particularly evident in the theme of Feminine Wiles. Men's fear of female powers of seduction was an important theme from the Middle Ages on. Eve, the original mother, was viewed as the instigator of the Fall and hence every woman was seen as a dangerous creature. Stories about the lust and deceit of women developed into popular *exempla contraria* with a warning function. The man is not depicted as a henpecked husband, but instead as a wise or physically powerful individual who, once taken in by the charms of a woman, can only expect ridicule and ruination. Lucas was the first artist to

Lucas van Leyden, *The Card Players*, ca. 1515. Oil on panel, 29.8 x 39.5 cm.© Museo Thyssen-Bornemisza, Madrid.

devote two series of prints to Feminine Wiles. However, his large woodcut of *Aristotle Ridden by Phyllis*, one of the best-known examples, does not belong to these series. Phyllis was the favourite courtesan of Alexander the Great, who put his duties before love, after warnings from his teacher Aristotle. Out of revenge for Alexander's rejection, Phyllis decided to seduce Aristotle. She walked around in the garden in front of the philosopher's window, with her skirts lifted high and her hair hanging loose until, burning with desire, he pandered to her whims and allowed her to use him as a mount. This humorous but instructive woodcut must have adorned the walls of many a home.

Lucas's first paintings, which he produced in around 1508, do not have religious subjects, but are small panels reflecting the daily lives of the citizenry. One particular group is devoted to gatherings of men and women in contemporary dress, sitting at a table and playing chess or cards, generally for money. The half-length composition of the figures ensures that all attention goes to the psychological interaction and also reduces the distance from the viewer. Lucas had a lot of success with this genre and his compositions were frequently copied or adapted. The satirical effect is often accentuated. The appeal of such depictions was undoubtedly the fact that men and women playing games together traditionally had erotic connotations and competition is an obvious factor. Betting and playing for money was officially banned in Leiden from 1508, but that seems to have had little effect in practice.

The painting *The Card Players* shows a woman playing a game of cards with a fashionable young man and a portly, older gentleman. The woman has just put some coins and the jack of spades on the table and is looking dreamily at the young man. He has conjured up a king of spades and is therefore the winner again, but the woman is only too pleased to lose to him. The older man has only an eight of spades and appears to have lost every hand. A woman with two men of different ages belongs to the pictorial tradition of the love triangle and the theme of unrequited love. The attractive young man is not only lucky in the game of cards, but also in the game of love, and the jackpot here is actually the woman.

Another use of playing cards is depicted in *The Fortune-Teller*, which shows a woman laying cards to predict the future for a well-dressed young man. Impressed, the man takes off his hat to the fortune-teller. However, her exposed bosom, the violets in her bodice and the large jug of wine are symbols of wantonness. To make the fortune-teller's deceit clear, Lucas has depicted a conspicuous image of a fool standing behind her, complete with an exotic fool's cap and bauble. In his prints, too, Lucas often introduces a fool as a commentator to draw the viewer's attention to the folly of the events. Interestingly, the fool nearly always appears in scenes that are related to sex, often illicit. The popularity of the figure of the fool was greatly enhanced by Sebastian Brant's lavishly illustrated *Das Narrenschiff* (The Ship of Fools, published in Basle in 1494). In addition to its entertainment value, this work had a didactic purpose: foolish people should be able to mend their ways when confronted with their own foolishness or that of others.

The relevance of paintings with religious themes

In 1526, Lucas received a commission from the children of timber merchant Claes Dircsz van Swieten to paint a memorial panel for the Pieterskerk in Leiden, in memory of their father. This resulted in one of the most impressive triptychs ever painted in the Netherlands. The exceptionally large format

Lucas van Leyden, *Triptych of the Last Judgement*, 1526-1527. Oil on panel, 269.5 x 184.8 cm (middle); 264 x 76 cm (volets). Museum de Lakenhal, Leiden. Photo by Rik Klein Gotink.

Lucas van Leyden, *The Fortune-Teller*. Oil on panel, 24 x 30.5 cm. Louvre, Paris.

demonstrates not only the availability of funds, but also the important public positions that Van Swieten had held. Remarkably, Van Swieten's actual likeness is missing from the memorial panel, which is very unusual; the work was, however, displayed close to the deceased's spacious crypt. The triptych shows Christ as Judge of the World on the Day of Judgement. The resurrection of humanity was a common theme for epitaphs, but never before had the theme been depicted so effectively. On weekdays, only the monumental exterior of the side panels could be seen, featuring the apostles Peter and Paul, the patron saints of the church, seated in a landscape. It must have made a great impact every time the panels were opened to reveal the large, naked figures rising from their graves and going up to heaven, lovingly guided by angels. Grim fiends lead other alarmed souls to the eternal torments of hell. Viewers are not quick to forget the woman sprawled in the foreground, struggling against a demon that has hold of her foot and is dragging her down to hell, or the man on the left of the central panel who is on his way to heaven and looks around to make sure his wife is following him. Another unforgettable figure is the angel on the left panel who, with his gaze focused on the viewer, wraps his arm around the buttocks of an attractive young man chosen to go to heaven.

Lucas made the unusual decision to depict an Old Testament theme, based on Exodus 17:1–7 and Numbers 20:2–12, in his painting *Moses Striking Water from the Rock* (1527), now in Boston, although the emphasis on the reaction of the bystanders is typical of his work. The Israelites do not seem to be aware of the miracle, but instead rush to fill their jugs with water and to satisfy their material needs. The picture appears to be an allegory of mankind's inability to truly believe. However, in another large triptych, *The Healing of the Blind Man of Jericho* (1531), now in St. Petersburg, Lucas depicts the power of individual faith by portraying the healing of blind Bartimaeus from Mark 10:46–52. This work was commissioned by the wealthy Leiden brickmaker Jacob Florisz van Montfoort and his wife.

Lucas van Leyden, *Triptych with the Dance around the Golden Calf*, 1531. Oil on panel, 93.5 x 6.9 cm (middle); 91.7 x 3 cm (volets). Rijksmuseum Amsterdam.

The Dance around the Golden Calf (painted around 1530) was also made for a private client. The story from Exodus 32 is an unusual theme for a triptych. Moses spent forty days on Mount Sinai, where he received the Ten Commandments from God, while his people, who had grown impatient, made a golden idol that they danced around and feasted. In the foreground, Lucas depicted men, women and children celebrating, while others dance around the Golden Calf in the background and, in the distance, Moses descends the mountain. Again, he is focusing primarily on the human tendency to place material desires and the satisfaction of basic needs above spiritual wellbeing, an inclination that is relevant to all eras.

So, Lucas's religious works may also be seen as an expression of a new and personal experience of faith which would be inconceivable without the influence of humanism (and perhaps the thinking of the Reformation). These works demonstrate that Lucas van Leyden was not only capable of creating appealing themes in his more intimate printed works, but that he was also a major innovator in his larger paintings, who captured the zeitgeist in a very personal way and used his art to bolster moral ideals. ■

Translated by Laura Watkinson

The exhibition *Lucas van Leyden and the Renaissance* will be held at Museum De Lakenhal in Leiden from 20 March to 26 June 2011. This exhibition, which will also feature other Leiden artists from ca. 1490–1550, is accompanied by a lavishly illustrated catalogue.

A Secret Uninhabited Corner of the Netherlands

Rottumerplaat and Rottumeroog

[MICHEL BAKKER]

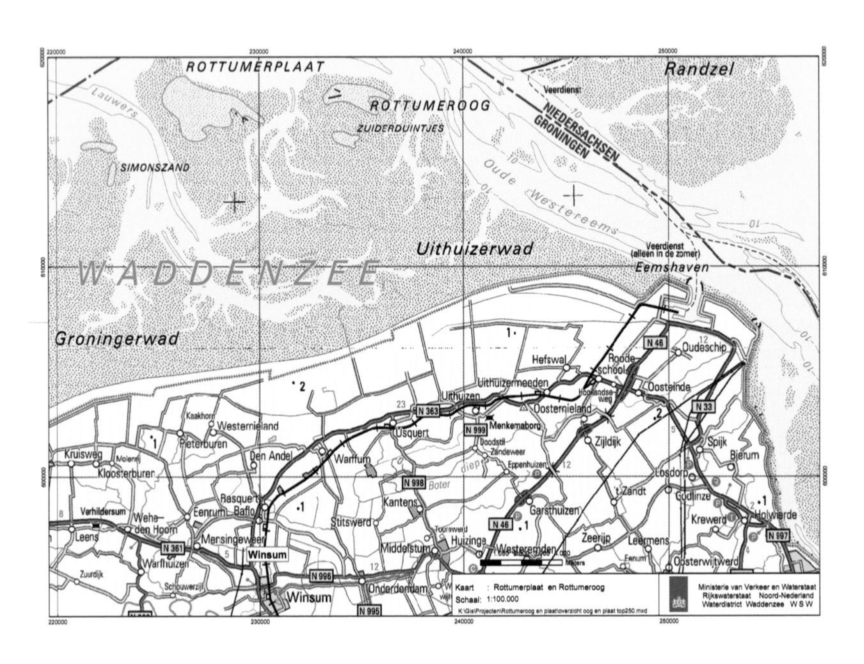

North-Groningen with Rottumerplaat and Rottumeroog in the Wadden Sea.

The battle against the water runs in the blood of the Dutch. And nowhere is that more true than on the Netherlands' northern coast. There has however been a subtle change, from the traditional 'fighting against the sea' to the broader notion of 'fighting with the sea'. Last year the Wadden Sea, the narrow intertidal strip that runs along the northern coast of the Netherlands and continues along the North Sea coasts of Germany and Denmark, was placed on the UNESCO World Heritage List. In all the area covers almost 10,000 square kilometres. The string of islands and sandbanks off the Dutch coast which marks the northern boundary of the Wadden Sea begins in the west with the Razende Bol sandbank, just off the island of Texel, and ends in the eastern Wadden Sea with the islands of Rottumerplaat and Rottumeroog, two jewels in this island necklace which lie uninhabited on the edge of one of the most densely populated regions in the world.

What follows is a story about history, culture and the last undiscovered natural treasures of the Netherlands. But it is also about an Irish earl and his women, about messages in bottles and left shoes.

The tiny islands of Rottumerplaat and Rottumeroog have for centuries formed part of the string of islands marking the northern edge of the Dutch Wadden Sea. As long ago as the Middle Ages, Rottumerplaat appeared on maps as 'Bosch'. Always more of a sandbank than an island, Rottumerplaat has never been inhabited. Its contours have been subject to continual change, although its location has remained more or less constant. Over the last thirty years, management of the island has resulted in the construction of a large

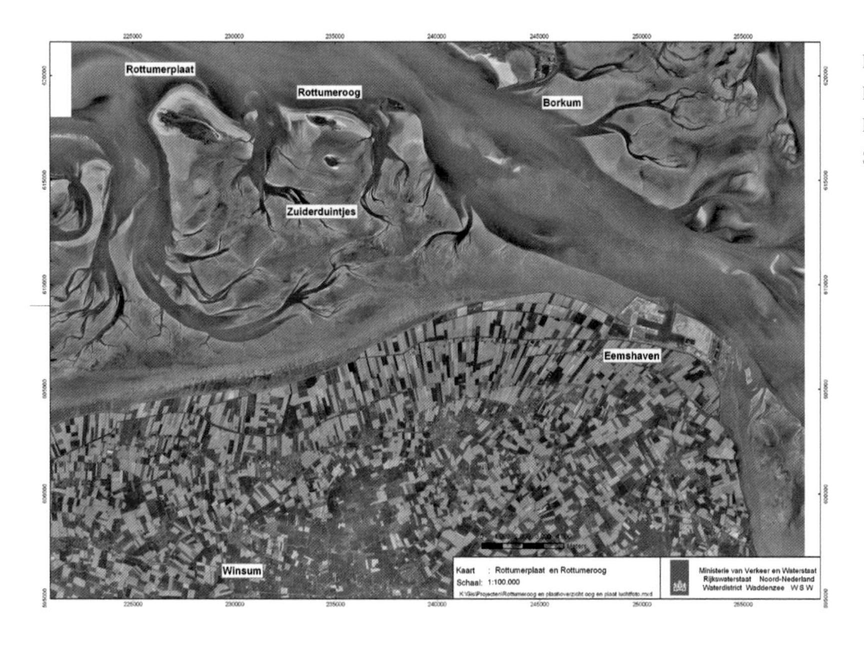

North-Groningen with Rottumerplaat and Rottumeroog in the Wadden Sea seen from the air.

drift dyke. Rottumeroog was much bigger in the past than it is today, and was in fact inhabited for hundreds of years. Its constant shrinking caused the higher central zone to shift east-south-eastwards. The dunes along the north-west coast were increasingly eroded by storm surges, while on the eastern side, partly under the influence of the wind, the landmass grew through a continual (if modest) process of accretion. One consequence of the movement of the island was that the home of the 'Warden' had to be relocated several times to a safer site further east. The way in which the dune formation 'walks' is nothing short of spectacular. At one point, very old - and very welcome - bottles of wine appeared on the western tip of the island; at some point in the past they must have washed up on the eastern shore and been buried by the shifting sands.

Cast-iron beacon on Rottumeroog.

A mad Irish earl

Maps from the 14th century name a further three small Wadden islands in addition to Rottumeroog: Bosch, Heffesant and Coornsant. It is likely that all three islands were used to graze cattle; Bosch may also have been inhabited. The only island about which much is really known is Rottumeroog. The island was formerly owned by two monasteries, a Benedictine monastery in Rottum, a village to the south of Usquert in the province of Groningen, and the Premonstratensian monastery in the municipality of De Marne, also in Groningen. A declaration by the pastors of the villages of Uithuizen and Uithuizermeeden in 1354 states that 'the people of Uithuizen may graze their cattle on Rottumeroog in return for payment and may also cut the marram grass on the island, but may not pull it up'. So there must already have been a sizeable area of meadowland at that time, though there were evidently fears of possible damage to the marram. In the late Middle Ages the island became a trading centre; the story goes that in 1483 goods on the island were stolen by raiders from Hamburg, who also set fire to the warehouses. In later years Rottumeroog became a safe haven for pirates. At the start of the Eighty Years War, the struggle for Dutch independence which began in 1568, the rebel *Watergeuzen* or Sea Beggars had a base there. In 1596 ownership of the island passed to the *Stad en Lande* (the city and province of Groningen), after which the ownership, leasehold rights and the right to flotsam and jetsam were traded many times over.

From 1707 the island was owned for some time by an Irish exile, Donough MacCarthy, fourth Earl of Clancarty. Many stories are told about this 'Mad Earl' ('Malle Graaf'). In the late 17th century he was a supporter of the last Catholic

king of England, James II. After the Glorious Revolution of 1688, in which James was deposed and succeeded by the Protestant William III of Orange and his wife Mary, Donough MacCarthy was first imprisoned in the Tower of London before being sent into exile in 1698 after the signing of the Treaty of Limerick.

Until his death in 1734 MacCarthy and his wife Elisabeth Spencer lived in the coastal area of the Northern Netherlands and North Germany, from Oudwoude in Friesland to Altona near Hamburg. In 1707 he purchased the island of Rottumeroog for 3,000 Dutch guilders; the price included a house, a horse and cart and the right to all articles found on the beach. The island of Bosch, which has since disappeared beneath the waves, also came into MacCarthy's possession. He finally settled in Praalshof, near Altona, where he died on 1 October 1734. Shortly before his death his title was restored

Planting brushwood on the West Side of Rottumeroog. Brushwood screens enhance dune formation.

This wandering Irish earl was probably regarded as a strange creature in his own day, as is borne out by his enduring nickname of 'the Mad Earl' and also by the many wild and sometimes legendary stories of smuggling and piracy, seal-catchers and serving wenches, barkeepers, adultery and debauchery. After his wife's death, he was said to have had three women around him: one with red hair, one with black and one with blonde. And the stories also say that the Mad Earl happened to be responsible for the start of the tradition of *wadlopen*, walking across the Wadden Sea at low tide. One of his servants on Rottumeroog was to be punished for misbehaviour. The Earl announced that he would be hanged next morning. The servant doubted whether his master really meant it, but had no desire to take his last look at his home village of Warffum dangling from the end of a rope. So early in the morning, at low water, he set off to walk across the Wadden Sea. To everyone's amazement, he arrived safe and sound in Warffum.

In 1738 the island again came into the hands of the province of Groningen, and in 1798 it became 'national property'. In 1876 the management and maintenance of the island passed permanently to the state under the aegis of the Ministry of Water Management.

Wardens and beacons

In 1637 a new post was created, that of Warden of Rottum. Between 1637 and 1965 the Wardens lived permanently - summer and winter - on Rottumeroog. The task of the Warden was to manage the island on behalf of the owner by maintaining and looking after it; he was also receiver of wrecks, with responsibility for goods washed up on the shore and had the right to collect gulls' eggs. When we bear in mind that the Warden also managed to run a farm, generally with a team of horses, cows, sheep, small livestock and pets, he clearly had to be a skilled and versatile worker.

The Warden was assisted in all this by his family and a number of male and female servants. In the eighteenth century a small contingent of soldiers temporarily swelled the population of the island. The Warden also had to protect stranded ships and cargoes and try to rescue victims of shipwrecks.

From 1743 to the present day, there have been a total of six Warden's houses on the island. The first was located on the eastern tip of Rottumerplaat, more than two kilometres as the crow flies from the present site. The last Warden, Jan Toxopeus, retired in 1965.

Since then Rottumeroog has remained uninhabited, though the Warden's house is still maintained. The new bungalow has since been upgraded and is still used during the summer months as a residence for the maintenance team which cares for the island.

And then there are the beacons, built as prominent landmarks to guide passing ships. There were originally two beacons on the island, serving shipping travelling up the Eems estuary. Until 1883 these cast-iron beacons had been preceded by wooden structures which had to be repaired and relocated every twenty to thirty years.

Because of the 'walking' of the island the western beacon eventually became separated from the land; it was demolished in 1931. By that time, advances in navigation technology meant that one beacon was sufficient. Today the remaining beacon, known as the *Emder kaap*, is still visible from afar, standing proud at 21.5 metres high; in 1999, though, it was moved to a new site 400 metres away. From 1910 to 1930 a lifeboat operated by the Noord- en Zuid-Hollandsche Redding Maatschappij, predecessor of the present-day Royal Netherlands Sea Rescue Institution, was also stationed on Rottumeroog.

Buildings on an uninhabited island

Until around 1920 Rottumerplaat was small (about 100 ha). It appeared at a spot which 300 years before had been approximately the centre of Rottumeroog. Between 1900 and 1940 the Boschplaat sandbank, originally to the west of Rottumerplaat, moved eastwards as a result of the encroaching Lauwers inlet. After 1940 it shrank rapidly and eventually merged with Rottumerplaat. Partly

because of this, and partly because another large sandbank to the north-west also attached itself to Rottumerplaat, by around 1950 Rottumerplaat had grown considerably. Between 1952 and 1980 a man-made drift dyke was created by extending an existing dune in the south-east of the island.

Installing sand stabiliser screens and planting marram and lyme-grass enabled this drift dyke to develop into a chain of dunes. The protection offered by this has enabled a rich area of salt marsh to develop in its lee. Spontaneous dune formation takes place in the western section of Rottumerplaat, but the island's present character is due in large part to the man-made drift dyke; if this were no longer maintained, Rottumerplaat would cease to be an island and revert to being a sandbank. Following the flood disaster in the south-western province of Zeeland in 1953, the Executive Agency of Transport and Water Management (*Rijkswaterstaat*) also took on the maintenance of Rottumerplaat.

The last Warden's house but one on Rottumeroog with belvedere. The last Warden Jan Toxopeues lived here with his family till 1957.

Rottumerplaat boasts a large and fairly luxurious dwelling-house. After the Second World War successive governments stressed the importance of agriculture in the Netherlands, and the prevailing opinion was that the country had to be able to produce some of its own food. A logical consequence of this was an increase in the area of land devoted to farming. The Mansholt Plan of 1968

Sandbank with seals on Rottumerplaat.

(named after the then European Commissioner for Agriculture, Sicco Mansholt, a native of Groningen) initially envisaged reclaiming the entire Wadden Sea for use as farmland. Later this was restricted to the eastern half, from the rudimentary dam which still exists to the island of Ameland up to and including Rottumeroog, roughly speaking that part of the Wadden Sea to the north of Groningen. A start was made by upgrading the Rottumerplaat sandbank into an island with a line of dunes along its northern edge.

Given the plans to reclaim the whole of the Wadden Sea, it made sense to have or create support stations at strategic points to act as links and as bases for workers. Rottumerplaat was regarded as a suitable site. Moreover, creating a drift dyke was a fairly cheap way of laying the basis for a dyke that would act as a defence against the sea. An important secondary-effect was the protection this was expected to provide for the mainland coast during storms, at least for so long as the Wadden Sea had not been reclaimed, protection that would of course become permanent thereafter. The thinking was that the new coastline would absorb the power of the North Sea, while in the lee of the island only wind-driven waves would be able to form, greatly reducing the impact on the mainland dykes.

There was already a small old dune in the south-eastern part of Rottumerplaat. This would now serve as an operating base and a site for the service buildings. In 1950/51 a hut known as 'De Pionier' was constructed; it was little more than a shed with room for a maximum of eleven people. It was small and very primitive; drinking water had to be brought in in milk churns and the only lighting was by gas. In around 1958 a second hut was built, large enough to sleep twenty people, along with a shed to house machinery and tools.

In 1965 a brand new accommodation block was opened; the building and its facilities are still in use today. A new wing was added in 1979, used exclusively as a dormitory. The original dormitory is now a recreation room, and improvements have been made to the furnishings, power supply, and so on.

Rottumerplaat.

Message in a bottle

Twice a year a small group of volunteers goes to live and work on Rottumerplaat and Rottumeroog. Among other things, they help to collect the rubbish that has washed up on the beaches. Each year around 20 million kilos of waste ends up in the North Sea, and recently global attention has focused on the vast amounts of plastic drifting around in the world's oceans. Three million kilos of waste wash up on the Dutch North Sea coast, mainly on the Wadden islands and the tip of the province of North Holland. This litter consists of everything from gloves, fish crates, light bulbs and rope to refrigerators and crates 'with contents'. While it is not uncommon to find messages in bottles, it always gives rise to mild celebration. These messages are often 'posted' from a German island, but there was also one from a Scottish vicar, trying a novel means of raising money for a new church organ.

One permanent component of this flotsam is shoes. For many years it has been claimed that more left shoes than right are washed up. In the case of shellfish such as the black clam this is a proven phenomenon: it is a demonstrable fact that more left than right shell-sections are washed up.

It is not all one-way traffic, however: post has also been sent from the island, though admittedly it was 'post by radio'. At the invitation of the Dutch broadcasting organisation VARA, the writers Godfried Bomans and Jan Wolkers each spent a week on Rottumerplaat in 1971. During their sojourn there, in total isolation, each of them kept a diary. From Hotel de Breedenburg in Warffum the radio presenter Willem Ruis kept in touch with them, and their conversations were broadcast to the nation.

'It would have been impossible to imagine two greater contrasts, and there was something nice about that', Bomans wrote later after the final broadcast in which the two writers featured together. Bomans did not feel at ease on Rottumerplaat. He was frightened at night (imagining that the sounds made by the seagulls were the mumbling voices of men) and quickly fell ill. He described himself as 'a man wearing a suit on the beach', and readily admitted that he would rather be back home in Haarlem. He appreciated the nature all round him, but did not really feel part of it. Wolkers, by contrast, was all energy: he went for long walks around the island, went swimming at night, lived largely from what nature provided, built an entrance gate, took an interest in the flora and fauna. His diary and radio fragments about the sick and dead seals that he found stick in the memory. A notable fact is that the tent where they both stayed was right in among the birds; Bomans even talks about a nest just five metres away.

A wayside restaurant

The islands Rottumerplaat and Rottumeroog are of great value in themselves. They help enclose the Wadden Sea and provide a degree of protection against the North Sea, while islands and Wadden Sea together protect the mainland from the full force of the sea's attack.

But there is more. The Wadden Sea has been described as the central wayside restaurant on the migration route between breeding grounds and winter quarters. Birds find an abundance of food there and on the exposed mudflats they can put on weight ready for the long flight ahead. It also offers them a safe resting place until they are ready to leave. And rare bird species breed there, such as the little tern and snowy plover.

The islands have their own value as nature reserves: the beaches, the tidal marshes and the dunes are each valuable in their own right, and there is a great diversity of flora and fauna. And they are not only a muddy Eldorado for wading birds, but also a haven for seals.

And both - now uninhabited - islands also bear the physical traces of particular histories which have become part of Dutch culture.

The islands having been placed under the protection of the Nature Conservancy Act in 1980, in the 1990s it was decided to leave them henceforth entirely to nature, given that the Act states that no work may be carried out in nature conservancy areas. This government policy came to the attention of Hendrik Toxopeus, the son of the last Warden, and he and his wife Jannie decided to occupy Rottumeroog. The occupation lasted two weeks and attracted the hoped-for publicity, extending as far as Parliament. The Friends of Rottumeroog and Rottumerplaat Foundation (Stichting Vrienden van Rottumeroog en Rottumerplaat) was founded in May 1991 with the aim of preserving these two important natural and cultural assets in the Wadden Sea. It works with volunteers to carry out maintenance, encourages research into protection techniques and works to increase awareness of the islands among the general public. The Foundation works closely with the statutory administrators of Rottumeroog and Rottumerplaat: the Water Management Agency, Forestry Commission, the Province of Groningen and the Ministry of Economic Affairs, Agriculture and Innovation.

To secure the future of the islands, with their natural and cultural treasures, reviving the post of Receiver of Wrecks would be an attractive option. Like his predecessors, this official could also monitor both islands as they migrate naturally towards the south-east.

The turbulent history of these two 'uninhabited islands' means they have come to feel very important to the Dutch. They appeal to the imagination, have a place in many people's dreams and are a source of inspiration for the visual arts, music and literature alike. Apart from the simple fact of their existence, their appeal lies in their inaccessibility. They are rightly and justifiably thought of as Wadden jewels. ■

www.rottumeroog.org
www.rottumerplaat.org

Translated by Julian Ross

(With thanks to Olga van der Klooster, Hendricus Kooi, Rita Renkema-Weerd, Dick Spijker, Wiepke Toxopeus).

Penetrations

The 'Art Needlework' of Michael Raedecker

[FRANK VAN DER PLOEG]

For years, visual artist Michael Raedecker (Amsterdam, 1963) was more popular outside the Netherlands than 'at home'. Art critics in the Netherlands often emphasise this. The fact is that Raedecker is barely represented in public collections in his home country. His work has been purchased by private individuals and for corporate collections but, in terms of museums, only the Van Abbemuseum in Eindhoven, the Scheringa Museum of Realist Art (until the collection was dismantled in 2009) and the Gemeentemuseum Den Haag own works by him. His exhibition *line-up* in 2009 was an opportunity to show what the Netherlands has been missing.

One of the main explanations for the fact that Raedecker is more famous outside the Netherlands is purely logistical. He has lived and worked in London since 1997, and that is where he has made a name for himself. He is also someone who seeks out boundaries in everything. After studying fashion at the Gerrit Rietveld Academie (1985-1990) in Amsterdam, he was briefly apprenticed to the Belgian fashion designer Martin Margiela. After this he changed direction and began working as an independent visual artist. He spent two years (1993/1994) at the increasingly internationally orientated Rijksakademie in Amsterdam. For the majority of artists, a period spent at the Rijksakademie studios is the springboard to an independent career. Participants from abroad usually keep Amsterdam as a base. But not Michael Raedecker. He studied to become a Master of Fine Arts (MFA) at Goldsmiths College in London and settled there in more than one respect. His name became firmly established when the famous gallery owner Charles Saatchi noticed his needlework. He showed Raedecker's work in a group exhibition entitled 'The New Neurotic Realism' (a 'movement' he branded in May 1998 with a publication by Dick Price). Michael Raedecker was nominated for the Turner Prize in 2000 and for more than a decade now he has been an internationally acclaimed artist who exhibits worldwide.

The difference between the acclaim at home and that abroad is also partly based on his choice of subject. The international character of his work manifests itself in his subjects. Raedecker often takes photographs of almost empty American landscapes and suburbs as source material and his visual memory takes him into equally American televisual worlds. At the same time, his work is rooted in the art history of the Netherlands. He chooses 'classic' genres such

Michael Raedecker, *superficial*, 2009. Acrylic and thread on canvas, 48 × 40 cm. ©The artist and Hauser & Wirth.

as still life and landscape, and quotes major figures such as Mondrian. As a result, it is the American influence in his work that was and is referred to in the Netherlands (even during his time at the Rijksakademie), whereas outside the Netherlands it is the Dutch derivations that are emphasised.

'On the bias'

In terms of technique, Raedecker strikes a balance between art and design, between Painting with a capital 'P' and handicraft with a small 'h'. He embroiders. Embroidery is not something that one associates with serious art. Yet the Netherlands has a couple of artists who have 'woven' this expression of popular culture into their work in such a way that it has become a visual medium with added value. In the flat plane, Berend Strik's stitching comes closest to Raedecker's. However, whereas Strik partially effaces and actually emphasises important visual elements by swamping them with machine stitching, Raedecker uses his thread as impasto and to sketch contours, sometimes very subtly and sometimes in large 'clusters'. Designer Hella Jongerius has embroidered the contours of images into vases, which means they can only be used for dried flowers, and in others she uses coloured silicone rubber to seal the holes that have been punched into the vases – and to suggest embroidery thread! – thereby making them waterproof anyway. A couple of years after that, she embroidered plates onto a tablecloth. Jongerius treats the functionality of her 'utensils' in the same way that Raedecker treats high art in his 'paintings'.

Raedecker once said in an interview: 'I've sort of entered [the art world] through the back door. I feel as if I am an intruder. Perhaps that's why I had to do something stupid, something deliberately wrong – marrying the rich and intense history of painting with accessible, clumsy, unfashionable handicraft." For Raedecker, the handicraft and the time he devotes to it are the *raison d'être* for his position in the art world. His paintings may be – no, they *must* be – time-consuming. He also sees it as a reaction to the more conceptual approach to art that preceded his period.

Raedecker's work method is fairly traditional. The starting point is usually a photograph he has found. Using a projector and a pencil, he transfers the outlines onto canvas, which he then places flat on the ground. He glues thread over the contours and paints parts of the image in acrylics. In earlier paintings he poured his paint over the canvas, often in different layers, which resulted in a rather impersonal skin of paint that contrasts strongly with the needlework. In his more recent work, paint plays a less prominent role. The acrylic paint is applied so thinly that the structure of the linen is just visible through it. If the paint plays a figurative role at all, then it is like an outline in a cartoon strip, just to provide a hint of shadow. Occasionally drips are visible, but the tactile structure comes from the appliquéd and stitched wool threads – this is the work that takes most time.

Deepening

In 2009, Raedecker created *simplicity* and *superficial*, both depicting an embroidered cloth on a table set for breakfast. The titles are only a superficial 'cover' (!). On closer inspection, deeper layers are visible. The works portray a table set for a meal. Using very few materials (various shades of grey) Raedecker suggests the folds of the cloths. The focal point of the painting is in the lower right-hand section, where the cloths are most detailed. At the edges, only the outline is visible. The cloth has a grid like the embroidery patterns in women's magazines. Over this we see a larger squared grid of slightly untidy thread. The grid is interesting. It features in other recent works, such as the floral piece *corrupt* (2008), which contains an allusion to an early Mondrian. Many of the squares in the tablecloths are embroidered in black, giving the appearance of a crossword puzzle.

Michael Raedecker claims not to want to 'steer' viewers too much, but his well-considered titles certainly point them in the right direction. Take *penetration* (2005), a painting of an umbelliferous plant with a noticeably phallic form. The erotic connotations of flowers have infiltrated art since Georgia O'Keeffe

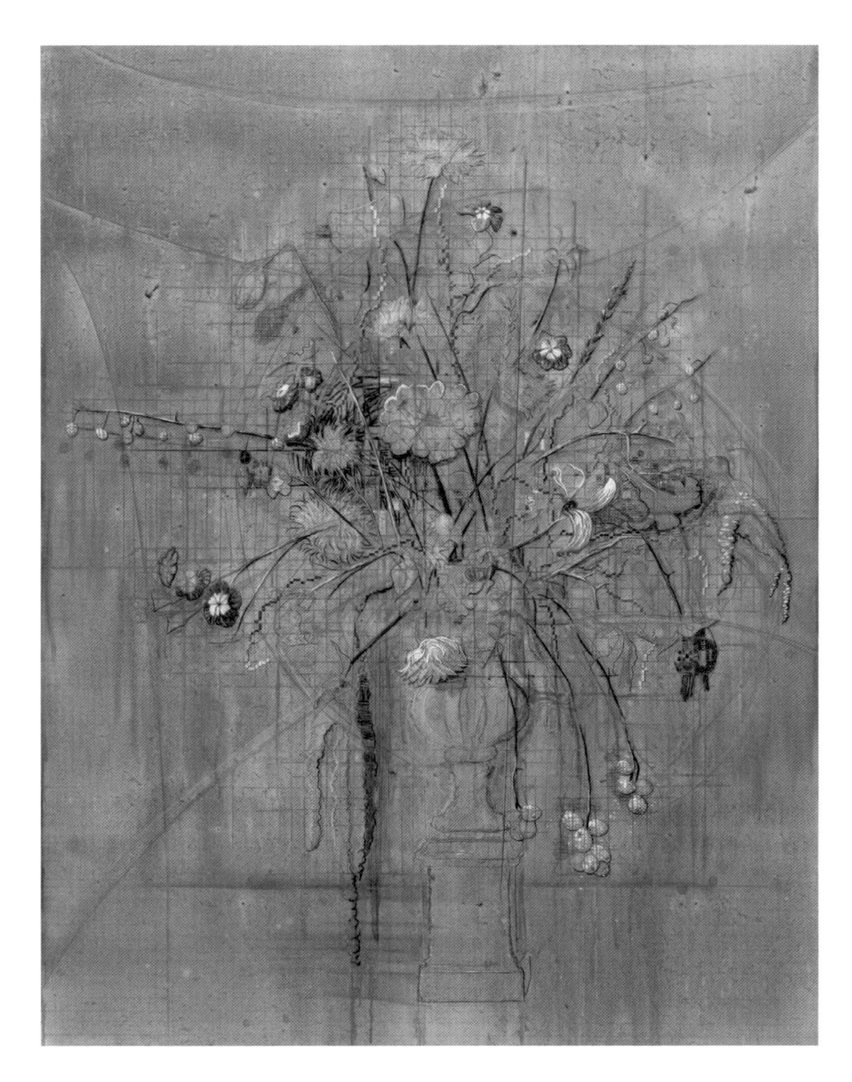

Michael Raedecker, *corrupt*, 2009. Acrylic and thread on canvas, 162 x 130 cm. © The artist and Hauser & Wirth.

(1887-1986). Raedecker emphasises that every plant needs penetration in order to emerge from the earth. He looks to himself, too: he constantly penetrates his canvases with his embroidery techniques, of course. It would be interesting to know whether he gives his works their titles once they are finished, or whether he has an idea for a title in mind when he begins. That seems to me to be a possibility. Raedecker himself explains that the title of his recent exhibition, *line-up* – a survey of the past five years of his career – refers to the 'line-up' of a music band and – with a little prompting from the interviewer – an identity parade at a police station.

His paintings have, almost without exception, a dark side. The use of colour, the choice of subject and titles all contribute to the sense of doom. Many of his landscapes and interiors have the appearance of deserted crime scenes. Raedecker isolates a limited number of visual elements - sometimes some walls, or one or two objects that would be too ordinary in a 'normal' still life. He uses colour sparingly. The use of many grey tints lends something sinister to his work. This is actually reinforced by sometimes subtle and sometimes vividly coloured elements that he adds with his needlework. It is an ambience that evokes – but much more subtly – the paintings of the Dutch artist Gé-Karel van der Sterren. Van der Sterren also plays with the skin of things, but in a slightly more direct way. His exuberant and candy-coloured paintings depict people or animals that have been skinned. Van der Sterren paints in acrylics, too, and uses oils for certain accents in the same way that Raedecker uses thread. Here we come to a singularity that evokes Raedecker's work – making comparisons with other artists. The emptiness and the focus are something he has in common with Luc Tuymans, and there are other examples of kindred spirits, nevertheless Raedecker's representations stand by themselves.

Raedecker's work seems remarkably easy to divide into historical genres: landscape, still life, interior and even portraiture. Apart from historical figures such as Hitler, Raedecker also presented a series of stereotypical heads: 'tronies', a genre often practised by Rembrandt. Raedecker has ignored the highest attainable genre of the Renaissance, historical painting. The ideal of incorporating as many figures as possible in complicated poses simply isn't his cup of tea. Raedecker's works are empty, deserted, devoid of human activity.

Development

Raedecker summarises his personal development as follows. In his first paintings his subjects are based on himself, as a child of his time. His youth was filled with images dominated by pop culture: television. There is something awkward about his paintings from 1993 and 1994 compared to works created a couple of years later. The lines and the stitching are deliberately clumsy, as Raedecker himself asserts. A good example of applying poured paint is an *untitled* painting from 1995. It represents a figure whose head is little more than a daub of paint. Five years later he painted the tronies, which are considerably more sophisticated.

This was followed by a longer period with work that has a surrealist undertone. A frightening example is *the reflex* (2003). We see a swan that has fallen forward in an eerie jet-black pool. We cannot escape the conclusion that the bird is a victim of an oil spill. This work shows Raedecker at his most proficient. The difference in rendering between this and the earlier works could hardly be greater. It is not only the plumage, foot, eye and beak that are realistically rendered in fleecy thread; he also paints the swan's reflection in the pool of oil with great panache. Obviously this was a subject that was waiting to be painted. A year earlier, the aforementioned Gé-Karel van der Sterren painted the swansong of a goose. The bird – most of its body already plucked – is running over a dark pond. Van der Sterren is not a man of small gestures.

Back to Raedecker. *Brilliant gloom* (2004) is a complex work. It depicts the type of solitary rural house we very often see in different forms in his paintings. It is night, and the viewer has the impression that there has been a party. Above the house hangs an enormous frame with cheerful lighting in every conceivable colour. The lighted spheres give out a misty glow. The frame – which has the appearance of overblown stage lighting – is in fact suspended in mid-air. The black 'drips' applied above it are not the essential structure from which the lights hang, but appear to be musical notes. In the foreground we see some floating lumps of stone and small bushes. It is a painting to lose oneself in.

Michael Raedecker, *therapy*, 2005. Acrylic and thread on canvas, 63 × 75 cm. ©The artist and Hauser & Wirth.

In *therapy* (2005), Raedecker takes on all his painting predecessors, from the classical painters – whose highest ambition was emulation, i.e. to improve on the work of the teacher – up to and including the magical realist Carel Willink, whose contemporaneous critics often complained that he knitted rather than painted the sweaters worn by his models. And what does Raedecker do in this painting? He 'knits' a coffee cup – literally. The rendering, the reflections in a fragment of mirror, the ability to make an embroidered glass look transparent; these are all examples of extraordinary skill.

In recent years, Raedecker has been inspired by the everyday. In 2007 and 2008 he painted grimy towels, washing hanging on a line, a table and chairs, a cake, the tables with embroidered cloths, but also, 'just like that', a section of an embroidery pattern – which he has already stitched. Even more than in the past, he reduces his visual information until only the absolutely essential remains. The tendency is to use less and less colour and a more outline-based approach. *On*, (2008), acquired by the Gemeentemuseum in The Hague, is an echo of *brilliant gloom*. A number of poles with electricity cables and illuminated spheres stand against a misty background. A fairy ring? A modern variant of megaliths? Latent surrealism.

Probably without realising it, Raedecker has an early soulmate in terms of material and also of ambience: Christine van Zeegen (1890-1973). Between 1915 and 1925, Van Zeegen mainly embroidered designs created by her brother – even then embroidery was for women. The result was anything but prim. She set her translations of nature (cockerels, fighting mantises, polyps), rendered in extravagances of thread, against almost monochrome backgrounds; to which the name 'art needlework' was given. Her *Opengespleten knotwilgstam* (Pollarded willow with split trunk) from 1914 is an explosion of woollen thread that, today, would certainly be regarded as erotic. It shares the unstoppable vigour depicted in Raedecker's *penetration*, but decay is inevitable: as the willow grows, the plant will eventually flower itself to death.

As a description, 'art needlework' perfectly expresses Raedecker's wish to fuse the 'high' with the 'low' – a fusion that is also reflected in the word picture. As Raedecker himself might put it, the vernacular 'penetrates' that which is higher – by first punching holes in the defences then lovingly binding the wounds. ■

Translated by Yvette Mead

FURTHER READING

MAXINE HODSON & ANNE-MARIE WATSON (ed.), *Michael Raedecker line-up*, Camden (Camden Arts Centre) / Harderwijk (d'jonge Hond), 2009, 87 p. Publication to accompany the exhibition in Camden Arts Centre; GEM, museum voor actuele kunst, The Hague; Carré d'Art - Musée d'art contemporain de Nîmes.

hael Raedecker, *iant gloom*, 2004. Acrylic thread on canvas, 190 o cm. © The artist and ser & Wirth.

Michael Raedecker, *reflex*, 2003. Acrylic and thread on canvas, 190 x 300 cm. Collection Gemeentemuseum Den Haag.

[ALEID TRUIJENS]

A Dutch Exotic in His Own Country

On the Writer Maarten 't Hart

Maarten 't Hart, Warmond, 2009. Photo by Klaas Koppe.

He is coming increasingly to resemble the prolific Simon Vestdijk (1898-1971) from Doorn, author of 52 novels, 23 collections of essays and thousands of poems, whom he greatly admired. Poems aside, the total output of Maarten 't Hart (1944) is getting fairly close: 19 novels, 9 collections of stories and over 20 works of non-fiction, including ethological studies, autobiographical works, books of essays and collected columns. And then there are thousands of uncollected articles, like the reviews he has written for newspapers and magazines. And in the midst of all this activity he has managed to reread and reappraise all 52 of Vestdijk's novels.

Certainly, 't Hart will have to continue writing a little longer to equal his model, who in the words of the poet Adriaan Roland Holst 'wrote faster than God can read'. But 't Hart isn't yet 73 (Vestdijk's age when he died): he reached the retirement age of 65 on 25 November 2009. He is unlikely to make much use of the reduced fares on public transport to which he is now entitled, since he is a fanatical cyclist. Moreover, he seems well-equipped to live to a ripe old age. Whereas Vestdijk sat thumping his typewriter for days on end (making a din that had to be drowned out by the whine of a vacuum cleaner), with a cigarette forever dangling from the corner of his mouth, and often suffered from depression, 't Hart radiates health and good cheer. He spends many hours in his vegetable garden, which provides him with the kind of frugal and unappetising food – turnips and carrots – that keeps you slim and tough. The writer promoted this pitiful diet in his last-but-one book *The Deaf Ears Diet* (Het Dovemansorendieet, 2007).

The two have other things in common too. Their precise scientific bent, for example. Many Dutch writers are historians, teachers or involved with literature, but not these two. Vestdijk studied medicine, worked as a doctor for a short time and remained fascinated by mental illnesses. As a biologist, 't Hart knows all about the behaviour of rats and aquatic animals: he wrote his doctoral thesis on the behaviour of the male three-spined stickleback, which 'creeps' repeatedly through the empty nest, and worked at Leiden University for a while as a researcher. He still regrets the fact that the university abolished his post as an ethologist and researcher – he could easily have handled that alongside his huge literary output and the work he did at home with plants and animals.

Even a scientifically-minded boy can be an avid reader. Ever since as a toddler in the library corner he opened a book about a dog called Tippeltje and an 'overwhelming feeling of happiness' flowed through him, 't Hart has read everything he could lay hands on – just hoovering it all up. As a reviewer for papers and magazines he seldom demolished books. Week after week he excitedly proclaimed his great loves: Faulkner, Trollope, Fontane, Roth, Conrad, Svevo and Proust.

In Dutch literature too he has his favourites: F.B. Hotz (1922-2000), for instance, the writer from Oegstgeest on whose door 't Hart knocked after Hotz's late début in 1976, to tell him how wonderful he thought his stories were. They became friends and 't Hart published a splendid book of reminiscences of Hotz, *The Man with the Glass* (De man met het glas , 2002).

Although in the 1970s and 1980s he wrote more for the press than many journalists or reviewers, 't Hart has a very low opinion of professional critics: he regularly makes it plain that he finds them a contemptible race, earning their living by demolishing what has been made with someone else's life's blood. They are loathsome pedants who are themselves incapable of writing a novel and take out their frustration at this in the newspaper. Within that despicable guild, in 't Hart's view, those who have studied Dutch make up the lowest caste. Those with a background in Dutch studies are crazy about narrative devices: they have learned nothing else in their stupid courses. They do not approve of a book unless it is 'layered', polyphonic or polyinterpretable; in short, they only like books that seem tailor-made for academic models to be tested out on them. It follows that authors who have studied Dutch write deadly dull books, in 't Hart's opinion.

He himself calls himself quite unconcernedly a storyteller. His main concern is the story he wants to tell, not so much the plot – which in his case is seldom ingenious – but the atmosphere, the dialogues and the characters' feelings.

Spectacular theatre with flowing robes

A great love of classical music also links 't Hart and Vestdijk. 't Hart enjoys playing the piano and the church organ, and Vestdijk also relaxed by playing the piano. Both are great aficionados of Bach and have written extensively on him and other composers, but Vestdijk liked Mahler while 't Hart loathes that composer's pathos. He prefers to listen to psalms.

Both of them took an anti-religious stance, although 't Hart's antipathy is more deep-seated and could also be called a love that has gone off the rails. In a series of columns for the daily *NRC Handelsblad*, collected as *Those who Abandon God Have Nothing to Fear* (Wie God verlaat heeft niets te vrezen, 1997) and *Through God's Eyes* (De bril van God, 2002), he attacks the many inconsistencies and contradictions in the Bible with the weapon of a close textual knowledge of the Scriptures; because 't Hart knows his Bible: at home, in a strictly Calvinist gravedigger's family in Maassluis, it was the only book. Yet for him Catholicism is still a degree or two worse than the faith of his forefathers: it is mainly the 'ritual mumbo-jumbo' of Rome that horrifies 't Hart: symbolic acts such as confirmation, confession and extreme unction. All 'accursed idolatry', in the view of the lapsed Calvinist, with as absolute low point 'the spectacular theatre of flowing robes' that the Roman Catholics call the Last Supper. The writer Gerard Reve, a Catholic convert, described such people, who are insensitive to the universal power of rituals and think that true believers feel that the Bible must be accepted as true, as suffering from 'symbol blindness'.

In 1947, when he published his collection of essays *The Future of Religion* (De toekomst der religie), Vestdijk felt that Christianity's great days were behind it: the future belonged to non-denominational, enlightened Christians in a just society. But for the anti-Bible campaigner 't Hart it is a great struggle just to cast off the literalness of faith. In 2000, in the older peoples' magazine *Plus*: 'I don't believe in Jesus as the son of God or in that old man with the beard; but I do believe in a supreme being, a shaping force behind the huge universe. My view comes quite close to that of the God of the Old Testament: a rather rancorous and tyrannical God, exalted above everything.'

Not completely free then. Only an ex-Calvinist can react to believers in such a fanatical, almost fundamentalist way. That was apparent in 2007, when 't Hart furiously demanded the resignation of Marianne Thieme, a Member of Parliament for the Animals' Party. 't Hart's was the final name on the party's list of candidates, because he feels strongly about animal suffering. Until he discovered that Thieme is a practising Seventh-Day Adventist. That Christian group expect the 'speedy Second Coming of Christ' at the End of Days. Hence Thieme was not fit to head an animals' party, he felt. Animals do not believe in the Second Coming or in the End of Days. Apart from which, why in that case should anyone get worked up about the future?

In 2010 't Hart's direct, principled way of reasoning produced a most satisfying result. The nurse Lucia de Berk, who had been sentenced to life imprisonment for the supposed murder of seven young patients in the hospital where she worked, was acquitted by the Supreme Court after serving almost seven years in prison. 't Hart had always believed in her innocence and found the evidence for her guilt, which was based on probabilities, utterly unconvincing. He, together with a number of other people, argued that there was insufficient proof that the children had died as a result of human intervention, and their perseverance led eventually to the conviction being overturned. 'After this judicial error I have lost all confidence in the rule of law in this country,' said 't Hart at the time.

There are also striking thematic parallels in the work of Vestdijk and 'Hart. Again and again the theme is love, which promises the fulfilment of every desire, but invariably ends in disillusion. Vestdijk wrote a great deal about his childhood in the small town of Lahringen, an anagram of his native Harlingen in Friesland. Here his literary alter ego Anton Wachter grew up, became an odd-man-out, a lonely boy, pampered by his mother and rejected by his first great love. Much of what 't Hart has written can also be traced back to the primal spring, the post-war poverty in a pious Calvinist family in Maassluis near Rotterdam. This beautiful town is the backdrop for novels set in the last century, especially the 1950s, such as *Stones for a Long-Eared Owl* (Stenen voor een ransuil), *Bearers of Bad Tidings* (De aansprekers), and *The Steep Slope* (De steile helling). But in the splendid historical novel *The Psalm Riot* (Het psalmenoproer, 2006) we are also in Maassluis, though now at the end of the eighteenth century. 't Hart describes the huge commotion caused when in 1773 a new rhyming version of the Psalms was introduced. The common people, the impoverished fishermen coping with falling herring catches, revolt. 't Hart identifies wholeheartedly with his main characters, and even puts eighteenth-century Dutch into their mouths.

On Tuesdays barley stew

Maassluis was also where his own revolt began. Although he was a quiet, well-behaved boy –albeit one who was very good at school – he was to free himself from rigid faith at an early age, and by wide reading, listening and studying develop into what he eventually became: an erudite writer and biologist, with a vast knowledge of music and literature.

The young Maarten, we read in essays, columns and autobiographical pieces – and the characters of his novels are made in his likeness – grew up in his Calvinist family with no toys, no books, no music, and in fact no money, but in the constant fear of the Lord. On Monday the family of five – see *The Deaf Ears Diet* – ate bread and milk, on Tuesdays barley stew and on Wednesday, traditionally the day for minced meat, there were gooey endives without mince. Thursday was the high point: brown beans with syrup! Father, the gravedigger, was inclined to hand out the occasional wallop, but his mother was very sweet. She let her son play with a doll from her own childhood and taught him to knit and embroider: 'With the same eagerness with which I now read, I clumsily knitted vests that sometimes constricted me like straitjackets, and sometimes came down far below my knees like dresses,' writes 't Hart in *The Sum of Misunderstandings* (De som van misverstanden). Is it really that odd, then, that in 1991 he came out of the closet with an aberration that had troubled him for years: the need to dress up in women's clothes? At that year's Dutch Literary Ball the writer appeared proudly, but with a charming diffidence, in a dress, with a curly wig and painted nails. Not that 't Hart had suddenly become a transvestite, and definitely not a homosexual. The need to disguise himself as a woman, he explained, issued from the desire to identify completely with the object of his love, the girls he adored. His highly polemical anti-feminist book *There's no Such Thing as Woman* (De vrouw bestaat niet), he told astonished interviewers, had been written in 1982 out of pure jealousy: didn't women, beautiful and unattainable, already have complete power over those puny men: why did they have to go and become feminists on top of that?

In 't Hart's *A Flight of Whimbrels* (Een vlucht regenwulpen) there is a description of an experience with one such unattainable girl. At a birthday party Maarten, a biologist of about thirty, still unmarried, meets someone with whom he makes a date. She turns out to be none other than the sister of his great childhood love Martha – to whom he was never able to declare his love; when he makes a last clumsy attempt the girl runs away in alarm. The rejection makes him doubt the existence of a heaven: 'What good was it to be saved by Christ and go to heaven after your death if she was just scared of you and ran away from you. You'd be in heaven for all eternity, or rather for all eternity feel the pain of her who was unattainable.' Maarten sees the girl he adores once more, at a primary school reunion. He studies her face intently – and is completely happy. That is all a lonely lover needs. He cherishes his loneliness, in which he can keep his desire intact. 'A person should be a cell,' the biologist thinks, 'a lump that divides into two, then there'd be no problem.'

Writing in a good humour

Finally, there is one further striking similarity between Simon Vestdijk and Maarten 't Hart: both are in some way underrated writers. With Vestdijk that did not seem to be the case during his lifetime. For years he was regarded as the obvious Dutch candidate for the Nobel Prize; according to Gerard Reve he had already written his acceptance speech. He gained many laurels and honours and was awarded all the great literary prizes: the P.C. Hooft Prize (1950), the Constantijn Huygens Prize (1955) and the State Prize for Dutch Literature (1971). But only ten years after his death he seemed to have been forgotten. School pupils no longer put his books on their exam reading lists and his books soon went out of print. Despite the immense amount her husband had written, in the 1990s Vestdijk's widow was unable to make ends meet from the royalties. Literary textbooks pay dutiful attention to Vestdijk. His versatility, erudition and productivity are praised, but his style, especially, comes in for severe criticism: his protracted descriptions lacking in sensuality, his meandering sentences endlessly weighing the pros and cons. The critics laid Vestdijk to rest: historically important, but very dated.

In 't Hart's case the underestimation takes a different form. His non-fiction works, on the Bible, on music, gardening and eating, are hugely popular. His novels have a fixed constituency of readers, who pay no attention to negative reviews. Secondary school pupils are still wild about the 'puberty book' *A Flight of Whimbrels*, but they also enjoy the thriller *Star Witness* (De kroongetuige) .

But he has not often been pampered with laudatory reviews. For years Dutch critics have said the same thing about almost every book: 't Hart's style is supposedly sloppy and garrulous, typical work of a prolific writer. It was felt that 't Hart repeated himself too often: we're back in oppressive Maassluis yet again.

Oddly enough, in the last forty years there has been little recognition of his great narrative gifts, but 't Hart certainly has the ability to evoke a past or alien world by identifying with it body and soul – like the Calvinist world of the 1950s or eighteenth-century Maastricht. This is an ability he shares with the much-admired F.B. Hotz. Apart from that, 't Hart is someone with a unique brand of humour: a mixture of exaggeration, self-irony and pseudo-logic and sometimes rage. Few Dutch writers are as witty as 't Hart. His humour is never sour or malevolent. 'I only write when I'm in a good mood,' he said once, and the reader senses that. In his latest book, *Engagement* (Verlovingtijd, 2009), that special humour is tangible on every page. It is the story of a remarkable friendship between Joeri and the first-person narrator. They are the sharpest boys in the class, and for half a lifetime Joeri manages to pinch every girlfriend from the narrator. The latter takes this serial theft calmly: his friend just is brilliant. This is also a novel about the bare, austere parental home, but the tone is more distanced and ironic than in *A Flight of Whimbrels*. The dialogues in this book are masterly, especially those between mother and son, in which they trump each other with appropriate commonplaces from the Bible, such as 'Golgotha is round the corner' and 'We bravely chew our bread of tears.' The novel was greeted with shrugs of the shoulders by the press: funny and entertaining, but oh dear, that Calvinist childhood again, again that gaucheness with girls.

As a result 't Hart has not been exactly deluged with literary prizes in his own country. He has received some modest awards but has never yet won a major commercial prize: his novels have not even made the shortlist.

Abroad, on the other hand, his work is appreciated and his prose has been translated into English, French, German, Swedish, Italian, Polish, Bulgarian, Hungarian and Russian and appears in quite large print runs. In Germany and Sweden particularly – countries with a rich Protestant heritage – he is very popular.

Perhaps it is because Dutch people know this writer so well from television: still with an enthusiastic or excited boyish voice, even at the age of 65.˙'t Hart says loudly and unashamedly what he thinks about the mistreatment of animals, about law and order in the Netherlands, about pious blockheads, about the great advantage of inferior wine (you don't get drunk quickly). Always benevolent, always good for an attention-grabbing quote. If a photographer calls for a portrait to accompany an interview and he happens to have his women's clothes on, he doesn't mind being photographed in them. 't Hart is so authentically and imperturbably himself, that one is inclined to see him as a 'type'. Something of an exotic in his own country, since these days you don't often see anyone so typically Dutch, so Christian through and through, so sober and openly thrifty. ■

Translated by Paul Vincent

Maarten 't Hart in drag at the Literary Ball, Amsterdam, 1991. Photo by Klaas Koppe.

Growing up in Public

Josse De Pauw, the Marlon Brando of Flemish Theatre

In Avignon they once called him 'the Marlon Brando of Flemish theatre'. Then what would one call Josse De Pauw (1952) as a film actor? Or as a writer, director or head of a theatre company? Underlying everything he does is a great sincerity.

His story is one of 'nature finding a way'. For many years the desire to do only what he wanted to do made De Pauw hesitant about joining large companies. He was afraid of becoming a pawn in someone else's game and afraid of having to make big compromises. On the other hand, his dream of setting up an organisation around himself and a few artistic kindred spirits came up against an economic reality. Requests for subsidies to fund such an organisation were rejected several times. Not productive enough, it was said.

Despite this, he has always continued to do his own thing, and in the way he wanted: not being thrown off balance by production pressures or the pursuit of profit. He has always considered integrity paramount. This has meant he has not always been financially secure. Even so, he has yet to do his first advertising spot.

There have been periods of intense theatrical activity, while at other times film has come to the fore, and sometimes writing. A busy bee? Not really. His guiding principle could easily be that talent shouldn't be strewn around too often, but when it is, it should be by the shovelful. Circumstances have turned De Pauw into something of a maverick, who has managed his entire career in such a way as to let him do what he likes. He needed the space to ventilate his mind and allow ideas to incubate.

This maverick approach defines the portrait of the artist. He allows others the same breathing space as he seeks for himself. Consequently, for him each artistic project begins with an alliance, with the various participants on an equal footing. This has an impact on his work as a director. More about that later. Another aspect of this maverick role is that there is nothing he is obliged to do. He doesn't have to strive too much for anything. This makes his artistic work restrained and pure. There is a great sincerity in everything he does. He is sincere towards himself, towards his subject and towards his audience.

Josse De Pauw and his wife Fumiyo Ikeda. Photo by Michiel Hendryckx.

'Light acting'

The artist's sincerity towards himself begins with a substantial dose of self-knowledge. Josse De Pauw knows that his technique has its limitations. He obtained his diploma in acting by the skin of his teeth: one mark fewer and... As a result, such skills as voice projection, breath control and body-movement are not his greatest concern when on stage. Nor is he the type of actor who sets up milestones in the course of a performance. He finds tricks and gimmicks too futile even to consider. He is not interested in transforming himself into some character or other and creating the illusion of being someone else. We have never been able to applaud him as Macbeth or Caligula. Whether on the stage or in front of a film camera, it was always very much Josse De Pauw who was standing there.

It is as if he had taken the acting style of contemporary theatre as his model. The character almost disappears. Such external features as costume or make-up are no longer used. And even the metamorphosis of the actor's physical behaviour is reduced to a minimum. I can hardly imagine Josse De Pauw on stage other than in a suit of neutral colour and contemporary cut. Usually with his left hand in his trouser pocket and gesticulating with his right, as if conducting his

Under the Volcano (2009)
by Malcolm Lowry.
Photo by Koen Broos.

thoughts. The actor makes himself available to allow the character to come to life within him. He adopts it and offers it temporary accommodation. He does not hide behind a role, but brings his whole personality onto the stage.

This sort of 'light acting' is sometimes associated with acting for film. On a set, an actor acts 'on a small scale'. He does not have to project his gestures or facial expressions out into the audience, as the camera comes and collects it all from him. It is not inconceivable that De Pauw's success in both theatre and film is because of his idiosyncratic interpretation of the actor's craft, which is far removed from the creation of an illusion. Yet it is often conveniently forgotten that film is a much more appropriate form for narrative realism. For this reason, perhaps, the reverse is the case, and it is far more the personality that De Pauw brings to bear that persuades film-makers to engage him. One might in fact call this a noble variation on typecasting.

De Pauw often appears as the incarnation of the 'rough exterior, heart of gold' type. In *Crazy Love* (1987) he played a man covered in hideous spots who is hopelessly in love with a girl. Ten years later, in *Hombres complicados*, he played the incorruptible customs officer who goes on a hike with his brother, a shady delinquent. And could anyone ever forget *Iedereen beroemd* (2000), in which a well-meaning underdog turns to violence to give his clearly under-talented daughter a chance in showbiz? This film by Dominique Deruddere was nominated for an Oscar in the 'best foreign film' category. Today Josse De Pauw has more than sixty films to his name.

In recent years, observing him on stage, I have sometimes wondered what his secret is. He is a rather static actor who commands respect through his formidable physical presence. He is a sturdy Brabant carthorse who impresses with his strength. He actually does very little: he hardly stirs, barely moves a step and makes virtually no gestures. In *Weg* he stands there producing funky musical theatre at a microphone. In *De versie Claus* he delivers a two-hour mon-

De versie Claus (2009). Photo by Koen Broos.

ologue using the words of Hugo Claus while staying more or less on the same spot. But in Malcolm Lowry's *Under the Volcano* we catch him out in a little show of frivolity. He plays Geoffrey, whose life is veiled in a mist of tequila. De Pauw depicts his drunken breakdowns with the elegant spiral movements of a corkscrew penetrating yet another bottle. So he *can* manage a trace of imitation, on condition that it is slightly stylised.

Voice coaches would probably prescribe him a refresher course; it is as if speaking loudly is hard work, and he rather has to force out the sounds. He balances this monumental strength with mental flexibility and alertness. Every sentence he pronounces has been carefully thought out. Which is why he is so palpably involved. And he is exceptionally fast at learning his lines. His stand-in role in *Mefisto for ever* at the Toneelhuis is the stuff of legend. Three weeks before the first night, one of the leading actors dropped out and De Pauw was called in to replace him. Day after day De Pauw crammed his way into the part and in the end came up with a truly impressive performance. It was for his Avignon performance in this production that the French press compared him to Marlon Brando.

A dilettante thinker

Whether it's a matter of learning lines, writing a play or working through the rehearsal process, it is always based on a thorough nosing through the material. Josse De Pauw is not an academic theoretician, he is a philosopher of life. Interviewing him is a treat. There are few topics he knows nothing about and on which he has not formed an opinion. De Pauw is a man for café discussions, for deep conversations. He keeps track of current affairs, is open to all the impressions of the metropolis and listens to life stories. He is an amateur thinker, in both senses: 'unschooled' and 'keen on thinking', and all this in the best sense of the word 'dilettantism'. Knowledge and intuition come together in him. All this has an effect on his acting. Someone who has often worked with him put it like this: 'Every sentence he speaks has the force of a point of view.'

Josse De Pauw's career can be summarised in the title of a CD by Lou Reed: *Growing Up in Public*. He has applied himself to several disciplines and in each has steadily undergone a substantial evolution. It was not a matter of quietly maturing and only then going public. His style was much more a question of quite openly trying things out in public. So it must certainly have taken courage to come out with a play for the first time or to opt wholeheartedly for musical theatre.

His first conquest was language. After all, in the beginning it was not the word. His first theatrical exploits, with the Radeis theatre company between 1976 and 1984, were not based on words. The trio was successful and went on long international tours. They performed humorous sketches and, to avoid them looking too much like mime, gave voice to occasional sounds and cries. One of De Pauw's first projects after Radeis, *Usurpation* (1985), consisted of a collage of well-known fragments of writing to which he added a connecting thread. This made him one of the first actors in Flanders to start writing for the stage. Those close to him could see how, after this production, he moved closer and closer to language. But it wasn't an easy process. Witnesses say that in the dressing room he was often extremely tense.

In the years that followed De Pauw evolved more and more towards speaking and writing. One of the catalysts was the Flemish Media Institute (FEMI), to which Erwin Provoost, now a successful film producer, had invited a Czech-American script doctor. His job was to boost the quality of Belgian scriptwriters, among them Jaco Van Dormael, Marion Hänsel, Marc Didden and Marc-Henri Wajnberg. And also Josse De Pauw and the youthful Peter Van Kraaij.

For these last two it was an important encounter. For material for the workshop De Pauw drew on recollections of his travels. He combined meticulous observation with evocative storytelling. He expanded his characters slightly to make them more interesting than they were in real life. The eight pages he handed in to the head of the course were to form the basis of his first full-length play, *Ward Comblez. He do the life in different voices* (sic). He asked Peter Van Kraaij to act as sounding board as he worked it up. Later they worked together on the play *Het kind van de smid*.

Alliances with kindred spirits

And so a writing career was launched. It took on a new dimension when he started applying himself to prose. At the request of a literary supplement, he wrote short pieces for the paper that were populated by his family, his life and Brussels characters (fictional or otherwise). All these pieces were ephemeral, but they were also highly recognisable and observed with a generous and fascinated eye. Here De Pauw showed himself to have the perfect philosophical approach to life, sometimes full of understanding and sometimes, as when faced with administrative hassle and short-sighted chauvinism, brimming over with impatience. Just as in his stage roles, he put his entire personality into his writing, revealing himself to be a magnanimous and broadminded individual whose

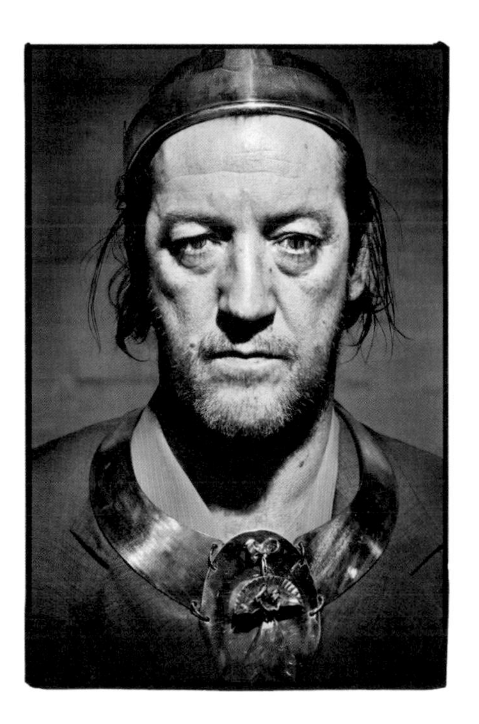

Larf (1999).
Photo by Phile Deprez.

basic principles are an acute sense of justice and an existential humanism. The two anthologies of these short pieces, *Werk* and *Nog*, brought him recognition and awards in the literary world.

Another steady evolution took place in regard to music. At the time of Radeis, De Pauw got to know the musician and composer Peter Vermeersch. Although Vermeersch had hardly ever been inside a theatre, he was promptly invited to write the music for *Echafaudages*. At that time musicians worked within their own personal limitations: they used the restricted number of chords that they knew. It signalled the start of a long artistic friendship. In *Usurpation* the music was closer to a free jazz idiom, and in *Ward Comblez* it was properly recorded on tape.

Until then, music had played a subordinate role in the productions. It was only in *Weg* (1998) that words, acting and music came together perfectly. One could no longer really call this spoken theatre, and in fact it was nothing less than a theatrical concert. Vermeersch had a soundtrack in mind for this production, because he found the scenes in the play so recognisable and familiar that he saw them as a film. The music sought to go along with these images. For *Larf* (2000) Vermeersch called up his big band. It was up to the actors to make themselves heard above this torrent of sound. In *Die siel van die mier* (2004) he proved that his music could be subtle and delicate too, in dialogues between the violin and cello played by George Van Dam and Jan Kuijken. In the Transparant production *Een nieuwe requiem* (2009), an adaptation of Mozart's famous work, he immersed himself in classical music.

Not only has Josse De Pauw thoroughly explored the worlds of words and music, but he has also steadily expanded his artistic alliances. Initially he was someone who preferred to work with kindred spirits, many of whose names have already been mentioned in this article. No entrance exam is needed for the job. Nor is proof of nobility or a shared background or age required. Several

Over de Bergen (2010).
Photo by Herman Sorgeloos.

people who have become involved say it was enough to make a few pertinent remarks. From then on they enjoyed his absolute trust. In the last few years this has been the case for the young theatre director Lotte van den Berg and the writer David Van Reybrouck.

Bestowing freedom is not difficult for someone who likes it so much himself. He set up many of his projects on the basis of a great sense of shared participation among their creators. In these cases a circle of kindred spirits would set to work almost like a jazz ensemble: 'does anyone else feel the urge to contribute anything?' But even in those productions where he was more distinctly the leader, he did not set himself up as the omniscient director. He was more like the man who created the right atmosphere and space. Instructing or directing others is not really part of the way he sees things. This has considerable consequences for what we understand as the traditional role of the director. For the theatre film *Übung* (2001) he came up with just a few suggestions for the script, by no means obligatory, which allowed the makers' club plenty of space. In that instance the result was miraculously good. But *Volk* (2006), a production based on teeming crowds of people in a city square, clearly suffered from the lack of a director's hand.

Open-minded mastery

Over the last decade, doing his own thing has no longer kept Josse De Pauw from engaging with existing organisations, even large ones. In the run-up to 'Bruges, Cultural Capital 2002', he accepted the artistic directorship of Het Net, an arts centre in that city. Partly because of the momentum of the 'Bruges 2002' event, he was able to set up the large-scale all-round production *SS* (2002), about Nazi sympathisers in the Second World War. After that, to many people's surprise, he turned up in *Death of a Salesman* (2004), a production by the Toneelhuis company in Antwerp directed by Luk Perceval. He had never done that before. After Perceval's departure for Germany, he even temporarily took on the job of director of that company for a year. And later, under the directorship of Guy Cassiers, he put in marvellous performances in *Mefisto for ever* and *Under the Volcano*.

Josse De Pauw has achieved a position where he can allow his skills in acting, writing and working with music to mature without losing any of his originality. He has attained a high degree of mastery while remaining entirely uninhibited. He is now so sure of himself that he is no longer averse to performing his public role in front of a wide audience. ■

Translated by Gregory Ball

Figureheads of State?

The Changing Face of the Monarchy in Belgium and the Netherlands

[RIEN EMMERY]

Queen Beatrix's Christmas Speech 2010. © Rijksvoorlichtingsdienst Communicatie Koninklijk Huis.

'King Albert refuses to accept Di Rupo's resignation', 'Queen Beatrix appoints a new coalition-forming adviser': recent headlines like these imply that the royal heads of state in Belgium and the Netherlands still exercise considerable political authority. And anyone who reads either country's constitution might be astonished at the apparent extent of the monarch's role in the legislature and the executive. It is a role that is debated with clockwork regularity in some sections of the political world and public opinion, because the Belgian and Dutch monarchies have indeed retained a certain measure of influence within the government. However, it is difficult to assess the precise extent of royal involvement. The monarch is not a president who can give interviews, talk publicly about politics, or become involved in public debate. This policy of discretion, which characterises the current function of the monarchy in the Low Countries, has important historical roots.

Political and public role

Both Belgium and the Netherlands are *constitutional* monarchies. A constitutional monarchy differs from absolute monarchy in that the sovereign's political and public role is rooted in the constitution, whereas in an absolute monarchy all powers are ultimately subject to the personal authority of the ruler. Although this form of government is mainly reminiscent of the *ancien régime* and Louis XIV's dictum *'L'état, c'est moi'*, absolutist regimes still exist to this day, though mainly in tiny states such as Brunei or Swaziland. But constitutional monarchies too come in all shapes and sizes. In some countries the sovereign still exercises considerable personal authority (Jordan, Morocco), while in others the monarchy has effectively been reduced to a ceremonial role with no real political power (Sweden).

Today in Belgium and the Netherlands the heads of state have a dual role. On the one hand they are actors in the political process, while on the other they have a broader symbolic role in society. The most important aspect of the political

Crown Prince Willem-Alexander in Afghanistan 2009-2010. © Rijksvoorlichtingsdienst Communicatie Koninklijk Huis.

role of the Dutch and Belgian monarchs is their inviolability, which is assured by the principle of ministerial responsibility. That does not mean that the monarch can do whatever he or she likes without being held responsible for their actions. On the contrary: every public act of the head of state is 'covered' by a minister who takes political responsibility, to ensure that the head of state does not act at cross-purposes with his government. This is most clearly apparent in the daily routine of signing laws and royal decrees, which is always done by the monarch and a government minister (the countersigner). The 1990 crisis in Belgium, when for reasons of conscience King Baudouin refused to sign the law legalising abortion, has been the only exception to this practice. The solution which was found at the time was for the King to proclaim that he was temporarily unable to rule and authorise the cabinet to ratify the abortion legislation. The parallels with the controversy surrounding his father and predecessor Leopold III's headstrong behaviour during and after the Second World War led to this episode being referred to subsequently as the 'little Royal Question'.

The current sovereigns, Albert and Beatrix, are regularly in contact with their prime minister or minister-president and sporadically with other political leaders and representatives of the economic, social, cultural, military and scientific worlds. Today, in 2010, the monarch no longer plays an active role but acts as a political mediator, a role comparable to what in the eighteenth century Adam Smith termed an 'impartial spectator'. The website of the Belgian monarchy puts it like this: 'In the political domain, the King's action does not consist in exercising personal power without the cooperation of ministers. The King interacts with players in the political arena by asking questions, expressing opinions, making suggestions, warning and giving encouragement. His perspective is that of continuity, long-term objectives, and major projects in which the country and the State must engage. The King exerts his influence through dialogue with all those involved in the political decision-making.'

In both Belgium and the Netherlands the head of state is probably most active during the process of government formation. He can refuse or accept the resignation of a government. If a new government has to be formed, he holds consultations and appoints the leader of one of the major parties to form a

Queen Wilhelmina on her bike in 1939.
© Koninlijke Bibliotheek, Den Haag, 53A27.

government (a *formateur*). In recent years, as forming coalitions has become more difficult, it has become usual to start with an *informateur,* an adviser to the crown who investigates which coalitions are possible and recommends a likely *formateur*. The *formateur* then sets about forming a government, drawing up an agreement with his coalition partners and agreeing a legislative programme. In Belgium the procedure is often so long-drawn-out that the Palace has introduced new posts such as a 'royal scout', a '*preformateur*', and even an 'elucidator' to defuse what can sometimes be tense political situations. Government formation is often tied up with wider political issues, of which in Belgium the most important is that of constitutional reform. However, in spite of this close involvement in the process of government formation the monarch may never impose his or her wishes or preferences – for instance for a specific coalition – on the political parties. Nor does the head of state play any part in choosing ministers or secretaries of state, only in swearing them in. In the Belgian constitutional reforms of 1993 the appointment of ministers and the dissolution of Parliament by the Crown were subjected to even stricter conditions, and the role of Parliament was increased.

The most visible activities of King Albert and Queen Beatrix are concerned with their wider social and public duties. The Dutch Royal House describes its role as 'cohesive, representative and encouraging'. It involves state visits abroad, receiving foreign heads of state and of government, bestowing patronage on certain organisations, conferring honours and titles of nobility, attending all manner of gatherings, celebrations and commemorations ... all of it with the aim of supporting 'positive initiatives in society' and contributing to 'social stability, continuity and progress in the country'. Audiences and visits to schools, museums or factories serve mainly to keep the monarch informed and provide him or her 'with a clear picture of the situation of the country – ongoing projects, problems, people who are suffering, their grievances, their demands and their hopes'. In addition, after national calamities (floods, mining disasters) or triumphs (Olympic medals) the monarch shares in the mourning or the celebrations. Finally, the monarch can also function as a last resort, an

King Leopold II on the beach in Ostend., ca. 1890.

ombudsman, for those who feel trapped in impossible bureaucratic situations. The symbolic and ceremonial role of the head of state is often said to be their most important function, and it has certainly increased in importance since the nineteenth century.

Belgium vs. the Netherlands

The big difference between the Belgian and Dutch monarchies is that the Belgian monarchy is recent and was chosen. When the Southern Netherlands (modern Belgium) broke away from the United Kingdom of the Netherlands in 1830, it was in large part because of the authoritarian behaviour of the Dutch King William I, who imposed a conservative constitution on the South by means of the notorious 'Dutch Arithmetic' (which overrode a Belgian majority against the constitution by counting all abstentions and non-voters as being in favour). Nevertheless, the Belgian National Congress voted to make their brand-new Belgium a monarchy, albeit a rather 'republican monarchy' with a more limited role for the head of state. Furthermore, the Dutch royal house of Oranje-Nassau was legally barred from ever holding power in Belgium by forbidding any marriage between the Belgian and Dutch royal houses, a decision that was only revoked a few years ago. When Leopold I accepted the Belgian throne, after reading through the constitution he remarked: 'Gentlemen, you have dealt harshly with royalty when it was not there to defend itself.' The comment reveals the strong liberal-democratic leanings of those who drew up the constitution.

Ever since the Burgundian era Belgium has had a long tradition of local or supra-national hereditary monarchy, but the dynasty established in 1831 was the country's first *national* monarchy. The Belgian royal house is not descended from an earlier absolutist ancestor, with its kings gradually having to give up more and more of their powers. The Dutch House of Oranje-Nassau, by contrast, has a tradition that goes back to the late Middle Ages. For two centuries before William I became King of both Netherlands after the Congress of

King Albert II
© FOD Kanselarij van de Eerste Minister - Algemene Directie Externe Communicatie.
Photo by P. Van der Elst.

Vienna in 1815, his ancestors had been Stadtholders in the Dutch provinces. Under the Habsburgs the Stadtholder had been a provincial governor with vice-regal powers, but during the Republic the Estates succeeded in reining back the Stadtholder's political role until by the eighteenth century his function was mainly military. William I, on the other hand, took sovereign political decisions on legislation and the appointment of ministers until his abdication. Only then, in 1840, was the ministerial countersignature introduced into the Netherlands. The spectre of revolution that swept through Europe in 1848 induced William II to make concessions to the liberal opposition and set up a committee headed by the politician and lawyer J.R. Thorbecke to revise the constitution. Since this constitutional reform the Dutch head of state too is inviolable and unaccountable, and government ministers answer to Parliament for the monarch's actions.

Of course, the role of the Crown in Belgium and the Netherlands has evolved further since the constitutions of 1831 and 1848. There has been a shift of power away from Parliament to the government, and within Government a shift from royal to ministerial power. In both countries supreme command of the army lies with the Crown, and at their coronation both monarchs swear to defend their national territory; in practice, though, it is the generals who control all military matters. Belgium's Leopold III was the last king to attempt to exercise a personal supreme command, and this contributed in large part to his abdication after the 'Royal Question'.

There have always been differences, large and small, between the Belgian and Dutch monarchies. In contrast to the Netherlands, which throughout the twentieth century had only queens (Wilhelmina (1890-1948), Juliana (1948-1980) and Beatrix (1980-)), in Belgium the so-called Salic law which excludes women from the succession was only repealed in the 1990s. In the Netherlands, the Queen chairs the Council of State, the highest advisory organ of the government, though its day-to-day work is left to a vice-chairman. On 'Prinsjesdag' [Prince's Day], which is specified in the constitution as the third Tuesday in September, the parliamentary year begins and the Queen delivers the Speech from the Throne. This is not a personal address but a statement of the government's policies for the coming political year. In Belgium, the Speech from the Throne fell into disuse after the reigns of Leopold II and Albert I in the late nineteenth and early twentieth century. Furthermore, the symbolic role of the Belgian king has become more important because of the country's progressive federalisation. The head of state is increasingly seen as a unifying factor for the different linguistic communities.

So there are striking similarities and fairly minor differences between the Belgian and Dutch monarchies. Observers sometimes whisper that the biggest difference is one of style, with the Belgian royal house labouring under a more old fashioned public image. Nevertheless, over the course of their history the two monarchies have evolved in much the same direction.

The monarchy's future

Monarchies do not have to be eternal or unchanging. As recently as 2008 the Nepalese monarchy was abolished, Bhutan changed from an absolute to a parliamentary monarchy, and the Grand Duke of Luxembourg lost a large part of his political power. Although recent polls show that monarchy as a constitutional form still enjoys widespread support in both Belgium and the Netherlands, that does not mean it is never questioned. In the past, financial and amorous scandals have given rise to sharp criticism of the royal houses. In 2009 there were even anonymous death threats against the Belgian Dowager, Queen Fabiola, as well as a failed attack on the Dutch royal family in Apeldoorn, which cost eight people their lives.

Radical republican parties are only to be found at the extremes of the political spectrum, even though almost all the traditional Belgian and Dutch political parties number some republican activists among their supporters. In recent years, many Belgian and Dutch politicians and academics have come to believe that a reduction in the power of the monarchy is inevitable, if only because the duties of the head of state, as defined in the constitution, no longer bear much relation to the real world. It is generally envisaged that the monarchy will develop into a Swedish-style ceremonial institution, in which the king or queen

Crown Prince Philippe as a fighter pilot.

no longer has any political role and retains only ceremonial and representative duties. The sovereign remains the head of state but no longer takes any part in government, no longer appoints ministers and no longer signs legislation. He or she is reduced to a 'figurehead of state'.

The long-drawn-out and difficult coalition negotiations of recent years have also played an important part in the debate. On the one hand they do nothing to improve the standing of the monarchy, since serious political crises automatically damage the prestige of the head of state as the guarantor of stability. And because circumstances push the head of state into the foreground, he or she is more vulnerable to criticism. The Dutch negotiations of 2010 were a striking illustration of this. Queen Beatrix came under fire because she turned too frequently for advice to her long-term political confidants such as Ruud Lubbers and Herman Tjeenk Willink. She was accused of obstructing the formation of a right-wing coalition between the Liberals (VVD), Christian Democrats (CDA) and Geert Wilders' anti-Islam party (PVV). When, during a parliamentary debate and without consulting Beatrix, the three parties expressed their intention of continuing their negotiations, the Dutch press even spoke of a 'republican moment'. Incidentally, the Queen reacted promptly, holding a discussion with the Liberal leader Mark Rutte and then re-appointing the Social Democrat Tjeenk Willink as interim adviser or *informateur*.

On the other hand, there are just as many commentators who argue that to form a viable coalition *without* an 'impartial spectator' would certainly be even more difficult. In Belgium particularly it is often said that a mediator who stands outside or above the communities can still be extremely useful. Yet in the negotiations in 2010 King Albert was accused of favouritism towards certain parties and politicians, especially by the N-VA, the Flemish nationalist and republican party who were the big winners in the election. Since the Second World War a paradoxical situation has developed in both Belgium and the Netherlands, with the traditionally republican Left finding itself increasingly obliged to defend the monarchy.

What might be a decisive factor in the debate on the monarchy is the fact that both royal houses face a succession issue in the near future. Beatrix and Albert are both well into their 70s and their heirs Willem-Alexander (Netherlands) and Philippe (Belgium) are not the most popular members of their families. The popularity of both princes has even declined in recent years. In Belgian political circles people have made no secret of their doubts about Philippe's qualities as the future king following some controversial statements that he made in interviews. In the middle of the latest government formation there was a rumour that the protracted negotiations had frustrated a plan for Albert to abdicate in favour of his son. And after a change of power it would only take a few indiscretions for the debate on the monarchy to flare up again with great intensity.

Hardcore royalists need not despair, however. Paradoxically, it is entirely possible that restricting the powers of the Crown will prove to be the best life insurance for the Belgian and Dutch royal houses. After all, a symbolic monarchy with a ceremonial 'figurehead of state' would prevent any possible conflict with the often capricious political system. ▪

Translated by Chris Emery

www.monarchie.be
www.koninklijkhuis.nl

FURTHER READING

D.J. Elzinga (ed.), *De Nederlandse constitutionele monarchie in een veranderend Europa* (Kluwer, Alphen aan de Rijn, 1996).

H. Hansen, *De koning komt! De toekomst der Oranjes en de ministeriële verantwoordelijkheid* (Van Gennep, Amsterdam, 1993).

A. Molitor, *La Fonction royale en Belgique* (CRISP, Brussel, 1994).

J. Stengers, *L'Action du Roi en Belgique. Pouvoir et influence* (Duculot, Brussel, 1996).

H. Van Goethem, *De monarchie en 'het einde van België'* (Lannoo, Tielt, 2007).

H.A. Van Wijnen, *De macht van de Kroon* (Balans, Amsterdam, 2001).

English in the Low Countries today

[REINIER SALVERDA]

About ten years ago Tom MacArthur, author of *The English Languages* (1998), carried out a simple test in the streets of Amsterdam. Walking from the central railway station into town, after every hundred yards he stopped a Dutch person and, without any introduction, asked them a question in English. And for about three kilometres, without fail or hesitation, they all answered straight back in good English.

What this test demonstrated was that in Amsterdam English is no longer a foreign tongue, but a completely natural second language. Recently, this finding has been confirmed in a study by Loulou Edelman of the linguistic landscape in Amsterdam. In the Kalverstraat shopping area in the centre of town she found that public signs and advertisements in Dutch and in English are present in nearly equal measure – visual evidence of the almost equal social status of the two languages.

In today's Amsterdam the English language is firmly established. International tourism, business and migration bring in very many people from all over the world, and the international English-speaking expat community is today the largest foreign presence in the Dutch capital. So, in a very Dutch show of linguistic accommodation, the D'66 political party recently proposed to regularise this state of affairs and turn Amsterdam into an officially bilingual town like Montreal (French-English), Brussels (Dutch-French) or Helsinki (Swedish-Finnish).

As it turned out, the proposal was unsuccessful. But shouldn't one think twice here? After all, in recent years South Korea and Chile have given English official status as their second language. So why not the Netherlands? As a small country dependent on global trade, international exports and world markets, the Netherlands is only too familiar with the increasing competition, in every market and in all sectors of the economy, of emerging powers such as India, China, Russia and Latin America.

The economic and political imperative of globalisation is that it requires English. India, for example, may be a multilingual country with 18 official languages, but at the same time it has some 300 English-speaking universities, and this massive investment is paying off. That is, India appears to be well positioned today for mass production in the digital world of the knowledge economy,

since it has an almost endless supply of skilled and highly qualified English-speaking IT workers who can do the same jobs as people in the first world - but a lot cheaper.

Attractive, available, useful

English today, as David Crystal has observed, is the first truly global language, with special status in almost every country in the world, either as an everyday second language or as a widely-known foreign language. This is the outcome of a linguistic revolution over the past half century that is linked with the rise of the United States to superpower predominance and driven by US media, entertainment and popular culture, the international scientific community (more than half the world's science journals are in English), the internet and communication technology, global trade and international finance, transport (the airline industry), tourism and mass consumption.

Today, it is estimated that some 2 billion people in the world know some form of English, and it is predicted that by 2050 half the world's population will be competent in English. English is already the language most widely learned by speakers of other languages, and also the most commonly taught foreign language all over the world. This business of teaching English as a foreign language is worth an estimated $ 7.8 billion a year, more than three times the comparable figure for German, and almost four times that for Spanish.

It is also a very attractive language, easily available everywhere, and offering people all over the world access to a wide range of highly desirable cultural goods: news, ideas, information, publications, films, music, entertainment, innovation and discoveries, social networking and job opportunities – all in English. English is also immensely useful, as it enables people from many very different linguistic backgrounds to enter into direct discussion with each other about common ideas, values, principles and policies.

So how do these global English developments affect the position and role of the Dutch language in the Netherlands? With its 21 million speakers the Dutch language ranks in the top forty of the world's approximately 6000 languages. Dutch has official status as a national language in the Netherlands, Belgium and Surinam, while the Afrikaans spoken in South Africa is a close relative. Dutch is an official language of the European Union (EU), and an official working language of the Union of South American Nations (UNASUR). Maintenance and professional support are provided by the Dutch Language Union, which was established jointly by the Netherlands and Belgium in 1980.

It is interesting to see what is happening in the Dutch education sector as it is going through a rapid and wide-ranging process of anglicisation. Dutch universities have by and large gone over to English as the international language of science and scholarship: PhD theses are now normally in English, and the scholarly output of Dutch academics is rated more highly if it is published in English. But despite a number of recent reports expressing concern about the quality and proficiency in English of both teachers and students, the Dutch Language Union has nothing to say about this development. Its main duty is restricted to supporting the Dutch language, while English remains the prerogative of more powerful government agencies such as the Department of Foreign Affairs and the Education Department.

Secondary schools are now following suit, and it is expected that within the next few years some 1500 schools will be offering the entire curriculum in Dutch and English. In primary schools, where English has been an obligatory subject in the upper two levels for almost 25 years, this will now be extended to level one. In playgroups English is starting up everywhere, with more and more kids taking half an hour or so of English per week.

'Everybody speaks English'

Education here provides a very strong stimulus, but the main reason why the Dutch are so good at English is not education but – according to the Groningen linguist Kees de Bot – the fact that the English language is so highly valued in mainstream Dutch culture. English is a pervasive part of Dutch life. Dutch TV offers very many English-language programmes, and these are not dubbed but subtitled. Hence, their near immersion in this huge daily supply of news, ads, shows, movies, quizzes, music, popsongs, soap operas – all in English - continuously reinforces and enhances what pupils learn in school. An interesting effect of this is that Dutch pupils acquire a lot of confidence as they go out and practise, and so all the time they are becoming better and better at English.

That is - and this is in line with David Graddol's prediction of 2006 - they are no longer learning English as a foreign language spoken in a faraway country, but rather as a second language, in everyday use in their own country.

This strong trend towards English within the Dutch education system has a clear link to developments in the international education market. A good example is the work of NUFFIC, the Netherlands organisation for international cooperation in higher education in The Hague. NUFFIC offers foreign students from all over the world information on the very many international study programmes and courses in Dutch universities, of which no fewer than 1543 are taught completely in English, ranging from agriculture, art and architecture through the humanities, engineering and social sciences all the way to mathematics and medicine. The Netherlands was the first country to offer such courses, and is still the front runner in this international market, as the continent's largest provider of good quality international English-language university education at Bachelors and Masters level.

Together with the international NUFFIC network of student recruitment offices in Brazil, India, Russia, China and Indonesia, this means that the Netherlands is well positioned for the increasingly competitive higher-education market for international students. Here NUFFIC's success is evident from recent figures: there are about 74,000 international students (including 17,000 from outside the EU) currently following courses at Dutch universities. New markets are being targeted and developed, also in Europe. In August 2010, for example, when British school exam results came out, it became apparent that thousands of British students were not going to find a place at British universities. So out came the Universities of Groningen and Maastricht with a massive PR campaign in the British media: If you can't find a university place in Britain, the message was, come to the Netherlands, where everybody speaks English, where the quality of higher education is very good, where the curriculum is taught entirely in English, and where you get far more teaching contact hours than in a British university. Add to this – as further selling points - that having studied abroad will in future look good on one's CV, and that it is a lot cheaper both to study and to live in the Netherlands than it is in Great Britain. The whole thing was spiced up with individual success stories of British students currently studying, for example, International Relations or Biomedical Sciences at Dutch universities.

Flanders – for reasons to do with the history of Belgium as an officially trilingual country - used to be far more restrictive in language matters and held on to the use of Dutch in education much more strongly than the Netherlands. But despite its proud tradition of strict legal and constitutional safeguards for the Dutch language, Flanders too is now going through a process of 'liberalisation' and from 2014 onwards will allow English to be much more widely used in its universities, especially at Masters level. Recently, the Education Minister Pascal Smet proposed the wholesale introduction across the national school system of English as the first foreign language instead of French. He was immediately censured. Going further, the historian Bruno de Wever has even suggested using English as the new national lingua franca, as this might help the Belgians to overcome their traditional linguistic-political conflicts and rivalries, and perhaps even to neutralise their long-standing tension over Brussels as the capital city of both Flanders and Belgium as well as the European Union.

Thus we are witnessing a rapid anglicisation in all sectors of society within the Low Countries. For many citizens, however, this is a cause of growing concern. Dutch language activists are taking Prime Minister Rutte to task for mixing too much English into his speeches. And in Flanders leading academic Wim Vandenbussche has pointed to the poor quality of English used in higher education, the concomitant loss of academic quality in the universities, and the consequent erosion in the position and function of Dutch as the language of education, knowledge and culture. It is interesting in this respect to note that student numbers in Dutch language and literature at universities in the Netherlands are in serious decline. At the same time, ironically, in the world outside the Low Countries there are today more than 180 universities in over forty countries where a total of more than 15,000 people are studying Dutch. At universities in Germany alone one can find more students of Dutch than in all the Dutch universities taken together.

This strong trend towards English does not, of course, only occur in Flanders and the Netherlands. What we see here are Europe-wide developments. Within the European Union (EU) English today comes top in the language hierarchy in their Brussels headquarters. The rise of English is overwhelming: more than 40% of the EU's population can now speak English in addition to their mother tongue, and ninety percent of European schoolchildren are learning English today. Of all EU texts, 45% are now drafted in English and no more than 30% in French, while working documents are seldom available in all the official languages.

At the same time, however, we witness the strong assertion in the various member states of national language policies aimed at monolingualism. In the Netherlands for example, proficiency in Dutch is a strict admission requirement for non-Western immigrants, and the teaching of immigrant native languages has been abolished. In fact, things really aren't all that rosy for other languages in the Netherlands. Teaching minority languages such as Turkish and Arabic is no longer allowed during school hours, and the teaching of foreign languages such as French and German, and even English, is in serious decline at university level - just as in the UK.

Within the various member states of the European Union, these and other such language issues give rise to wide-ranging debates, cultural and political differences and divergent trends in policy-making. As a result, the European language situation has become a sensitive political issue, as Phillipson has noted. Official EU language policy, under the motto of 'Unity in Diversity', recognises the value of the linguistic diversity as one of the cornerstones of European culture. But in actual fact, as the Amsterdam sociologist Bram de Swaan has argued, the more languages are officially recognised in the EU, the more this will work to the advantage of English.

Everything seems geared to a massive language shift towards English. The airline KLM and other Dutch multinational companies are leading the way here, and many policy-makers in the Netherlands appear to expect a monolingual future, with the EU using English as the single, common lingua franca for the whole of Europe. Some people may even think that since we now have this global lingua franca, there is no need for other languages any more. But in a world that is marked by an all-pervasive multilingualism, we will always need other languages besides English, and people who know two or more languages will always be in demand as go-betweens and intermediaries between the very many different languages, peoples and cultures.

The Internet points the way here. English has been the medium of the Internet revolution, and this has given a very strong boost to the English language. India, China and other massive populations may have been slow to come on to the Internet, but usage is growing rapidly today, and Chinese is set to become the dominant language on the web before long, while English – as Nick Ostler predicts – may already have peaked. The fact of the matter is that the future of the Internet will be multilingual.

My point here is that English is a dominant, pervasive and growing presence all around the world today; it is necessary, useful and beneficial as a global lingua franca; but there is and will always be linguistic diversity and multilingualism, with many other lingua francas used throughout the world language system; so English will never be enough, and it makes no sense to lock oneself into just this particular language, however widespread it may be. This is as true for the Low Countries as it is for Europe with its very many different languages, and here I quote the Paris-based French-Lebanese European writer Amin Maalouf, who states in his essay *On identity* (2000) that '... whatever the future of Europe, whatever form the Union adopts and whatever countries are included among its members, one question presents itself now and will still present itself to future generations: how are all the scores of human languages to be managed?' ■

Photos by Klaas Koppe.

FURTHER READING

CRYSTAL, DAVID (2003). *English as a Global Language*. Cambridge: Canto.

DE SWAAN, ABRAM (2002). *Words of the World.* Cambridge: Polity.

EDELMAN, LOULOU (2010). *Linguistic Landscapes in the Netherlands. A Study of Multilingualism in the Netherlands*. Utrecht: LOT.

GRADDOL, DAVID (2006). *English Next*. London: British Council.

MCARTHUR, TOM (1998). *The English Languages*. Cambridge: Canto.

OSTLER, NICHOLAS (2010). *The Last Lingua Franca: English Until the Return of Babel.* London: Allen Lane.

PHILLIPSON (2009). *Linguistic imperialism continued.* London: Routledge.

SPOLSKY, BERNARD (2009). *Language Management*. Cambridge: Cambridge University Press.

VANDENBUSSCHE, WIM (2010). ''. In: Albert Oosterhof et al. (eds.), *Nederlands in hoger onderwijs en wetenschap?* Ghent: Academia Press, pp. 15-18.

Marcel Broodthaers,
Miroir d'époque regency, 1973.
Convex mirror in frame
(gilded wood), 142 x 77.3 cm.
Collection S.M.A.K., Ghent.

Photo by Dirk Pauwels.

Chronicle

Architecture

The *Selexyz* bookshop in Maastricht.

Religious Heritage and More

At this point in time it is still unthinkable that cathedrals such as the Notre Dame de Paris, the *Kölner* Dom or the *Duomo di Milano* will become redundant. However, many less spectacular church buildings will, all over Western Europe. This article explores the challenges associated with the current and increasing redundancy of Christian church buildings in the Low Countries. Two thousand years of Christianity have left a deep imprint on our culture and, although membership of established religious communities is decreasing, Christian conventions and cultural values are still present in our society. Nonetheless, fewer churchgoers need fewer church buildings, leaving us with countless church buildings that are out of use. In the Netherlands, for example, the expectations are that about 1200 church buildings will become redundant in the next ten years. Yet religious redundancy does not necessarily equal physical, social or spatial redundancy. This gives rise to a debate on the (im)possibility of using and re-using these (soon to be) surplus church buildings.

Almost every 'old' - from medieval to gothic revival - church building in a city centre nowadays seems pre-eminently to be an example of cultural heritage rather than a religious artefact. The religious function of many inner-city church buildings is slowly diminishing; however their historical and cultural significance, as well as their architectural shape and their position in and relation to the urban tissue, continue to be of value. City councils and developers are starting to recognise the commercial, cultural and social power of such buildings. The church gets 'culturalized'; it becomes a tourist attraction or is turned into a museum, bookstore or boutique to start a whole new life that isn't religious at all. Some famous examples are *De Nieuwe Kerk* in Amsterdam, which is now a centre of cultural life with large exhibitions, the *Selexyz* bookshop in the *Dominicanen Kerk* in Maastricht or the *Wolweverskapel* in Ghent, which is currently a clothes store.

The re-use of church buildings is not a new phenomenon; *De Nieuwe Kerk*, for example, became a cultural centre back in the nineteen eighties. Ever since the *Nieuwe Kerk* foundation was set up it has been used for cultural events, lectures and exhibitions. The monumental church building is situated at Dam Square, next to the Royal Palace. It will still be used for the coronation of future Heads of State and was the location for the wedding of the Prince of Orange and Princess Máxima. This is an interesting example of non-religious re-use, not only because it's a successful cultural centre, but also because this type of conversion is reasonably acceptable to the religious

Tapestry exhibition in the *Kunsthal Sint-Pietersabdij* in Ghent.

communities. Since its new programme is cultural the re-use is considered 'neutral'. It could only be considered 'fitting' if the new function were at least partly religious. This 'cultural centre recipe' has often been used, for example the concert hall of AMUZ in the former convent church of St Augustine (Antwerp), the *Kunsthal Sint-Pietersabdij* and the Provincial Cultural Centre *Caermersklooster* (both in Ghent). Other forms of profane re-use, such as the *Sint-Josephkerk* ('s-Hertogenbosch), which was transformed into a party centre, or the *Bernadettekerk* (Helmond, in North Brabant), which has become a supermarket, are much less acceptable and have actually led to a reduction in the willingness of religious communities to consider re-use unless they have control over the new program.

A commercial programme is often considered 'unworthy' or inappropriate. This is an issue with the *Wolweverskapel*, too. Having had all sorts of functions, this listed building is now a clothing shop. The question is how long a religious building keeps its religious connotations, as this one has not been used for religious purposes since the beginning of the nineteenth century. In heritage terms the new program has been designed to be reversible, meaning that it can be removed without damaging the building. At the same time it leaves the space intact. The same thing has been done in the *Selexyz* bookshop in Maastricht, in the by now famous former Dominican church. A three-story high-rise full of books, designed by *Merkx + Girod* architects, provides us with a new perspective on the church building and is fully reversible.

These are all listed buildings that are, by their age and location, very much embedded in the surrounding urban tissue. Most of the churches that will become redundant, however, are probably the less famous, smaller and more locally oriented church buildings. The ones you'll find next door, the neighbourhood church, the house church, the place to go for the local community. The size of the problem is greatest here and since the buildings are often not listed their existence in the future is not ensured, the solutions need more subtlety. Can they become apartments, or should they retain their public function in some way? Should we support 'co-housing', multifunctional and religious re-use, or is that a hopeless task? Should we demolish them or will there be a revival of religion in time? Is it better to demolish than to re-use a church building in an inappropriate manner? And if we only want to re-use them in a way we deem suitable, how many cultural centres, libraries, health centres, neighbourhood centres etc. do we need? Many questions, which only time will answer.

Whatever the answer is, we should keep in mind that the church building is a special type of heritage. Not only because we are confronted with a high level of church redundancy and will subsequently have to deal with these churches, whether we want to or not, but also because of the fact that a church building represents much more than just its own history. It is an expression of religion, but it is also an architectural and urban element with tangible and intangible cultural and socio-historical values. All these aspects should be considered in the discussion on the (im)possibility of re-use; it is not only a question of how to respect religious, theological or liturgical values, but also of how to deal with their significance as a cultural and urban element, an essential part of a city or neighbourhood.

Through the ages, above-average attention, vigour and care have been devoted to the designing, building and rebuilding of churches. From the Middle Ages until quite recently the erection of a church building played a significant and often leading part in the development and growth of a city. In addition, a church building in itself is also a centuries-old and very powerful building typology, and in this case the label 'church' reaches far beyond its function. Formal symbolism, such as a church tower or a cross, and other spatial and ornamental elements determine the religious connotations of a church building. A church building that has been turned into apartments for example, does not simply become an apartment building. No, it is a church in which people live; the converted church continues to refer to its religious past.

This, however, is all rather theoretical. Closing down a church is first and foremost an emotional process and a difficult decision for the (local) religious community. Next, there are many different interests and points of view when it comes to the question of 're-using or removing' once a church has been closed down. The differences nearly all relate to how one perceives a church building. Is it nothing more than another pile of stones or is it saleable property? Does it have a vital connection to the contemporary socio-cultural status quo or is it an historical artefact? Is it a symbolic representation of a specific religious community or of a Christian world view in general? It all depends on the position of the people involved in the process of redevelopment. Are they active church members or more 'cultural' Christians, neighbours or architecture lovers, policy makers or developers? They all have different points of view.

Religious communities tend to place the emphasis on minimising emotional confrontation in combination with maximising financial gain in order to maintain the buildings they do still own and use, leading to a preference for removal. Cultural and governmental players, on the other hand, often emphasise cultural and historical relevance and therefore plead for re-use instead. This frequently leads to a delicate situation. It is a contested space, where religious beliefs, commercial interests, cultural consciousness and emotions set the agenda.

It is rather difficult to come to a conclusion. Religious heritage is and will remain a tense subject as long as the church has both a cultural and religious presence in society. It is, however, possible to reconsider our views when it comes to the preservation and re-use of heritage. By taking into account that a building can be valuable for very different reasons and by letting go of the idea that it can only be preserved in the form of the stones it was built from and can only be re-used by giving it a new function we widen all perspectives.

Loes Veldpaus

Film and Theatre

A Western in Italy

Anton Corbijn's *The American*

The American, the second feature film by the Dutch photographer and director Anton Corbijn (° 1955), tells the story of Jack, an American contract killer (played by the superstar George Clooney), who, after a dramatic shoot-out somewhere in the snow-covered countryside in Sweden, goes on the run and finds a temporary home-cum-hiding place in the desolate Abruzzo region of Italy. But the past continues to haunt him...

On the basis of this brief summary and the atmosphere of suspenseful tragedy and resigned gloom, *The American* can best be described as a melancholy gangster thriller. But in his superb photo book *Inside The American*, a photographic diary of the whole production, Corbijn says that in fact the main model for the film was his favourite film genre, the Western: a man murders someone, goes on the run and hides out in a small western town. As an outsider he comes into contact with the priest (the spiritual element) and the whore (the carnal). But the past catches up with him. There is a shoot-out and he leaves the town again. A 'classic' scenario, in other words.

Neo-western or not, the least one can say of *The American* is that it is not exactly the sort of film one would expect from Anton Corbijn. But by now he is used to doing unusual things. He certainly cannot stand being labelled. Although he had been acclaimed worldwide for his photos of U2, David Bowie, Elvis Costello, R.E.M. and others, he was gradually getting absolutely sick of invariably being called a 'rock photographer'. He was a photographer plain and simple. So when, after directing several dozen music videos for the likes of Nirvana, Metallica, Nick Cave and Depeche Mode, he felt like making a real film, it was definitely not going to be a 'music film'. Even so, he made his debut in 2007 with *Control*, a black and white film on the prematurely truncated life and self-inflicted death of the Joy Division singer Ian Curtis.

It was the Joy Division's first album, *Unknown Pleasures*, that prompted Corbijn to come to London then. He felt the urge to live in the place where this music originated, and at the time his explanation was that he wanted, after all, to make a music film. But he himself did not want to call *Control* simply a biography of a rock musician. To be more specific, he said, it was in the first place a tragic love story. In any case, it was considered good enough to open the prestigious *Quinzaine des Réalisateurs* section at the 2007 Cannes Film Festival.

After such a successful debut, it seemed inevitable that Corbijn would continue to make films. Or not? In the photo book mentioned above, he writes that making *Control* had been 'a life-changing experience', but also that the unavoidable promotional tour for the film had been 'so soul-destroying' that immediately afterwards he returned, at least for a while, to photography, his first love. But it was not long before he realised he had irrevocably caught the film bug. And so he went in search of 'another adventure, another story'. One thing was for sure: it certainly would not be another story of

England in the 70s or about a dead musician, though of course these were exactly the scenarios people were sending him. On the contrary, it had to be a completely different genre of film, a piece of real fiction, something contemporary and something in colour too.

Then Corbijn received a scenario based on the novel *A Very Private Gentleman* by the English author Martin Booth. It appealed to him somehow. He left for Italy with the scenarist Rowan Joffe, more specifically for the little-visited region of Abruzzo (where Booth's story was set) to find the locations and inspiration needed.

The leading character in *A Very Private Gentleman* is an eccentric Englishman who combines his job as a contract killer with one as a gunsmith. However, it was decided to make this Englishman an American, and the possibility was mooted of trying to interest George Clooney in the part. But on the very day of his appointment with Clooney, he woke up to a nightmare: he saw on the television news that the Abruzzo region, and in particular the town of L'Aquila, which he had selected as the main location, had been struck by an extremely destructive earthquake. 6th April 2009 became one of those days he would never forget. He was convinced that the whole project was dead and buried.

But George Clooney was interested in the scenario and agreed to do it. And after some extra exploration of Abruzzo new locations were found. L'Aquila was replaced by Sulmona and scenes were also shot in the mountain towns of Castel del Monte and Castelvecchio. Scenes had to be framed carefully so as to keep the buildings destroyed or damaged by the earthquake out of shot.

The plot of *The American* cannot be called particularly original or innovative (the silent loner, the whore with a heart of gold, the final contract), but this is more than compensated for by the marvellous photography (though fortunately it does not lapse into postcard aesthetics) and meticulous compositions. Even so, the *dénouement* remains (relatively) surprising. But before that point is reached, several major characters have crossed the silent Jack's path, including a mysterious client called Pavel (played by Johan Leysen) and a female client (Thekla Reuten) who apparently needs a very specific weapon.

Anyone expecting a typically frantic action film about a hit man on the run will be disappointed. There are a couple of shoot-outs and action sequences, of course, including a chase on a Vespa, but the narrative tempo of the film remains largely calm, almost contemplative and melancholy, and stays focused above all on the restrained yet intense performance by George Clooney. Yes, Jack is in someone's sights, and he is the first to realise it, but Clooney is able, in almost all circumstances, to simultaneously control the stress and paranoia this brings while yet making them palpable.

A final comment on the Western references: at a certain point we see Jack in a café drinking an 'Americano' coffee, and on the television there's an excerpt from *Once upon a Time in the West*, with Henry Fonda in the lead and a soundtrack by Ennio Morricone. For those viewing *The American* who do not immediately recognise the excerpt, the director Anton Corbijn has provided a regular who proudly gives the name of the director: 'Sergio Leone. Italiano!'

Jan Temmerman
Translated by Gregory Ball

www.corbijn.co.uk

Peter Missotten, *Montezuma*, 2010 © Peter Missotten / De Filmfabriek.

Radical Space

Theatre Producer Peter Missotten

In the normal course of events this is how it goes: a theatre producer chooses a play and the decor flows from his interpretation of the piece. Not so with Peter Missotten. He has an image in his mind and so selects a specific play. 'Most people find that an illogical way of working, but don't you make the park first before you let the children play in it?'

Missotten (b.1963) began working in the theatre when he was nineteen, as a lighting technician in a production of *The Cement Garden*, based on the well-known novel by Ian McEwan which has also been filmed, by the Flemish producer Guy Cassiers (since to gain international renown). After that first experience in the theatre Missotten went off to study video art at Sint Lukas in Brussels, where he received tuition from, among others, Chris Dercon, who became the new director of Tate Modern in London in the Spring of 2011. The plastic arts have always been what fascinated and inspired Missotten the most, including in his work in the theatre that seeks to associate itself closely with performing and installation art.

To start with Missotten mostly did video installations. This was how he came to create *The Mind Machine of Dr. Forsythe* with Anne Quirijnen and An Marie Lambrechts. The idea was to make a utopian machine that could replace the choreographer William Forsythe, of whom Missotten is a great admirer, and which could create 'Forsythe choreographies' autonomously, like a machine. The video work, projections on six large glass panels borne by cranes was shown in the context of Antwerp European Cultural Capital 1993. The Filmfabriek, an independent production house for video and digital media that offers a home to a variety of artists, was also born out of that project in 1994.

Missotten had a stroke of luck with *Expect Poison from Standing Water*, which was created for the Pleinmuseum in Utrecht and toured alongside Les Nuits Blanches in Paris and at the Venice Biennial. This consisted of a video installation in which he projected image and text on to a water curtain, which hung like a digital water mirror above the space beneath. That new take on a landscape, the auditorium, is also apparent in his theatre work. For Missotten the accommodation counts as space.

For the last 27 years Missotten has continued to work closely with Guy Cassiers. He designed the set-

Peter Missotten, *Kwartet*, 2006
© Koen Broos.

ting and/or video work for a number of the latter's theatre and opera productions, including *The Woman Who Walked into Doors* (from the book by Roddy Doyle). In 2006 he was also responsible for the staging of *Sunken Red* (from the novel by Jeroen Brouwers), which was chosen for the Avignon Festival. When Cassiers was artistic director of the Toneelhuis in Antwerp in 2006 he asked Missotten, as one of the seven producers at that time, to create and present his own work under the wing of the city theatre.

Even though Missotten did not create any exceptional location theatre such as Serre (2007), which was played in a park, he did, as it were, create location theatre in the theatre. With Heiner Müller's *Kwartet* (*Quartet*, 2006) the public slumped on bean bags to look up under the rafters of the theatre attic where two performers on a glass platform were gradually being covered in snow. With *Weerslechtweer* (2010, could be translated as Badweatheragain) the set was immersed in light and the sound of T.S. Elliot's poem 'The Waste Land'. Does the 'normal' theatre auditorium fail to hold any interest for Missotten? 'On the contrary, I make very good use of the auditorium. You see the radical approach but also the space.' That was extremely obvious in his 2008 creation *De wilde wilde weg* (the title is a wordplay that can be read as *The Wild One Wanted to go Away* or as *The Wild Wild Road*), in which he sent his actors up a wooden footbridge, a catwalk that stretched from the back of the stage to the first balcony in the *Bourlaschouwburg* in Antwerp.

In addition to being a producer Missotten is also a tutor at the *Toneelacademie* (Stage School) in Maastricht, where he teaches on the performing arts course. 'I see the *Toneelacademie* not just as a school but also as a place for productions where young people can try things out – together with the staff'. These are no careless words. That 'creating things together' goes from small performances such as *ILLBEGONE* (a co-production between the Toneelacademie and Manchester Metropolitan University that won the award for the best foreign production at the ITs festival in Amsterdam) to huge productions of operas such as Philip Glass's *Kepler* (Linz, 2009), or Bernhard Lang's *Montezuma* (Mannheim, 2010). When, in 2009, Missotten was given the prestigious commission to direct and stage the composer Philip Glass's new opera *Kepler* for Linz European City of Culture 2009, he was confident enough to let Karel van Laere – one of the first year performing arts students take care of the costumes.

Glass invited Missotten to produce after he had heard him highly praised by the director Russel Davies for the production of *Kwartet*. 'At the time there was still no music, only fragments of libretto. But I think in imagery, not in text. I rarely let the setting be determined by the narrative, which means there is an interesting tension between text and space that also makes it interesting for the performers to work on it with me. What fascinated me about Kepler, the mathematician and astronomer, was not his life but his way of thinking. When he discovered the planets move on an elliptical path he was disappointed that it was such a simple, ugly form', laughs Missotten. 'I showed

Peter Missotten, *Bezonken rood*, 2006 © Peter Missotten / De Filmfabriek.

Glass my design and immediately warned him that it was unlikely that I would change it much after that. That's how it turned out too, the copper sculptures that drift down on to the stage, the singers moving like the orbit of a planet on it. I kept all these ideas. Glass had also written music for during the scenery changes, but there weren't any changes of scenery. We didn't do each other any favours in that respect, with the result that the 'change music' created an alienating tension on the stage.'

In the Spring of 2010 the cooperation between Cassiers and Missotten that had gone on for years came to a (temporary?) end on account of 'differences of artistic opinion', and Missotten left the Toneelhuis. 'Apart from the personal friendship I find it a great pity, especially from the point of view of theatre. I love the big auditorium and everything it's got to offer, which seems to have frightened off a lot of producers in Flanders in the past. Flemish theatre has far too many medium size productions and hands the large auditorium over to commercial productions and musicals. That's a shame, because I'm convinced that you can attract a broad public to the large auditorium as well if you have fascinating images.'

Liv Laveyne
Translated by Sheila M. Dale

Belgium and its Language Border

Running right across the middle of Belgium is a horizontal line, stretching from the border with France in the west to the German border in the east. As it approaches the German border, the line bends quite sharply southwards, running vertically towards the Grand Duchy of Luxembourg. This is the 'language border', a frontier which divides Belgium into three distinct language areas: Flanders (the northern, Dutch-speaking area of Belgium), Wallonia (the French-speaking region in the south of Belgium) and, close to the German border, German-speaking Belgium. There is actually a fourth language area, right in the centre of the country: the Brussels Capital Region. Officially bilingual (French and Dutch), this region is in reality highly Europeanised and intercultural. The Brussels Capital Region lies in the midst of Flanders like an oasis. It is entirely surrounded by Flemish territory, though French speakers living in some of the peripheral municipalities around Brussels have been granted individual rights, or 'facilities'. Broadly speaking, these give them the right to use French in contacts with the authorities. A comparable system is in existence in a number of Walloon and Flemish municipalities along the language frontier.

In round numbers, there are around six million inhabitants in Flanders, four million in Wallonia, 75,000 in German-speaking Belgium and 1.1 million in Brussels, taking the total population of Belgium to just over 11 million. These figures do not however include the very large presence of embassy staff, EU officials, NATO personnel, asylum-seekers and illegal immigrants in and around Brussels (the capital of Europe and headquarters of the European Commission). When all these groups are included, the real figure for the number of residents in the Brussels Capital Region is several tens of thousands higher.

The driving force behind the division of Belgium into language regions (and in fact behind the entire process of Belgian state reform) was and remains Flanders. Belgium was created in 1830, when it separated from the Netherlands. Until the end of the 20th century, it was governed as if it were in reality a monolingual - French-speaking - state. This led to protests in Flanders, ultimately resulting in the division of the country into distinct language areas.

The first language law dates from 1873, and allowed the use of Dutch in court cases. In practice, however, this law was rarely applied, based on the argument that 'the right of one party - the Flemish defendant - to use his own language did not imply a duty on the part of the other party - the French-speaking judge or lawyer - to understand that language'. The 1873 law was somewhat symptomatic of the way in which the unfolding language legislation in Belgium was systematically held back and boycotted by French-speaking Belgium, which was keen to retain its hegemony throughout the whole country.

Belgium's wealth at that time was generated almost exclusively by heavy industry. That industry was located in Wallonia, which was also where the political power was concentrated. It is no coincidence that the 'Flemish movement' only began to achieve real success from the 1960s onwards, which among other things was the period when the division of the country into language areas was established. Heavy industry then relocated to the major port areas, which were located in Flanders. Step by step, separate parliaments and governments were gradually installed within the different language regions, sometimes with differing powers (a fact that regularly leads to confusion). In addition to the Federal (or national) government seated in Brussels, Belgium also has a Flemish government (also seated in Brussels) and a Walloon government (with its seat in Namur), the government of German-speaking Belgium (with its seat in Eupen), the Brussels government (again seated in Brussels) and, to top it off, a separate government for the French Community (with its seat in Brussels). The Belgians themselves still sometimes have trouble working out who is who in this plethora of institutions.

German-speaking Belgium is a case apart. After the end of the First World War Belgium, which was on the winning side and had fought bravely in battles on the river Ijzer, in the extreme west of the country, had requested the 'return' of the province of Zeeland (containing the Scheldt estuary) and Luxembourg (the Grand Duchy). These requests were not successful but, by way of consolation, under the Treaty of Versailles in 1919 three German *cantons* in the east of the country were ceded to Belgium: the German-language cantons of Eupen and Sankt-Vith and the Walloon canton of Malmedy. No one had asked for this, and the integration of Eupen and Sankt-Vith into Belgium proved to be a very lengthy and difficult process. Today, however, these 'newest Belgians' are proud to be so.

The division of Belgium into language areas was

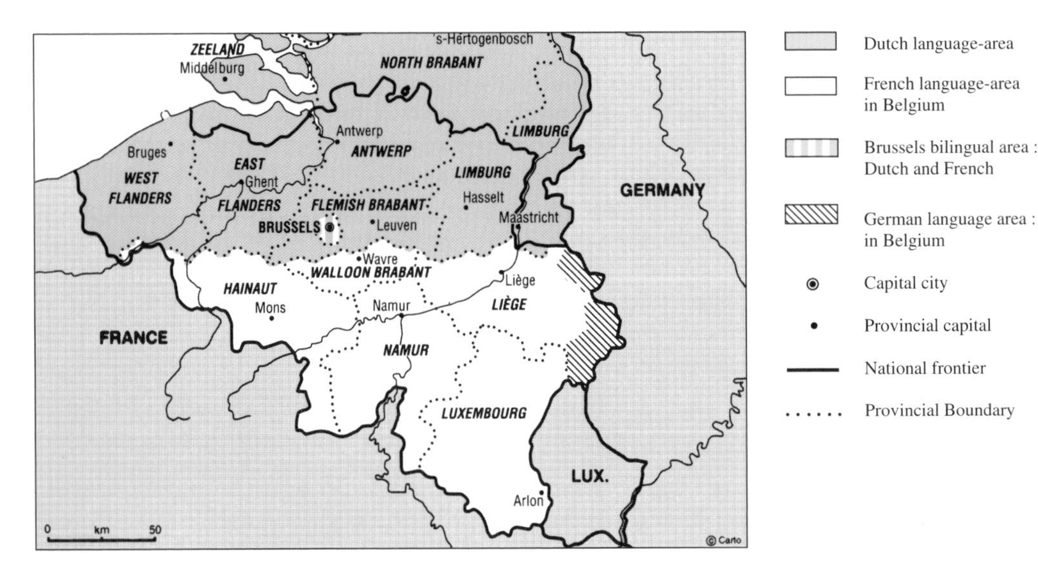

given official form in 1962/1963, when both houses of parliament passed a series of laws on the use of the different languages (Dutch, French and German). This event had been preceded by a long history of language disputes, but the debate also continued thereafter, and in fact still rages today. Walloons, Flemings, natives of Brussels and German-speaking Belgians are still engaged in a quest for an internal Belgian equilibrium. While that process is by no means complete, it has the great merit of being conducted peacefully, without violence, weapons or secret armies (such as, until recently, the IRA in Northern Ireland or ETA in the Basque country). Each step in this internal Belgian reform process undergoes thorough and lengthy preparation, sometimes leading to frustrations, as well as to endless and not always particularly interesting debates between politicians and between opinion-makers in the media.

The international press has written frequently, especially recently, about the impending demise of Belgium, but that is still a long way off. The process of state reform is simply continuing, and the likelihood that it will never result in the complete break up of the country into four language zones has a great deal to do with Brussels. Both Flanders and Wallonia are closely interwoven with the Belgian capital: Flanders because Brussels is like an enclave surrounded by Flemish territory; Wallonia because Brussels has a very large number of French-speaking residents. Immigration from Brussels also means that in some 'peripheral communities' - Flemish municipalities surrounding Brussels with facilities for French-speaking inhabitants - French speakers now make up the majority, and French-speaking politicians consequently regularly demand that Brussels be enlarged by absorbing these municipalities into the Capital Region. However, the Flemish will not hear of this; they believe that these French speakers should adapt to the language of their new region, and should therefore learn Dutch.

And so the debate goes on.

Guido Fonteyn
Translated by Julian Ross

Belgian Money and Finance during World War II

A Magisterial Survey

Financial historians have only recently begun a serious examination of banks and banking on the European continent during the Second World War. As often as not the impetus for this research has come from outside, the result of pressure exerted by representatives of clients robbed by the Germans through the banking system. The result has been a wave of publications which has entirely changed our perception. From an understudied sector of the wartime economy, banks and banking have become one of the best known, creating a new kind of bias: what happened in banking now risks being taken as an example of business behaviour under dictatorship simply because we know so little about other key sectors, such as construction, mining, textiles, transport or communications.

Though not prompted by outside pressure, the book under review, a comprehensively rewritten and condensed English edition of a Dutch volume published in 2005 as part of the Belgian national bank's history series, therefore forms part of the ongoing examination of European wartime banking. It amounts to an outstanding achievement. Two historians in their late seventies publishing a substantial book based on extensive research in archives at home and abroad is remarkable enough in itself. But for them to use their combined experience to present an object lesson in composition gives cause for rejoicing. Anyone who has ever tried to weave the many different strands of a large company into a satisfactory narrative knows just how difficult that is. Now imagine doing that for two companies performing roughly similar semi-public services in the name of the same country, yet under entirely different circumstances and facing fundamentally different challenges: one in occupied Belgium juggling to balance the increasingly pressing demands and peremptory orders of the Nazi regime with the needs of the population and the economy at large, the other improvising to keep the government in exile financed and manage Belgian economic and financial interests outside occupied Europe.

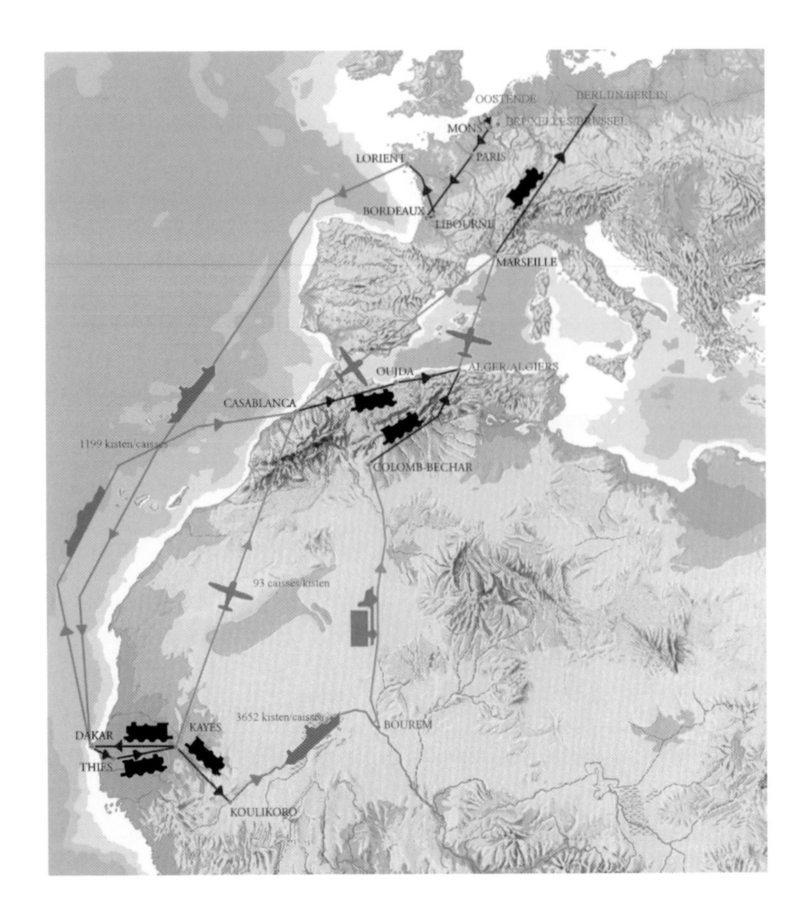

The Mysterious Ways of Belgian Gold during World War II, © Lannoo / Nationale Bank België.

The very wealth of themes clamouring for attention might easily have led to a sprawling book, but Van der Wee and Verbreyt have succeeded marvellously in composing a compelling storyline, moving effortlessly from occupied Belgium to London or New York and back, from fundamental macro-economic problems to the logistics of transporting gold, or from conflicts between Nazi officials and bank directors to personal portraits of the main protagonists, flavouring the narrative with telling quotations from original documents and using quantitative data sparingly and effectively. The often painful dilemmas of business under dictatorship are discussed frankly and fairly, without the facile guilty verdicts of some historians, but also without glossing over clear mistakes and misjudgements.

Rather than a conventional history of the Nationale Bank van België/Banque Nationale de Belgique, the book therefore offers a comprehensive account of money, monetary policy, banking and finance during the Second World War on both sides of the front lines. Interestingly, the two parts remained in remarkably close contact with each other, enabling a considerable degree of coordination between them. When faced with difficult decisions about Nazi demands bank officials could consult the government in exile and determine their position accordingly. Conversely, Belgian officials in London knew what was happening in the country, which helped them materially in planning the return of the government and preparing key policy decisions such as the currency purge. By contrast, the Nederlandsche Bank in occupied Amsterdam and the Dutch government in exile, for instance, exchanged information only intermittently, so the bank's board was out on a limb when faced with Nazi demands, and the government knew next to nothing about the situation in the country. This created considerable friction following the return of the government after the liberation.

In showing how Belgium managed it, this magisterial survey presents a model history of finance during the Second World War which other countries would do well to follow: dispassionate yet fully committed, wide-ranging without being exhaustive, giving fair criticism but not picking every bone. If only we all possessed such powers of composition.

Joost Jonker

HERMAN VAN DER WEE AND MONIQUE VERBREYT,
A Small Nation in the Turmoil of the Second World War, Money, Finance and Occupation, (Belgium, its Enemies, its Friends, 1939-1945),
Leuven University Press, 2009, 494 pages.

M - STAM - MAS
City Museums

Three Flemish cities, Antwerp, Ghent and Leuven, all have a new museum. The Leuven museum was the first to open, launching out with a large exhibition on the 15th century painter Rogier van der Weyden. The Ghent museum opened its doors to the general public on 9 October 2010, and the opening of the Antwerp museum is planned for 17 May 2011. Three new museums within two years - that really is quite remarkable.

These museums have certain common characteristics. All of them are municipal museums. They make use of collections that have existed in their cities for quite a considerable time and are now being provided with a more updated presentation. All three of them are housed in new or renovated premises. Lastly, all three have a snappy, catchy name: M, STAM and MAS. But that is where the similarities end.

M is Leuven's municipal museum. It is situated in the city centre, not far from the Gothic city hall and the university library. A city museum had already existed there since the early 20th century: *Museum Vander Kelen*. Architect Stephane Beel was given the task of making a new, spacious and airy museum out of this old building, along with that of the former academy. Old and new had to be forged into a whole new entity. Beel has created a striking white building in which there is an eye-catching abundance of travertine and the original columned frontage has been preserved as some kind of symbol.

Furthermore, the new museum houses an original collection that is most interesting for its unique collection of late-Gothic paintings and sculptures, including works by such artists as Dirc Bouts, as well as for 19th century paintings by various Flemish masters and sculptures by such artists as Constantin Meunier and George Minne. In addition, M wants to let present-day and classical art enter into a dialogue. This has been achieved via an abundance of exhibitions that have a rich mixture of classical and contemporary art. Works by such present-day artists as Jan Vercruysse, Angus Fairhurst, Matthew Brannon, Robert Devriendt have already been on show. The exhibition of work by

M in Leuven.

Rogier van der Weyden has commanded international attention. The ritual objects of the Congolese region of Mayombe or the magnificent, ornamented pages of the Anjou Bible have also featured in successful exhibitions. With this combination of contemporary and classical art, M seeks to attract a public from way beyond the boundaries of the Leuven region. One year after opening, it has at any rate gained a solid position in the cultural life of Flanders.

STAM, Ghent's new city museum (*STAdsMuseum*), is housed in the former *Bijlokeabdij*. For a museum that wishes to show the history of the city of Ghent, this abbey, whose earliest history goes back to the 13th century, is a dream location. The abbey houses, for example, one of the finest medieval refectories in Western Europe. Furthermore, an art college is situated in the immediate vicinity of the museum, really making this a venue for art and culture. Here, too, serious conversion has taken place, although the architecture is less spectacular than in the case of M and certainly than the new museum in Antwerp. The city architect, Koen Van Nieuwenhuyse, has primarily created a new reception pavilion, adapting the rest of the existing buildings to the needs of a contemporary museum. An

STAM in Ghent.

important part of the STAM collection consists of items from the former *Bijlokemuseum*. From the more than 17,000 artefacts in this collection, STAM has made a selection that narrates the history of the city of Ghent. It makes intelligent use of multimedia, too. It is possible, for example, to walk over a large map of the city and almost explore it house by house. A scale-model allows you to sense how the city has evolved through the ages. There are, though, real highlights worth admiring: medieval manuscripts and documents, paintings and sculptures. The history of the city is told chronologically. There is also enough room in STAM for contemporary exhibitions, although here - unlike M - the accent is on the permanent collection and on showing the history of the city.

MAS stands for the museum on the river (*Museum Aan de Stroom*). The river in question is of course the Scheldt and the city is Antwerp. The new building is without a doubt the most spectacular of the three new museums. The internationally recognised Dutch firm of architects Neutelings Riedijk has designed a sixty-metre-high tower with large exhibition spaces. There are magnificent views of the city of Antwerp and the old harbour from the large glass sections of the building, which features references to the 16th century warehouse or *Hanzehuis*. At the foot of the museum lies a 1600 m² square, for which the well-known artist Luc Tuymans has designed a large mosaic. MAS tells the story of the city of Antwerp, the river, the port and the world. To do this, it makes use of three existing collections: the ethnographical museum, the national maritime museum and the folklore museum. In addition, sections of the *Vleeshuis* Museum collection will be moved to MAS. And there will also be a place for the unique collection of pre-Columbian art from the estate of the Flemish industrialist Paul Janssen, which has been acquired by the Flemish Community.

A maximum of 5% of all the artefacts from the collection will be able to be put on show. The intention is to display new items in regularly changing temporary exhibitions. At present, however, MAS is not yet open to the general public, which will first be able to ascend the tower on 17 May 2011. Until then, it can sample the pavilion in front of MAS. That is where this large-scale project is being presented and where there is a temporary exhibition illustrating contacts between Antwerp and China.

MAS in Antwerp.

Three venues, three new museums, three different ways of tackling a project. In each case, existing old collections are given a new, engaging presentation. Important items are being dusted off, once more being made accessible and sometimes being placed in a different perspective via the use of new media. With their collections, new exhibitions and, especially, their new settings, these museums will also become major tourist attractions for their respective cities and regions.

Dirk Van Assche
Translated by John Irons

www.mleuven.be
www.stamgent.be
www.mas.be

'A Dutch Political Novel'
Max Havelaar in English

The British public's very first acquaintance with Multatuli's *Max Havelaar* dates back to 1867. A long contribution about *Max Havelaar* entitled 'A Dutch Political Novel' appeared in *The North British Review* in the context of 'the great question of the day in the Netherlands – the government of the Dutch colonies'. The article offered the reader acerbic quotes about the Dutch colonial administration in Java, ending with Multatuli's furious appeal to King William III.

Although the reviewer agreed with him on many points, the end was, in his eyes, Multatuli's 'greatest mistake', because in a constitutional monarchy it was, of course, impossible for the king to reply. The critic also censured the style of the Saïdjah story, which may have been appropriate for 'poetical fiction' but was absolutely not suited to a serious discussion of the accusations *Max Havelaar* contained. Multatuli had no-one but himself to blame, then, that with his 'sensational romance' and 'talented writing' he was now generally looked upon as a gifted writer rather than as a reformer of the Dutch East Indies.

The first complete English translation by Baron Alphonse van Nahuys followed in 1868. Within a century there were another two: Willem Siebenhaar's in 1927 and Roy Edwards's in 1967. The first time *Max Havelaar* was translated mainly as a colonial document, the second time as satire, and finally as the classic work of the Dutch literary canon.

Nahuys was primarily concerned with the colonial facts and the irrefutable indictment that forms the core of the book. He moved to London specifically to acquire a good mastery of the English language for it. Not unusually for those days he adapted Multatuli's text, making it shorter and more pointed, for the benefit of English readers and their reading pleasure.

In his foreword Nahuys referred explicitly to the American writer Harriet Beecher Stowe and her famous antislavery novel, *Uncle Tom's Cabin* (1852). Multatuli himself had also mentioned her name in his novel in 1860, immediately after Saïdjah's story. Remember, though, that slavery had barely or not been abolished in the Dutch Empire – only in 1859 in the Dutch East Indies and, finally, in 1863 in Suriname. On this point then Multatuli took a highly topical position against the exploitation that marked the Dutch Kingdom as a conservative Christian, anti-liberal, slave-owning power, in contrast to the British Empire (which had already abolished the slave trade in 1807 and slavery in 1833).

Nahuys's translation continued to make waves for a long time. In 1921 it was reprinted for the edification of the British proletariat as a serial in *The Worker's Dreadnought*, under the editorship of Sylvia Pankhurst. And in 1926 'The Story of Saïdjah' was included in the anthology *Great Short Stories of the World*, which has been reprinted many times since then. It was an appropriate selection because, beyond the sentimental setting, what Multatuli did here was revolutionary. He was the first writer to put an ordinary Javanese village boy centre stage, with his own name, his feelings, ideas, experiences, reflections, dreams and desires - a person, just like you and me, who at the end discovers his great love, Adinda, abused and murdered by Dutch soldiers who had come to bring law and order to the Lampung District. A shocking story in which Multatuli completely wiped the floor with the image of the Netherlands as a civilised and enlightened model coloniser.

In total we know of ten British reviews from 1868. The verdict of the *Westminster Review* on 1 April 1868 was definitely positive: 'It is difficult to say whether *Max Havelaar* is more interesting as a novel or powerful as a political pamphlet. From either point of view it is of rare and first-rate excellence'. And, according to the progressive *Contemporary Review* of the same date, Multatuli's criticism of the Dutch Trading Company (of which the Dutch King was the largest shareholder) showed how misguided the praises of the British colonial expert, John William Bailey Money, concerning the efficient exploitation of Java by the Dutch government, in his much-read work Java, or *How to Manage a Colony* (1861), really were.

In contrast, in 1869 the well-known British naturalist, Alfred Russel Wallace, who had just spent eight years travelling around the Dutch East Indies, after strongly recommending Money's 'exceptional and in-

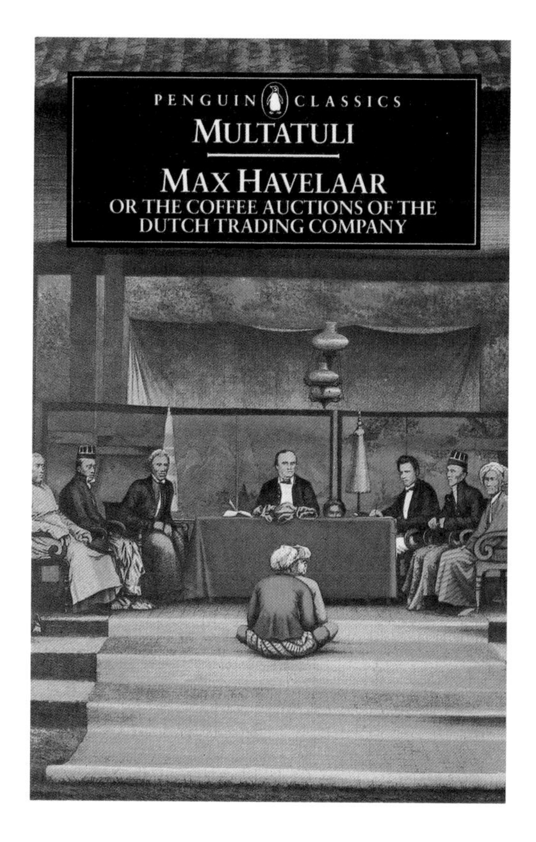

teresting' book in his *The Malay Archipelago*, was critical of the *Max Havelaar*: 'a very tedious and long-winded story, full of rambling digression'; 'exaggerated', 'neither dates, figures nor details are ever given, it is impossible to verify or answer them.'

Via Wallace's book, though, Nahuy's translation did have an important literary impact, influencing the writer Joseph Conrad in particular. *The Malay Archipelago* was one of his favourite books and he is supposed to have read *Max Havelaar* in the Raffles library in Singapore.

The translator of the second English *Max Havelaar*, Willem Siebenhaar, was an idealistic and anti-imperialist Dutch anarchist, who left for Australia in 1891 because of his political ideas. In Perth, in 1922, he met the writer D.H. Lawrence, who vigorously encouraged him to finish his *Max Havelaar* translation, which was finally published in 1927 by Knopf in New York.

The third English translation, by Roy Edwards, is currently the most widespread. In 1982 it was included in Eric Montague Beekman's *Library of the Indies* and, with an introduction by Reinder P. Meijer, in the prestigious *Penguin Classics* in 1987. The Beekman edition has been reprinted by Periplus in Singapore since 1993 and can now also be read on Google Books.

Edwards's translation was very faithful to the text and, in comparison to Nahuys's, he made it much more direct, with his lively everyday style and regular appeals to the reader.

Multatuli raised the theme of exploitation by showing the price the Javanese had to pay for what in the Netherlands was an ordinary consumer good – a cup of coffee. His novel put the conflict between Dutch ethical ideals and Dutch East Indian colonial practices on the table in no uncertain terms, and the question has come up regularly in international discussion ever since.

What is interesting in this context is to see how and with what literary analogies the translators have tried, in their important role as intercultural intermediaries, to position Multatuli for English readers. Whereas Nahuys, in 1868, emphasised Beecher Stowe's anti-slavery motif, in his foreword a century later Edwards pointed to Multatuli's genius and the vitality which, as a writer, he has in common with that other great nineteenth century autodidact, Vincent van Gogh. Nowadays the (post)colonial view of *Max Havelaar* dominates, but historically we find that it was for his humour that he was praised.

Not for nothing is *Max Havelaar* counted, even now, 151 years after it was published, as the greatest and most important work of all the literature written in Dutch. But in the wider context? Is *Max Havelaar* in translation capable of transcending its form as the text of a novel to become a figure of universal eloquence?

The answer to that comes from Anthony Wild in his *Coffee: a dark history* (2004), and it very clearly lies beyond literature: 'the name *Max Havelaar* has become the call to action of the global Fair Trade movement'. Seen from the critical postcolonial perspective it is a political novel that has put the dark underside of globalisation on the agenda in a way no other has.

So, even now, Multatuli and his *Max Havelaar* continue to inspire the worldwide struggle for humanity and justice.

Reinier Salverda
Translated by Lindsay Edwards

Death in a Cathedral

A Dog of Flanders

© Twentieth Century Fox Film Corporation, 1960.

How many literature-lovers still remember the oeuvre of Marie Louise de la Ramée? Yet, writing under the pseudonym 'Ouida', this author created an English-language novel which recounts what without exaggeration can be hailed as the best-known story about Flanders and the Flemings. *A Dog of Flanders* was published in 1872 and became a bestseller. To date, millions of copies have been sold, and in Japan alone there have been some 500 reprints.

The main character in *A Dog of Flanders* is an orphan boy called Nello. He is initially taken in by his grandfather, a poor dairy farmer. Each day, they go to Antwerp together to sell milk to the wealthy burghers. One day, however, his grandfather dies and Nello is abandoned by virtually everyone. Only one faithful friend remains, his dog Patrasche. Yet Nello refuses to be discouraged. He is very talented in drawing and enters a drawing competition which offers a substantial monetary prize. Sadly, he fails to win the contest. In desperation, he goes to the city one last time with Patrasche. On Christmas Eve he dies from his hardships, in Antwerp Cathedral, lying in front of Pieter Paul Rubens' famous depiction of *The Descent from the Cross*, with Patrasche in his arms.

Japan, in particular, still seems to be completely enchanted by this story with its strong theme of being alone in the world. Each year, the Cathedral of Our Lady draws huge numbers of visitors from Japan who are prepared to undertake the long flight in order to visit the place where Nello lost his life. The characters from *A Dog of Flanders* appear to form part of the collective memory in the land of the rising sun, partly because of a popular animation series which was first broadcast on Japanese television in 1975 and which has been re-broadcast every year since then. Apparently, the sad ending is very appealing to the average Japanese person. With a little imagination, Nello can be seen as a sort of Samurai who, until his last breath and against his better judgment, fights against his undeserved fate and dies a courageous death.

But Japan is not the only country where *A Dog of Flanders* is well known. There have been several occasions when the United States, in particular, has also been charmed by the story of Nello and Patrasche. Hollywood produced no fewer than five films of the story, the first appearing as early as 1914. The reviews of this film by Howell Hansel reveal something of a puzzle. Evidently there were two versions, one with a happy ending and one in which Nello died in the snow just outside the Cathedral. This second version would also turn out to be the only one in which Nello and Patrasche came to a bad ending. The fact that Hollywood dislikes death and hardship was also clear in the second film portrayal. In this 1924 version, directed by Victor Schertzinger, Nello and Patrasche are adopted by a wealthy painter; and of course they live happily ever afterwards. The main character was played by the talented Jackie Coogan, only ten years old at the time but already one of the biggest stars in Hollywood. Yet another film version of the story appeared before the Second World War, this time directed by Edward Slowman, and according to aficionados one of the many uninspired products to come out of the Hollywood film factory.

It was to be 1960 before the next film version appeared, directed by James B. Clark and showing Nello & Co. in colour for the first time. Part of the film was shot on location in the Low Countries, in Antwerp of course, but strangely enough also at a number of picturesque locations in the Netherlands. The cast contained a few Dutch actors, some of whom enjoyed

Facsimile of picture which appeared in the first print of A Dog of Flanders
© Cambridge University Library.

a certain fame. The last (for the time being) version filmed in America appeared in 1999. For a while, it seemed as if this film, directed by Kevin Brodi, would remain faithful to the book. However, shortly after his death in the Cathedral, we see Nello in heaven where his prematurely dead mother and his grandfather are sitting waiting for him. A member of the jury for the great drawing contest informs Nello that he was really the deserving winner of the competition. Moreover, from his place high up in heaven, Nello is able to watch over his own funeral and it comes as no surprise that everyone attending had found him a very likeable boy. The desire of filmmakers to tailor films to the expectations of American audiences appears indefatigable; because it turns out, of course, that everything had just been a bad dream - what else had the viewer expected? So it is quickly back to the earthly existence, where we see how Nello wakes up in the Cathedral, with all the characters standing around him in a circle. It is the perfect moment for a group hug, and a good moment for the closing credits to start rolling across the screen.

What about the story in the Low Countries themselves? It is almost as if there is some kind of strange curse there on stories that give them a presence in the outside world. Ask the average Dutchman to describe the plot of *The Flying Dutchman* and he is likely to sigh and shrug his shoulders. And apart from a few bar owners near the Cathedral of Our Lady in Antwerp, virtually no one in Flanders has ever heard of Nello and Patrasche. It is not that attempts have never been made to bring the boy and his dog to life. Well-versed comic strip aficionados will know that Album 201 from the *Spike and Suzy* series, which is widely read in Flanders, was inspired entirely by *A Dog of Flanders*. In Hoboken, near Antwerp - and according to local worthies the village where Nello grew up - there stands a small bronze statue erected especially for the pilgrims from Japan. And in 2007, Didier Volckaert and An Van Dienderen made a fascinating TV documentary based on the story.

The Flemish publishing house Lannoo also recently jumped on the bandwagon with *A Dog of Flanders. Een nooit geziene kijk op Vlaanderen*[1] (*A Dog of Flanders. Flanders seen as never before*). The 'pièce de résistance' in this book is the faithful translation of the very rare first edition of the novel. The original version and a translation by the contemporary Flemish writer Tom Naegels are printed alongside each other. Different collaborators focus among other things on the Japanese animation series and the Hollywood films, as well as on life in Flanders in 1870 and the turbulent life and tragic death of the writer herself. Highly original is the article about dogcarts in the Low Countries, and of course there is no avoiding the question of why the story arouses so little interest in Flanders itself. The book is also beautifully illustrated, using stills from the animation series and films, as well as pictures from the *Spike and Suzy* comic strips, for example.

Hans Vanacker
Translated by Julian Ross

NOTE

1. An Van Dienderen & Didier Volckaert (eds.), *A Dog of Flanders. Een nooit geziene kijk op Vlaanderen (A Dog of Flanders. Flanders seen as never before)*, Tielt: Lannoo, 2010, 265 pp.
ISBN 978 90 209 8852 9

So Universal, yet so Dutch

Gerbrand Bakker's *The Twin*

In Gerbrand Bakker's *The Twin* (transl. David Colmer, 2008, original: *Boven is het stil*, 2006) Helmer van Wonderen has 'put Father upstairs'. That means the 55-year-old farmer is making a literal and figurative move. A power shift takes place on the West Frisian farm in the North of Holland (the province Holland that is). The old man who took control over Helmer's life and autocratically reigned over the farmhouse's ground floor, has now been moved upstairs. Father is tired and worn out; he will soon die. In the meantime, his son Helmer starts redecorating, and buys a new double bed.

Behind the move hides a tragedy, subtly expressed in *The Twin*. Slowly, taking his time, Bakker reveals a tale of loneliness and repressed passion. 35 years before, Helmer lost his twin brother, Henk, in a car accident; his father lost his favourite son. At that point Father decided that Helmer was 'done there in Amsterdam'. He orders Helmer to quit his Literature studies in the big city, and to start working on the farm now that Henk – the natural farm heir – is gone. A 'life milking cows', full of unspoken frustrations between father and son, follows. Yet the move of the aging family tyrant initiates change. So does the sudden reappearance of Riet, brother Henk's former fiancée, who was driving the car in which Henk lost his life.

This Summer *The Twin* received the International IMPAC Dublin Literary Award 2010, a cash prize of 100,000 euros. This is the most valuable literary award for a single work of literature published in English. *The Twin* clearly appeals to an international audience - 163 international libraries in 43 countries nominated 156 novels for the IMPAC long list, which was cut down to a shortlist of eight. Bakker's novel had to compete with the likes of Zoë Heller and Joseph O'Neill, who are both widely known; whereas Gerbrand Bakker from Wieringerwaard in the Netherlands seemed to many so obscure that the international press kept stubbornly referring to *The Twin* as 'his literary debut'. The book was Bakker's second literary brainchild.

Besides receiving the IMPAC award, *The Twin* also won the French Prix Initiales 2010 and has been nominated for the Prix Cevennes. The novel gained international press coverage and has been translated into seven languages. What is it about *The Twin* that is so attractive to the international reader?

Is the story not too Dutch, taking place in a culturally limited setting? In an interview with the *Irish Times* Bakker says boldly: 'A Dutch writer should write about Dutch characters. I ask why would a Dutch writer write about a Russian?' What then accounts for the novel's international appeal?

I wonder if the appeal is in the confirmation of an image of the Netherlands that reigns abroad, an image of country landscapes, cows and ice skating. It extends even to the object that Father uses to hit the twin brothers with - a wooden clog, no less. It is a recognizable Dutch picture, repeated on the book covers at home and abroad. On his website, Bakker confesses that when his publisher asked him about ideas for cover images, he answered: 'something with sheep'. Yet four cows are shown on the Dutch edition, staring at the reader from beneath a blue sky with greyish white clouds.

The choice for this visual seems to be inspired by the works of Dutch landscape painters such as Ruysdael. Ruysdael used cattle as a signifier of Dutch prosperity. It is no surprise that several international reviewers of *The Twin* choose the word 'landscape' when referring to the vivid descriptions of nature in the book. Bakker's work certainly evokes thoughts of landscape painting. His writing is observant, with a great attention to surroundings; the setting is rural and the animals – subtly 'painted' – can easily be seen as literary characters in their own right.

The Twin's strength is also in the intimacy created between reader and narrator. The reader is invited to peek into a normally closed farmhouse. The scope of the cold Dutch landscape becomes manageable as the (foreign) reader gets to know the secrets hidden behind the closed doors. It is a joyous voyeurism, comparable to the feeling of looking at a Vermeer painting, such as his *Milk Maid*. The motif of voyeurism is unforgettably symbolised in the novel when Helmer and neighbour Ada stare at each other from behind their living room windows, both slowly lowering their binoculars.

Hendrick Avercamp, *Ice-skating in a Village*, c. 1610, Oil on panel, 36 x 71 cm, © Mauritshuis, The Hague.

Vermeer, as well as other Dutch painters such as Pieter de Hooch, often includes a window or door that looks out from the intimate interior onto the street. There is the city where other things happen. In Bakker's work there is a similar 'vista': the outlook on Helmer's broken dream of studying literature in Amsterdam, serving as a reminder of a life not lived.

Though Bakker says he wants to write about Dutch characters, his themes are universal: loneliness, loss, taking control of one's own life and ageing. These themes may be more appealing to international readers because of *The Twin*'s overlap with visual representations of Dutch culture: landscape paintings, intimate interiors and vistas.

There is the icescape, too - lively Dutch winter scenes depicting young and old enjoying winter, skating, playing ice hockey etc. This genre is probably best represented by Hendrick Avercamp who painted *Ice-skating in a Village* (early 17th century). Several scenes in *The Twin* are reminiscent of Avercamp's painting. For example, Helmer learned to skate without his brother. While his mother skated pirouettes on the ice, the farmhand safely pushed young Helmer forward. Another 'icescape picture' is the twins' dad daringly driving his car at high speed over a frozen lake, with Helmer and Henk in the back seat.

In Avercamp's *Ice-skating in a Village* most people are enjoying winter together. They are all part of a group of some sort - couples, a sports team, a family. Or they skate by themselves, focused, eyes forward like marathon runners. However, in the middle of the painting there is a little girl. She seems both lost and in place in the busy surroundings, standing steadily on her skates, a small pale creature that stands out and fits in at the same time. Bakker's novel, *The Twin*, is similar to this strange little girl; it is a coming-of-age novel about a 55-year-old; it is both typically Dutch and reaches out to the wider world; and it takes place on a small farm but is recognizably cosmopolitan.

Stefanie van Gemert

Gerbrand Bakker, *The Twin*, Archipelago Books, 2009, 343 pages.

Belgian Designer Pop

Charming Chameleon Daan Stuyven

A child that quickly gets bored with its toys and is forever in need of new stimuli – that's the picture that's left in the mind whenever one considers the multi-faceted career of Daan Stuyven (b. 1969). The uninitiated would never suspect that one and the same person are behind the euphoric dance of 'Swedish Designer Drugs', the shadowy country of 'Icon', the scissors-and-paste rock of 'Woods', the crooner jazz of 'The Player' (piano version) and the soundtrack of films such as *Verboden te zuchten (I Know I'll See Your Face Again*, 2001) and *Meisje (Girl*, 2002) – to name just a few of Daan Stuyven's songs.

Nevertheless initially his career followed a fairly unambiguous path - indeed an almost stereotypical one according to the 'handbook for would-be musicians'. At the end of the eighties, with his group Citizen Kane, he took part in Humo's Rock Rally (*the* springboard for Flemish musicians), and nudged open the door to success with bands such as Volt and Running Cow, whose 'Gasoline on Fire' was a hit on radio. But Stuyven only really began to attract attention in 1996 with Dead Man Ray, an avant-gardist rock group that was perfectly attuned to the Flemish musical landscape at that time. Shortly before this, after years of worthy efforts doing the circuits in the shadow of the cathedral tower, this scene was finally deflowered once and for all by the Antwerp band dEUS, whose ex-guitarist Rudy Trouvé, moreover, was Daan's sparring partner in Dead Man Ray.

In the light of how he was to develop later this would seem to have been a bad move on Stuyven's part: what was this pop fanatic doing in such strange company as Dead Man Ray? But if you listened carefully you could hear clear pop melodies behind the noise of the guitar and the clipped computer sounds. The taut design and the exaggerated allusion to pop kitsch in 'Bee Gee' were also writing on the wall that Stuyven was after more than success in a cult. However it was with Dead man Ray that he made a first attempt to break out of the alternative circles: in 1999 this group was responsible for the making of a new soundtrack for the comedy of the absurd *At the Drop of a Head*, dating from 1962. That project brought together a whole spectrum of things that fascinated Daan Stuyven – you can trace lines from it that criss-cross his whole artistic career.

Firstly, Daan Stuyven as man of the image. Not only is he a film fan who has composed soundtracks for diverse films (of which a selection is brought together on the CD *Cinema*), but for a long time he worked mainly as a designer. His background in graphics works its way through into more or less everything Stuyven does, most obviously in his immediately recognizable self-designed CD cases with the characteristic block capitals. But Daan also makes stylized images of himself, of his music and of his lyrics too. Whatever he creates always benefits from this clarity, the fact that it can be recognized immediately. To illustrate this: for virtually every new phase of his musical career he comes up, chameleon-like, with a new look, frequently a variant on that old classic, the gentleman's suit – which earned him the official title of 'the best dressed artist in Belgium' in the Flemish musical press. On his solo records (released under his first name 'Daan') many of his hits seem to be style practices, almost a pastiche (the electro-fiddling in 'Housewife'). His lyrics reverberate from the florid images, such as 'they liked the sting but not the cactus' in *Exes*, about the women in his life who seem unable to stay with him for long.

Daan's second great fascination is Bobbejaan Schoepen (1925-2010), a remarkable figure who owes his legendary status in Flanders to a long career in the ballad circuit, variety, film (among others *At the Drop of a Head*, mentioned above), and also the business world, with the Bobbejaanland amusement park as his best-known creation. It's probably Schoepen's combination of artistic and commercial talent, his gift for making a business success of his ideas, that appeals so much to Daan, because actually he is doing exactly the same thing, so many years later, as a solo artist: turning mad ideas into products in a way that means they are appreciated by a broad public.

Daan's obsession with Schoepen – occasionally he has even been called Bobbedaan – reached its peak in 2007-2008, when he was one of the people working on the Bobbejaan Schoepen come-back record (that

Daan Stuyven (1969-).

would also seem to be the latter's testament) and he won a popular competition on national television with a cover for Schoepen's *De lichtjes van de Schelde*.

At about the same time Daan took a shy at the Eurovision Song Contest, at which he wanted to represent Belgium. It turned out to be little more than a joke that got out of hand, but it might have succeeded all the same. With his songs and image tending to become more and more kitsch, as a somewhat louche but nonetheless charming singer, he certainly wasn't the odd one out at this high mass of camp. It was also the pinnacle of his obsession with pop culture, which was strongly geared to images, as well as of his third fascination, which is connected to this, Belgitude. This is an artistic attitude that rejects regionalism (in particular Flemish Nationalism) and takes the tradition of, among others, James Ensor and René Magritte and the musicians Jacques Brel and Toots Thielemans as its points of reference. Mockery, the grotesque, absurdism, surrealism and intractability are typical of artistic expression in Belgium. In imitation of Arno, Daan shows himself to be a true follower of Belgitude, witness his participation in the Belgavox-concerts, an initiative to promote 'solidarity, dialogue and respect between Flemings and Walloons.' We have already discussed Daan's tendency towards visual and musical kitsch, but his lyrics also overflow with grotesque and surreal images. We cite the Scandinavian slapstick from one of his greatest hits, *Swedish Designer Drugs*: 'It's hard to be strong/depending on northern refineries, how deep is your fjord/how shallow thy watery eyes/how could I recupe/surrounded by 95 dogmas/like a reindeer I'm struck by Swedish designer drugs'.

Relatively speaking, Daan also includes rather a lot of French language numbers in his version of Belgitude – something that's unusual for a Flemish artist – and, when questioned by a newspaper about his favourite food, he even admitted that he can enjoy a *mitraillette*. That's Daan all over: when famous personalities being interviewed by the media constantly show off with refined dishes and fancy restaurants, he extols this greasy Brussels snack consisting of chips and a sausage and a piece of fried meat stuffed in a roll. Stuyven loves to play with people's expectations, enjoys wrong-footing them with music and things he says that you suspect are ironic, though you can never be sure. (Indeed a bit later Daan confessed to a newspaper that he loves raw fish.)

That game's amusing, but you can get tired of it. And Daan seems to have realised that himself. He turned forty recently and is playing with words and images less and less. You can hear this on his CD *Manhay* from 2009. Gone are the campy electro and allusions to tacky hits from the eighties. Instead you get relatively simple pop with a traditional feel. There's no misunderstanding lyrics like those of *Icon* either: '(...) So don't try to be an icon/con the i inside of you/ that picture you've been painting/doesn't look a thing like you (...).' In interviews, too, Daan says that he has changed. 'I've come to terms with myself. I'm an idiot, but I can be satisfied with myself,' he said in a Belgian newspaper at the end of 2010.

You can get a foretaste of how this new Daan, without musical masquerades, sounds on his latest CD, from 2010, entitled (not insignificantly) *Simple*, where he's given old numbers a new jacket – and by no means always an expensive designer model. It seems we still haven't heard the last, and the best, from this charming chameleon.

Pieter Coupé
Translated by Sheila M. Dale

www.daan.be

Netherlands Bach Society Celebrates its 90th Birthday

It was conductor Willem Mengelberg who in the early twentieth century established the Dutch tradition of annual performances of Bach's *St. Matthew Passion*. In his interpretations with the *Concertgebouw Orchestra* Mengelberg opted for richly scored choral and orchestral parts. He hardly used original instruments. Instead of the harpsichord, for example, he used a 'nail piano' which had thumb tacks in the felt of the hammers. Besides that, he employed all sorts of excessive romantic techniques to accentuate the dramatic impact of the music, like sudden changes of tempo and huge dynamic contrasts. A severe reduction of aria's and recitatives was considered necessary as a matter of course; otherwise the audience would not sit through the performance without falling asleep.

In the decades that followed, these ponderous productions caused more and more controversy. In 1921 the foundation of the Netherlands Bach Society was the most visible evidence of a tendency to revise the 'massive' performance practice with Mengelberg as its icon. The Netherlands Bach Society took a position that was diametrically opposed to Mengelberg's performance ideals and, as of 1922, performed its own annual production of the *St. Matthew Passion*.

The ambition was to move away from a lavish nineteenth century performance practice back to the 'concert style' of Bach's own era. As a rule the Bach Society performed the *St. Matthew Passion* not in a concert hall but in a church, the *Grote Kerk* in Naarden (a quaint moated city between Utrecht and Amsterdam). The performance of the sacred work in a church was welcomed by many and by opting for a performance on Good Friday instead of Palm Sunday - Mengelberg's preferred moment - the newcomer emphasized the difference with the Mengelberg tradition. In 2011 the Netherlands Bach Society celebrates its 90th anniversary. It is now the oldest early music ensemble in the Netherlands and perhaps even in the whole world. The fundamental principles referred to above are still intact, although the Society has gone through many changes. The musicians do not limit their performances to Bach, since the repertoire has broadened considerably over the years. Yet its pulsing heart (and irreplaceable money maker) continues to be the annual performances of the *St. Matthew Passion*, now an entire concert series performed at diverse locations in the run-up to Easter.

In its infancy, the Bach Society hardly ever collaborated with baroque specialists. On the contrary, the vocal soloists sang with as much passion with the Bach Society as under Mengelberg. Only when Evert Cornelis became its director in 1927 did a more modern notion of 'authenticity' become part of the Society's profile. To achieve this, Cornelis studied the orginal manuscripts. He also (re)introduced the uncut *Matthew Passion*, considering leaving out passages as nothing less than a criminal offence.

The Netherlands Bach Society became a well respected and integral part of the musical infrastructure of the Netherlands. In the fifties its leader - by that time Anthon van der Horst – even conducted the annual *St. Matthew Passion* of the *Concertgebouw Orchestra* twice, when Mengelberg's successor, Eduard van Beinum, was seriously ill. Charles de Wolff became the next conductor of the Bach Society and kept his position for nearly twenty years. In the mid-eighties yet another course was set. Inspired by the initiators of the historic performance movement, for example Nikolaus Harnoncourt and Gustav Leonhardt, the new leader Jos van Veldhoven reorganized the Bach Society into a Baroque orchestra with a smaller choir of specialized singers. At the beginning of the new millennium van Veldhoven even reduced his choir to one or two soloists per part.

Over the years the Bach Society has become a well respected brand with international fame, even impressing the critics of *The New York Times*. Van Veldhoven conducts the series of *Matthew Passions* only every other year; in the seasons in between the Bach Society invites other acclaimed conductors to enrich the interpretation.

The 90th anniversary of the Netherlands Bach Society will be used as a kick off season leading eventually to the festive celebration of its 100th anniversary in 2021 as programming nowadays looks far, far ahead. In this case such planning is an absolute necessity. In anticipation of its first century of existence, the Society has set itself the challenge of performing all the works by Johann Sebastian Bach over the next decade. A major enterprise this, as Bach's compositions include more than 1100 works, of which the *St. Matthew Passion* is but one ...

Emile Wennekes

www.bachvereniging.nl

Jos van Veldhoven (1952-).

The Flanders Recorder Quartet

Ambassadors of a Forgotten Instrument

We are in London, at the court of Henry VIII, in the year 1539. The King has had the five Bassano brothers from the Venice area brought over to work for him. Their task? To play the recorder for the King every day, as well as making instruments and giving him music lessons. It is widely known that, in addition to his penchant for feminine beauty, Henry VIII also had a passion for music, played music himself and wrote several compositions, too. However, his interest in instrumental music was uncharacteristic of his era, especially in England.

In the 16th and 17th centuries, Europe's musical centre of gravity was Italy, where such renowned composers as Monteverdi and Caccini were engaged in the transition from the Renaissance to the Baroque. Whereas the Renaissance was predominantly a period of vocal music (sometimes accompanied by instruments), from the time of the Baroque there was increasing interest in purely instrumental music. One of the instruments that gained a greater degree of independence was the recorder. It had been played by professional musicians since the 1500s and groups of several recorder-players were formed, which came to be known as consorts. It was a fact, however, that many recorder players played violin or oboe first, and took up the recorder as their second instrument. The importance of the recorder declined towards the end of the 17th century in favour of the flute.

In the 18th and 19th centuries, the recorder actually disappeared altogether until interest in it was renewed in the 20th century. On the one hand there was the Early Music movement, which viewed music from the Renaissance and the Baroque with a revived interest

The Flanders Recorder Quartet.
From left to right:
Joris Van Goethem, Tom Beets,
Paul Van Loey and Bart Spanhove.

in historical playing techniques. The use of original instruments or historically correct copies played a major part. On the other hand, a lot of modern composers have rediscovered the potential of the recorder in all its forms, from sopranino to contrabass, and have even expanded this potential.

The Flanders Recorder Quartet, known in Dutch as *Vier op 'n Rij* (Four in a Row), is considered internationally as the very best in both aspects of recorder music. Its four members are Bart Spanhove, Tom Beets, Paul Van Loey and Joris Van Goethem. Their performances of Early Music are renowned for their spontaneity and the apparent naturalness with which a centuries-old score comes to life. The quartet aims to make the dead notes sound as if they were devised on the spur of the moment. They try to find the perfect instrument, or perfect combination of instruments, for every concert programme, based on the historical background to the music. Together, these four musicians have a range of instruments of which even Henry VIII would have been envious. But the Flanders Recorder Quartet is not only an Early Music ensemble, since plenty of contemporary composers also write music for them. To keep right up to date, they have conceived one of their most recent concert programmes as a jukebox, with a choice of 80 numbers (old and new) to which the audience can zap at will using voice computers. The success of the Flanders Recorder Quartet is undoubtedly due to the combination of a broad range of musical interests, boundless commitment to each project and the close ties between the four members. The quartet also regularly shares the concert platform with other leading musicians.

The Flanders Recorder Quartet is probably one of Belgium's best cultural exports. They have appeared on concert platforms at home and abroad more than 1500 times. From Belgium to Seoul, from the United States to South Africa, the sound of their recorders has been heard all over the world. They have also recorded about 20 CDs for several well-known record companies including *Deutsche Grammophon* and *Harmonia Mundi*. But their impact extends further still. Bart Spanhove has written a book on ensemble playing (*The Finishing Touch of Ensemble Playing*[1]), which in the meantime has been translated into German and even Chinese. Since the quartet plays so much unfamiliar music, the German publisher *Heinrichshofen* has brought out a series of scores of new and unknown works for the recorder repertoire: *The Flanders Recorder Quartet Series*.

To conclude, this bold assertion: although the Flanders Recorder Quartet does not work by order of any royal court, its efforts on behalf of recorder music may have just as significant an impact on the future of the instrument as the work of the Bassano brothers in the 16th century.

Klaas Coulembier
Translated by Gregory Ball

www.flanders-recorder-quartet. be

NOTE

1. Published by Alamire, Peer (Belgium), ISBN 90 6853 144 1.

A tribe, supposedly untouched by civilisation, discovered by an airplane that flew over the Amazon rainforest in 2008.

Ton Lemaire

Philosopher of Earthly Spirituality

There are only a few great Dutch philosophers. After the Enlightenment and Erasmus, Spinoza and Grotius, that was it. Since then, partly because of the Netherlands' natural orientation towards the outside world, Dutch philosophy has turned unilaterally to other countries and has built up no real tradition of its own. One of the few modern Dutch thinkers who constitute an exception to the rule is Ton Lemaire (b.1941). His work covers a broad spectrum yet is still highly coherent, allowing him to develop his own theme without relying solely on references to other writers.

Lemaire is not just a philosopher, he is also an anthropologist and is profoundly concerned with the relationship between man and nature. His focus on 'primitive peoples' has led him to kindred thinkers like Jean-Jacques Rousseau, Claude Lévi-Strauss and Henry-David Thoreau, on whose work he is an expert. But Lemaire's own programme, as we can see in retrospect, is determined by a highly individualistic approach: who is man in his landscape?

Lemaire's *Philosophy of the landscape* (originally *Filosophie van het landschap)* was published in 1979. A bestseller in its genre, it is still being reprinted today. In fact the essay is an introduction to everything that was to follow. Lemaire's research focuses on the relationship between modern Western man and the landscape, a landscape Petrarch discovered in the fourteenth century as he enjoyed the view after climbing the Mont Ventoux. The landscape has since been exploited on a large scale by the modern tourist industry. Its discovery has meant that Western man has lost his natural (in the sense of self-evident) connection with the land. A degree of objectivity has been introduced and with it a degree of alienation. After a personal crisis in the nineties Lemaire left the university and now lives in the French countryside.

In the much later work *With open senses, Nature, landscape, earth (Met open zinnen. Natuur, landschap, aarde*, 2002) Lemaire searches for a strategy that will allow man to return to his own land. He develops an extremely individual philosophy of the sensory affinity between man and earth. This affinity with the elements is the source of an earthly spirituality that, inspired by Nietzsche's Zarathustra, led Lemaire to the term 'spiritual naturalism'. In his major recent work on the darker sides of progress, *The Fall of* Prometheus (*De val van Prometheus*, 2010), he describes in minute detail how in the course of history, and particularly as a result of the Enlightenment, this spirituality has been forced further and further into the background. The economic growth scenario is not only exhausting the earth's resources but also the human spirit.

The study *On wings of the soul (Op vleugels van de ziel*, 2007), as original as it is scholarly, shows another side of Lemaire: the art historian. He charts what the variety of kinds of birds has meant for art, including the art of poetry. In this way he shows that biodiversity is of importance not only biologically but also culturally. The bond with earth and nature is a rich source of metaphor that also feeds the imagination. The loss of religion may have led to the demystification of the world, but the romantic and artistic bewitchment that comes from a certain destiny shared by man and nature has refused to let itself be eradicated. Lemaire himself accuses the monotheistic religions, especially, of being the greatest 'debunkers'.

Closely related to this vision is Lemaire's conviction that man has experienced a kind of ecological utopia which really did exist. Lemaire situates this in the Palaeolithic period, when homo sapiens was a hunter-gatherer. The struggle for daily existence was minimal, man must have been fairly healthy, there was no productivity or consumer pressure and weal and woe were fairly distributed. The bond between man and nature was experienced as magical. It is a utopia that pops up all over his work. This primitive being is the being that still truly lives *in* his landscape. For Lemaire he is an allusion to the *Paradise Lost* motif. This was partly the source of inspiration for his book *The Indian in our consciousness* (*De indiaan in ons bewustzijn*, 1986), in which he depicts the way in which the culture of the original inhabitants of the American continent was represented by those who took over the country. But in *On the value of cultures* (*Over de waarden van kulturen*, 1976) the full extent of his admiration for the first forms of human civilisation is also to be heard. From his self-chosen position of solitariness Lemaire continues to hold up the ideal of the hunter-gatherer to the urbanised Netherlands like a modern Zarathustra. And at the same time that gives rise to surprising new perspectives on the philosophy of culture.

Jan-Hendrik Bakker
Translated by Sheila M. Dale

The Neuro Calvinist who Discovered the 'Homo Lobe'

Dick Swaab and the Netherlands Brain Bank

Brain researcher Dick Swaab (b.1944), the 'homo lobe' man and founder in 1985 of the Netherlands Brain Bank, recently retired from his post as professor of neurobiology at the University of Amsterdam. But there was no question of giving up working; the following morning he went about his business again as usual. His research group continues in full swing, he carries on lecturing and, until the end of 2014, he is still *jus promovendi* (in charge of postgraduate students) and will continue to hand out the appropriate doctoral degrees. He will also retain his professorial chairs in China and at Stanford University in California.

Dick Swaab, (1944 -).
© Nederlandse Hersenbank, NIN, Amsterdam.

In his valedictory lecture Swaab took advantage of the opportunity to broach a subject that has fascinated him for a long time: death. Both the medical profession and the public need to be better prepared for this. He is disturbed by the fact that families only begin to think about euthanasia once a parent is suffering from dementia, without having given it any serious consideration at an earlier stage. Alzheimer's patients are often no longer capable of making an independent decision to end their life. According to Swaab, their wishes should be made known as soon as the process of dementia begins, otherwise it is simply too late. Moreover, the patient should discuss the matter first with his or her doctor to find out how s/he feels about it. That avoids problems. During his valedictory symposium, Swaab ran a course with colleagues entitled *Dead common.* For his part Swaab took the plunge a long time ago: 'If I have to go down the Alzheimer's path, I'm getting out.'

Apart from Alzheimer's, Swaab also undertakes research into depression, schizophrenia and sexual differentiation in relation to psychiatric disturbances. Why are men more frequently troubled by ADHD and autism, whereas women are more afflicted by depression and eating disorders? Swaab has little time for the belief that individuals can take care of themselves, considering that the influence of social environment and upbringing, will-power and a sense of responsibility is very limited. The title of the book he published last October, *We are our brain*, leaves no room for misunderstandings. 'The only environment that counts', he said in an interview, 'is the chemical environment in the womb'.

In 1989 Swaab caused a stir on the international scene with his announcement that the brains of homosexual men differ from those of heterosexuals. One area – quickly dubbed 'the homo lobe' by the media, although it is only a minute part of the hypothalamus – is larger in homosexuals. Feminists and sexologists fell over each other to state their aversion to this repulsive idea, the university considered it wise to provide surveillance for Swaab's lectures and there were even threatening letters. At the same time transsexuals, in whom the male and female areas of the brain seem to have been reversed, rejoiced in the fact that it was not a perverted upbringing or a weak character that was the 'culprit', but testosterone asserting its influence in the womb. Twenty years after the consternation over the homo lobe a number of research studies have confirmed Swaab's findings unequivocally: it is difficult to overestimate the influence of sex hormones on brain development. It occurs before birth, and goes on into the first couple of years of life. 'Neuro Calvinist' Swaab refers to it as 'biological predestination'.

In 1985 Swaab established the Brain Bank. What led to this was the problem he had in obtaining the brains

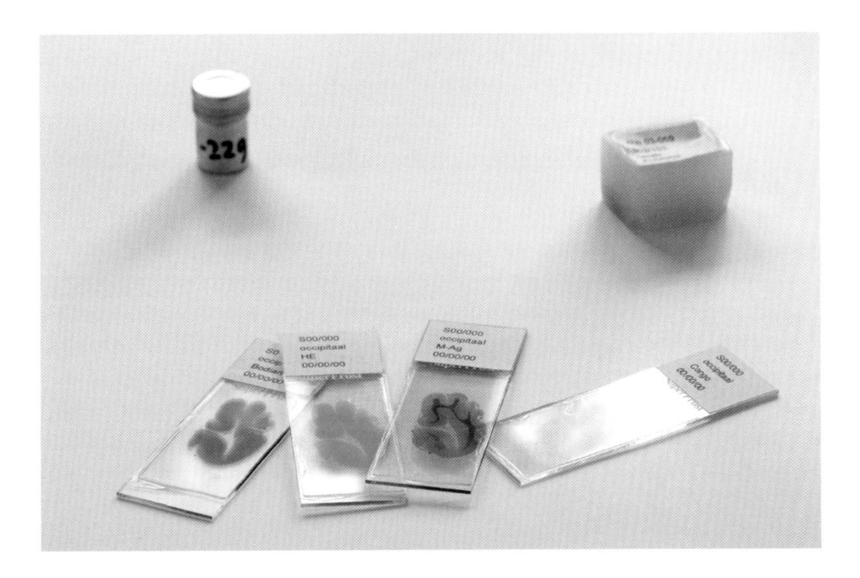

Brain tissue samples, © Nederlandse Hersenbank, NIN, Amsterdam.

of well documented Alzheimer's patients: four years for five specimens. The reason was that they often died at home or in a nursing home – not handy places for a post-mortem. The bank has now expanded to hold three thousand tissue samples – and the same number of registered donors. Specimens are taken from over eighty different areas of every brain acquired. They are then prepared for diagnostics and research and frozen at -80^{0}C. Every precaution is taken to safeguard privacy. Hundreds of research groups in many countries are grateful to be able to use this facility for their research. Swaab himself is also in the card index. There is a great shortage of donors.

Dick Swaab, child of the Hunger Winter of 1944-5, chanced on brain research when, in 1966, he was a student assistant at the Brain Institute in Amsterdam (the present Netherlands Institute for Neurosciences). His parents would have supported him, but he wanted to pay for his studies himself. In common with his father, Swaab feels a need to explain his research to society at large and to tell people about it. On one occasion he accompanied his father, a gynaecologist, to a meeting where information was being given on the contraceptive pill, which was brand new at the time. He was jeered at, just as his son was jeered at when he published on the homo lobe. But neither bomb scares nor threats had any effect on Swaab.

Life is largely a matter of chance, according to him, and we can have little influence on it. Character is established in the early years; then we have to manage with what is there. We are our brain; our spirit is the product of a hundred million brain cells – including numerous possibilities of derangement. 'Environment and hormones are only responsible for small variations within narrow margins, and in a manner that is already predetermined', says Swaab.

Dirk van Delft
Translated by Sheila M. Dale

Things Fall Apart The New Kingdom of the Netherlands

At midnight between October 9 and October 10, 2010, the flag of the Netherlands Antilles, part of the Kingdom of the Netherlands in the Caribbean, was lowered for the last time on the West Indian islands of Curaçao, Bonaire, St Martin, St Eustatius and Saba. These islands, which used to constitute the Netherlands Antilles, a separate 'state' within the Kingdom of the Netherlands, started 10-10-10 as new entities within it. Curaçao and St Martin became autonomous 'states' within the Kingdom, whereas the so-called BES islands, Bonaire, St Eustatius and Saba, became special municipalities within (the 'state' of) the Netherlands. Erroneously, the 'state' of the Netherlands is commonly identified with the Kingdom of the Netherlands. Even though the 'state' of the Netherlands is the biggest player within the Kingdom, it is only one of the constituent parts of the Kingdom.

The dissolution of the Netherlands Antilles is a compromise that has been agreed upon as a solution to long-running dissatisfaction with the central influence of Curaçao in the Netherlands Antilles and the desire of the islands of Curaçao and St Martin to receive the same autonomous status as Aruba, another Caribbean island 'state' within the Kingdom of the Netherlands, without them having to take the step of becoming completely independent. Because the Dutch Antillean constellation is one of the last remnants of the Dutch colonial period, these new developments need to be seen from the perspective of (post-) decolonization. After the Indonesian colony claimed independence in 1945, the need to establish a new relationship between the Netherlands and the remaining colonies became very clear. As a consequence the Charter for the Kingdom of the Netherlands, originally intended as a decolonization document, came into force in 1954, granting the West Indian territories, i.e. Suriname and the Netherlands Antilles, self-government. Suriname

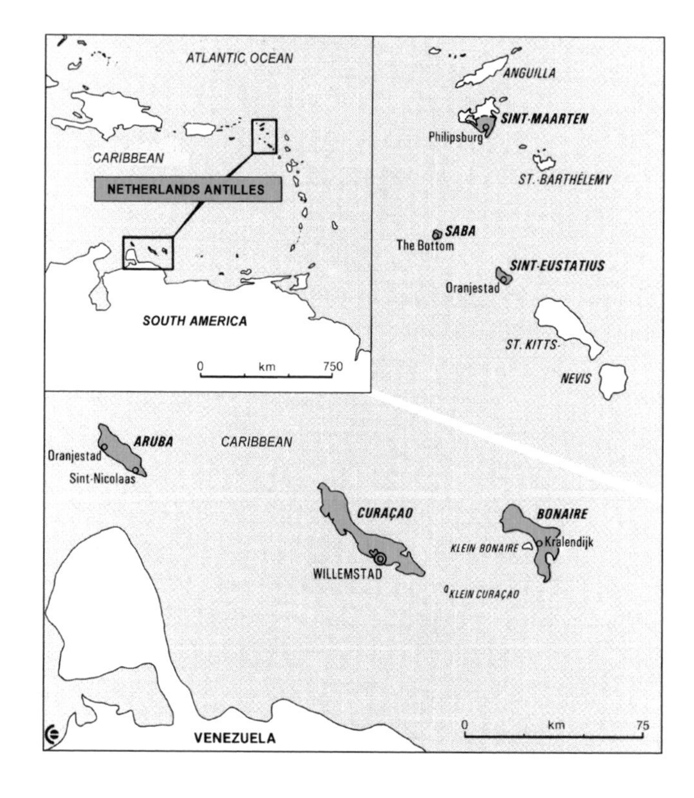

was granted full independence in 1975 and Aruba seceded from the Netherlands Antilles in 1986, becoming an autonomous entity within the Kingdom on the condition that it would get full independence in 1996.

In fact Aruba never did become independent, preferring to remain within the Kingdom in exchange for a number of concessions on good governance and inspiring the drive for other islands of the Netherlands Antilles to attain the same level of autonomy. During the ensuing twenty years, different strategies were explored and tested in referenda. These have resulted in the recent new structure in which the Kingdom of the Netherlands consists of four 'states' - the Netherlands, Aruba, Curaçao and St Martin - and, since the 10th of October of this year, the 'state' of the Netherlands includes three special Caribbean municipalities - Bonaire, St Eustatius and Saba (BES).

This new political construction has created an interesting transition period for the partner 'states' within the Kingdom of the Netherlands: new relations have to be built up, new governments have to be established and new legislation has to be drafted and implemented. Illustrative of this process is the complexity of the legal construction in the BES islands. Though officially they are a municipality of the Netherlands and one would expect Dutch law to apply there, large parts of old Antillean law still remain in effect. Having become part of an EU Member State, i.e. the European part of the Kingdom of the Netherlands, one would also expect the BES islands to be part of the European Union. On the contrary, the BES islands remain OCTs (Overseas Countries and Territories), countries which are related to an EU Member State. The new structure of the Kingdom implies huge legislative and administrative transformation within the new 'states' and within the new municipalities of the Netherlands; this transformation can only be achieved by gradually bringing existing law and administrative structures into conformity with the new situation.

The re-engineered relations between the 'states' of the Kingdom of the Netherlands will probably have a big influence on the exchange of Dutch and West Indian culture. Due to the dissolution of the Netherlands Antilles, the different islands have more direct relations with the Kingdom; as a consequence the relations between, for example, Curaçao and the Netherlands could become closer, resulting perhaps in increased exchanges of cultural, educational and social projects, which could lead to an improvement in mutual understanding. On the other hand, the complexity of the new construction could also put more distance between the partners within the Kingdom

At present the Kingdom of the Netherlands acts as the binding factor between the Netherlands and the West Indian islands. This relationship between the Kingdom and the 'states' which constitute the Kingdom is re-enforced in the current political construction, but it is very clear that the Caribbean discussion about autonomy and independence is not yet finished, and that the Dutch call for political and budgetary transparency within the Caribbean territories of the Kingdom still exists. The new construction leaves some parties dissatisfied, and these parties will continue to raise their voices and to question their responsibilities within the Kingdom and the responsibilities of the Kingdom towards the Caribbean 'states'.

Eric Mijts and Viola van Bogaert

Surrealism Comes to the Low Countries

The Difficult Political Situation in Belgium and the Netherlands.

Belgium and the Netherlands have a chaotic political year behind them. The magic of the polder model, which used to be so highly commended, and the famous democracy of consensus seem to have lost their efficacy. At one time the Low Countries were known for the hidden talent that enabled them to find an ingenious compromise in the most hopeless situations, which would long since have caused other political systems to collapse into argument, division and chaos. The Dutch political scientist Arend Lijphart, who won international recognition for his fascinating work on the politics of accommodation, attributed the stability in the divided Belgian and Dutch societies to an original game of co-operation, arising from a highly specific political culture aimed at consensus and broad agreements.

At present there is no such political stability in the Low Countries. Holland is now back on track, albeit in a locomotive with a two-stroke engine that could come off the rails at the slightest provocation. In the Netherlands many people are currently wondering how long the teetering cabinet can survive, particularly as the reason for its existence – Geert Wilders' PVV party is proving to be a fickle and unstable partner. Sure enough the Belgians are even worse off, though in the land of Magritte people are used to a fair dose of surrealism. There people are wondering if there is any possibility of a government by the summer of 2011 as a result of the June 2010 elections. The formation of the Belgian government threatens to be the slowest in history, they have only the Iraqis to beat. Because of this quite a lot of people are wondering whether in the Netherlands and Belgium, too, in the logic of the majority, ideas of power, confrontation politics and populism have gradually taken over from efforts to reach an agreement.

In both Belgium and the Netherlands the government fell before the end of the legal term of office. The reason for the premature dissolution of the cabinets was not the same, but in both cases the initiator had party political motives in view. In both countries politics seems to have increasingly become a consumer product and statesmanship has to be a match for the opinion polls.

Balkenende IV (the Christian Democratic CDA / the Socialist PvdA / the austere Protestant Christian Union) fell on the 20th of February 2010 as a result of the decision-making process concerning the possible extension of the Dutch military mission in the Afghanistan province of Uruzgan. CDA wanted to keep open the option of extending this mission, but Deputy Prime Minister Wouter Bos (PvdA) wanted to be out of Uruzgan for good by the end of 2010. Indeed the coalition partners had agreed on this in 2007. However, according to some commentators the PvdA hoped it would be able to count on the sympathy of the electorate if it allowed the government to fall over Uruzgan. The PvdA had done very badly in the opinion polls at the beginning of 2010 and the general prediction was that it would be badly damaged in the municipal elections on 3rd March 2010. Moreover Bos's strategy seemed to work, because an electoral massacre was avoided. According to the PvdA leader the party was back, something that also appeared to be the case from the relatively good election result in the Second Chamber elections, in which the PvdA was the second largest party in the Netherlands.

In Belgium the initiator of the fall of the government fared less well. The Flemish liberals, Open VLD, wanted out of the Leterme II government because the party was failing to put a liberal stamp on policy. The new young chairman, Alexander de Croo, and his spin doctor, Minister Vincent Van Quickenborne, wanted to get a clearer liberal alternative going and could do this better from the opposition than from inside a government in which Open VLD were languishing. The persistent community negotiations to do with the Brussels-Halle-Vilvoorde (BHV)[1] question were a useful excuse for the Flemish liberals to demonstrate their decisiveness by quitting the government. The reason they gave was that the deadline to shelve the BHV problem for all time had not been respected. "Alea iacta est", tweeted Van Quickenborne from the corridors of the Wetstraat/

SHAME- protest in Brussels on January 23rd 2011, demanding a government, around 200 days after the elections.

rue de la Loi. There was no longer any option then but to bring forward the election dates.

The results of the Belgian elections were very clear. The Flemish Nationalists of the N-VA continued the positive trend of the previous year and improved upon it, to be delineated as the largest Flemish party. The chairman, De Wever, himself collected one of the highest personal returns in Belgian history. The French-speaking socialist Elio Di Rupo (PS) had a similar triumph in French-speaking Belgium. The result: two legitimate leaders who had a *once in a lifetime opportunity* to break through a period of institutional blockade. In addition to a clear mandate from the electorate it also appeared during the campaign that all parties saw the need for a solution to the BHV problem and a thorough reorganization of the state. In French-speaking Belgium too, with the exception of a few acid outpourings from community quibblers such as Olivier Maingain (FDF) and Joëlle Milquet (CDH), a new mentality seemed to be showing itself in embryonic form. The *'on est demandeur de rien'* of 2007, in which every reform of the state was rejected in advance, gave way to a pragmatic attempt at 'balanced reforms'. Thus in Belgium, from day one after the elections, it was evident that there was the potential to unravel the community knot and that the new government would be formed round a PS-N-VA axis.

In the Netherlands it was all more obscure. The electorate had left a totally fragmented political landscape in which the liberal VVD only just had a majority over the PvdA and in which Geert Wilders' Islamaphobic PVV made the traditional government combinations difficult. It was far from clear which parties could unite to form a government. It was a long and sometimes chaotic courtship dance with no natural leaders, in which from time to time no one knew which way to turn anymore. Besides the VVD almost every party could be part of the government, even the PVV. The most frequently suggested combinations were a centrist cabinet made up of the three traditional parties, a centre-right coalition of VVD, CDA and PVV and the so-called Purple-Plus Variant with VVD, PvdA, the leftist liberal D66 and the environmentalist GroenLinks. But none of the combinations was obvious, which meant that VVD leader Rutte's campaign wish to form a new cabinet by the 1st of July suddenly sounded very hollow.

In contrast, the time scale proposed by De Wever in Belgium of having a federal government on its feet by the 1st of September sounded courageous but, oddly enough, less unrealistic. There were clear leaders on both sides of the language barrier with the shared am-

The Dutch political leaders Maxime Verhagen (CDA), Mark Rutte (VVD) and Geert Wilders (PVV) at the start of the Rutte cabinet in 2010.

bition of carrying out a substantial reform. The only problem was, as became evident much later during the actual discussions, they each meant something different by this. But in the intoxication of the first few weeks following the elections there was the prospect of a rapid formation. Since then we have come to know better: the Belgian record of 194 days without a government was broken easily at Christmas 2010. Meanwhile it seems Belgians are aiming for the Iraqi world record of 248 days. The Dutch formation period, however, was much quicker, taking 'only' 127 days.

Despite the faster formation the Netherlands also experienced a problem that had surfaced very clearly in Belgium during the formation of the 2007 government: a lessening of the institutional desire for consensus. The politics of accommodation, in which the political elite manages to find a way to even out the contradictions in society, is not working so well. In the Low Countries the polarization has become so great that political leaders are no longer able to meet each other in private. The talent for understanding your political opponent and respecting each other's sensitivities seems to be withering. Together with the breaking down of pillarization, the blurring of ideological differences, the personalization and above all the huge mediatization of politics, the increased volatility of the electorate is causing the political system to draw its horns in nervously. The outcome is interminable discussions on formation with whole series of people charged with forming a new government and cabinet, and other royal envoys.

Meanwhile, in the Netherlands the Rutte cabinet rules, but the viability of this minority government of VVD and CDA supported by the PVV seems limited. The majority of 76 seats out of 150 is extremely narrow. One vote the wrong way is sufficient to give the government problems. That is no figment of the imagination, given that the one-man Wilders[2] outfit is a group full of uncertain and unstable people. Moreover the fact that a number of CDA people are putting the Rutte cabinet's hard-line migration policy under a magnifying glass is not a good sign. It will be nothing short of a miracle if Rutte I goes the full term.

Despite these sombre prospects a look over the southern border may provide some comfort for the Dutch: at the end of January 2011 the Belgians were still without a government. All the difficult discussions about asylum, pensions etc still have to be held there. In Absurdistan (Belgium) everyone is so used to a government of unfinished business and crisis that no one bats an eyelid. And when, on 23 January, a bare 40,000 demonstrators in the streets of Brussels gave a signal that there must be a government soon, this signal was nuanced out of existence by the political class. A few days after the demonstration the nth round of negotiations ended and the impasse is total. Only external pressure, in the form of international speculation on the extent of Belgian debt, will give rise to a greater 'sense of urgency'.

At the time of writing this article, in early 2011, it is impossible to say how the future coalition will look. Maybe there will be fresh elections in 2011. Meanwhile there are already reports in the Belgian media of the demise of Belgium. It won't come to that, but the alienation of minds that Belgium experienced in 2010 will push consensus democracy ever further away. In the Netherlands, too, we shall have to wait to see whether the Rutte cabinet achieves integration or division. The Low Countries are going through a difficult period in politics.

Carl Devos and Nicolas Bouteca
Translated by Sheila M. Dale

NOTES

1. BHV is an electoral constituency for federal and European elections which is unique in that it extends across two linguistic areas: the 19 bilingual municipalities of Brussels and the 35 Flemish municipalities of Halle-Vilvoorde, a part of the Province of Flemish Brabant. The numerous French speakers in the Flemish suburbs are thereby able to vote for the same Francophone parties as Francophones in Brussels. They are the only voters in Belgium that can vote across the language border that divides unilingual Flanders from bilingual Brussels and unilingual Wallonia. In 2003 BHV became a legal problem when the Constitutional Court decided that the new electoral law of 2002 was unconstitutional because provincial constituencies had been created to replace the former district constituencies everywhere except in Flemish Brabant (which completely surrounds Brussels). The Constitutional Court ruled that the combination of BHV with provincial constituencies elsewhere had to go, otherwise the Federal elections would no longer be legal. The Flemish parties regard the judgement as vindicating their demand that the existing constituency be broken up. The Francophone parties stress that the Court has not ordered the break-up of the constituency and consider that a return to the old district electoral system is the best solution. They will only agree to the break-up of BHV in exchange for large concessions by the Flemish. It is the terms of that exchange, the break-up of BHV for concessions to the Francophone community that have still not been agreed upon. In April 2010 this question led to premature elections after the liberals quit the discussions over BHV and the Leterme II government.

2. The PVV has only one member, Geert Wilders himself. Sympathizers can only apply as volunteers or donors.

Koenraad Tinel,
Flandria Catholica, 2009,

The Church Loses its Stranglehold

Annus Horribilis for the Catholic Church in Belgium

On the 24th of June 2010 the relationship between the Church and state in Belgium changed once and for all. Following an order from an examining magistrate in Brussels, the Public Prosecutor's Office broke open the grave of Cardinal Désiré-Joseph Mercier (1851-1926) in the St Rombout's Cathedral in Mechelen, looking for hidden files on child abuse. Nothing was found. The police also raided the home of the retired archbishop, Danneels, in the same town. In Leuven they visited the committee that was tasked by the Catholic Church with looking into child abuse in its ranks. Almost the entire archives of the archbishopric, all the computers and the committee papers, too, were seized. The operation was named Chalice. The press was involved and the images were relayed around the world.

The reason for the raid was the bombshell that exploded on the 23rd of April of that same year when the Bishop of Bruges, Roger Vangheluwe, confessed to sexually abusing his underage nephew for years more than two decades earlier. The bishop resigned and went into hiding. The brand new Archbishop Léonard subsequently called upon all victims of sexual abuse within the Church to identify themselves to the committee which the Church itself had established in 2000 to hear and help victims. Up to 2009, 34 cases were handled. In the ensuing weeks a total of 475 complaints came in, spanning a period of around fifty years. In September the chairman of the committee, the well-known child psychiatrist Peter Adriaenssens, brought out the final report of the committee, whose members had resigned following the seizure of its papers.

The facts date mainly from the years 1950 to 1980 and two thirds of the victims are boys. The abuse flourished in a context of power. At the time priests and monks ran the show in both day and boarding schools, and in youth movements. They seemed untouchable. The Church was a privileged caste that was highly respected by society. There was a culture of keeping quiet and turning a blind eye when sexual abuse was detected. Victims did not dare to come out into the open. If they did, frequently no one would believe them. Peter Adriaenssens compared the silence of the Church to a mother who learns from her daughter that she is being sexually abused by her father. Although the mother is convinced that the abuse must stop, at the same time she is completely astounded that it is her own husband who is involved. She tells the daughter she cannot believe it. Moreover, according to the committee, the Church had no language for discussing this abuse of power. A priest, a bishop, works virtually independently with little supervision. In addition they had to shoulder the considerable burden of ensuring that the Church was not damaged. The indignation and moral revulsion in Belgium, and particularly in Flanders, which is Catholic by tradition, was enormous. The institution that for so long had taken a stern view of the moral misdeeds of believers was dealt with severely.

The legal situation is complex. Many of the offenders have grown old or died in the intervening period. Frequently the facts date from too long ago for a case to be pursued in a court of law. However there is a call for the term of limitation for sexual abuse by those who have reached the age of majority to be extended. In mid-November 2010 a parliamentary committee was established in the Belgian Federal Parliament to examine sexual abuse and matters pertaining to paedophilia 'within a relationship of authority, especially within the Church'. The bishops and the former and present archbishops, Danneels and Léonard, appeared before it. Danneels admitted that the institution had paid too much attention to self-preservation, but neither of the Church leaders took moral responsibility for the behaviour of those who served under them. They were clearly afraid of a flood of demands for compensation, as happened in the U.S.A. A great many members of Parliament, members of the committee of inquiry, believe there is a deliberate hush-up operation by the Church hierarchy. Flemish lawyers representing a number of victims of sexual abuse are even preparing a writ against Pope Benedict XVI. Their argument goes that the Pope bears the ultimate responsibility for the abuse, because the Holy See would have given bishops and other kindred spirits instructions 'to organise the cover-up'. Contact has already been made with American confrères who have summonsed the Vatican before.

As mentioned earlier, the legal situation is complex. Although the Church has given the impression that it is capable of developing its own system for administering justice, it is now emphasizing that the victims must turn first and foremost to the justice system, thus to the 'state'. But in the meantime the Public Prosecutor has decided that the examining magistrate who set up Operation Chalice went beyond his remit in seizing the papers of the Adriaenssens committee. He is not allowed to use them in his legal research and must return them to the victims. Exactly how that is to be done remains to be seen.

This *annus horribilis* in the Catholic Church in Belgium should be seen against the background of galloping secularization which started in the mid 1960s, in Flanders especially. In 1976, 36 percent of Flemings between the ages of 5 and 69 still attended Sunday mass every week. In 1998 the figure was 13 percent and in 2009 that dwindled to 5.4 percent. If this trend continues the churches will be empty on a Sunday in 2016. In contrast to the falling 'normal' church attendance, though, baptisms and burials remain popular. The figures for the last few years have stayed at more or less the same level. 71 percent of all those who died received a church burial, and 67 percent of Flemish children were baptized. Church marriages, however, have declined from 30 percent in 2006 to 26 percent in 2009.

Nonetheless the Church still has a strong base in Flemish education: almost 70 percent of all pupils in primary and secondary education are in subsidized (i.e. 'state' funded) 'free' education, and that is Catholic education – in name at least. The Catholic pillar still exerts an influence in the unions, health insurance and the entire care sector, too. In short, Flanders is no longer 'Catholic', but the culture of Catholicism still persists.

The new Archbishop of Belgium, who was appointed in 2009, the conservative French-speaking Léonard (who also speaks perfect Dutch) has brought about a change of culture as well. Whereas his predecessor, Danneels, had led the Belgian Church for decades by diplomacy and had papered over conflicts – a strategy which did not win him any praise in Rome – his successor is a strictly orthodox shepherd who does not shrink from challenging those who think differently from himself with his pronouncements on homosexuality and Aids, among other subjects. Léonard wants a Church that can take on the world, his message is clear, unremitting and transparent. The patience for which Danneels was formerly praised is long gone, but it is now coming back to haunt him.

Be things as they may, a new relationship is being forged between Church and state in Belgium. The Church has lost its stranglehold forever and will have to find a new place in this secularized society. Some dream of a Church of an orthodox minority, a Noah's Ark. Others believe in a chastened Church more in keeping with modern times, a Church that is more than the sum of its leaders, more than the hierarchy of pope and bishops, a grass roots Church of believers.

Luc Devoldere
Translated by Sheila M. Dale

The Mayor of Rotterdam Is from Morocco

Mayor of Rotterdam since early 2009, Ahmed Aboutaleb was born in 1961 in Beni Sidel, a small clay hut village in the Atlas Mountains in Morocco. He came to the Netherlands in the 1970s and now he's in charge of one of the largest ports in the world. He is a practising Muslim, a Dutchman and a Moroccan. This is the first time that a Dutch municipality has a mayor of Moroccan origin.

Aboutaleb is a member of the social-democratic *Partij van de Arbeid* (PvdA - Workers Party). Before he became mayor, he was Secretary of State for Social Affairs, a position he held for almost two years. Over the past few years, Aboutaleb has changed job quite often. He was an alderman in Amsterdam and before that a civil servant in the Dutch capital. He was head of Forum Institute for Multicultural Development and has also held various jobs in journalism and counselling. He was a TV reporter for the commercial channel RTL, for example, and a spokesperson for the Dutch Minister of Culture.

Aboutaleb came to the Netherlands when he was fifteen. As he himself stated in a newspaper interview, he left behind 'a cow, a donkey, a well and an awful lot of rocks'. He wanted to become assimilated into Dutch society as quickly as possible from lower technical school through secondary technical school to technical college. Eight years ago already, the former leader of the PvdA, Felix Rottenberg, had the following to say about Aboutaleb: '...Ahmed's CV is the result of a sense of discipline, self awareness and perseverance that's almost pre-war in nature'. He added that Aboutaleb could easily become a minister or the mayor of Amsterdam. In the same interview, Aboutaleb's wife remarked that the Netherlands was not quite ready for that yet: 'it will probably take twenty years before someone like Ahmed can become mayor of Amsterdam'.

The Aboutaleb family didn't have to wait that long. Though it wasn't Amsterdam but Rotterdam he became mayor of. Aboutaleb's political career did begin in the capital, however. He was elected alderman there and

Ahmed Aboutaleb (second person from the left, 1961-).

attracted a lot of media attention following the murder of the film director Theo van Gogh in November 2004. Van Gogh was murdered by a Moroccan. Following the murder, Aboutaleb said that young Muslims who didn't share core Dutch values should better leave. Ever since that moment he has been threatened and has had to be protected.

And now he's the mayor of Rotterdam, a city of almost 600,000 inhabitants of 174 different nationalities. When he was being sworn in as mayor, Aboutaleb remarked that his security should not be a cause for concern regarding his contact with ordinary Rotterdammers: 'I'll meet unannounced with workers, pub-goers, business people when walking through a neighbourhood or if I ring someone's doorbell and ask for a cup of coffee or call by at a school. That will happen without the press.'

When Aboutaleb became mayor, *Leefbaar Rotterdam* (Pim Fortuyn's political heirs) demanded that he give up his Moroccan passport. During his inauguration they severely criticised the new mayor's dual nationality. He was handed an envelope addressed to the King of Morocco. Aboutaleb was supposed to put his passport in it, but he left the envelope untouched.

Aboutaleb said that he refused to accept that his loyalty towards the Netherlands should be called into question. But he did add that the 'New Dutch would have to rid themselves of any feelings of victimisation. You've chosen to belong to the Netherlands and to participate. But that doesn't mean that you have to burn all your bridges behind you.'

During his first years in office Aboutaleb wished to be known as a strict but just mayor, as someone who isn't shy of taking strong measures. *Feyenoord* supporters were not allowed to go to Amsterdam for the game against their sworn enemies *Ajax*. They had to pay for any damage they caused during a game themselves.

Rotterdam plans to save 600 million euros in the next four years. The new mayor's approach is dynamic. *Blijdorp Zoo* hardly receives funding any more, for example. Aboutaleb set out these measures himself and hardly moved an inch from his original position during the negotiations that followed. This hard line seems to be appreciated by the port city's dwellers. Seldom does one ever hear severe criticism of the mayor in Rotterdam.

Aboutaleb is proud to have held various important positions in public office in the Netherlands; as he once stated when he was appointed Secretary of State: 'As a Muslim and as the child of a simple immigrant from the Atlas Mountains, I've been accepted as a member of this country's government. This is extraordinary, extraordinary, extraordinary. I'll cherish this moment. And I am very proud of the Netherlands, where this is possible. I am proud of all the Dutch people who have put their trust in me.'

Joris van de Kerkhof
Translated by Peter Flynn

Gabriel Metsu,
Man Writing a Letter,
c. 1664-1666.
Oil on canvas, 52 x 40.5 cm.
National Gallery of Ireland, Dublin.
Photo by Roy Hewson.

Gabriel Metsu Once More Famous than Vermeer

Nowadays, the name Gabriel Metsu (1629-1667) is not the first to be associated with the Golden Age of 'Dutch' painting, a period which more or less coincides with the seventeenth century. There was a time when things were different. In his day, Metsu was certainly one of the most valued painters and a trendsetter in Dutch cities. After his death his star rose even higher and during the eighteenth century Metsu's work was considered to far outstrip - and as a result was much more expensive - than his contemporary Johannes Vermeer's. In those days one clearly wondered why one would buy a Vermeer if there was a Metsu available. Later on, appreciation for the old masters underwent drastic changes and for a long time Metsu faded into the background. The last time there was an exhibition dedicated to his work was back in 1966 in the city of his birth, Leiden. The last monograph on Metsu to be published was in 1974.

At the moment the artist is enjoying somewhat of a

Gabriel Metsu,
The Old Drinker,
c. 1663. Oil on canvas,
22 x 19.5 cm.
Rijksmuseum,
Amsterdam.

comeback. In 2007 Adriaan Waiboer got his PhD from the Institute of Fine Arts at New York University with a substantial dissertation on Gabriel Metsu. As curator of North European Art at the National Gallery of Ireland, Waiboer put on an exhibition that included approximately forty works by Gabriel Metsu. Afterwards the exhibition travelled to the Rijksmuseum in Amsterdam and from 17 April till 24 July 2011 it will be on show at the National Gallery of Art in Washington DC. Featuring some 35 paintings, this exhibition is the first monographic exhibition of Metsu's work ever mounted in the United States.

Little is known of Gabriel Metsu's life. He was born in Leiden in 1629. His parents had arrived there separately as children, moving from the present border area between South West Flanders and Northern France. Gabriel's father was also a painter and a designer of tapestries but he died before Gabriel was born. Gabriel Metsu may well have inherited his talent from his father but learned the art of painting from others outside his immediate family circle. How this actually happened we do not know but one thing is certain, the well known fine artist Gerard Dou from Leiden was influential in this respect, as was the work of the prominent genre painter, Gerard ter Borch, who worked in Deventer. It is possible that Metsu served a short period of apprenticeship in Utrecht.

In 1654 Metsu set himself up as a self-employed painter in Amsterdam. He specialised in genre scenes and paintings with a narrative, often moralist theme which people could emulate. These works probably allowed him to find a niche in the Amsterdam art market. He combined Dou's formal language with Ter Borch's subjects, as it were, but in this respect often chose more distinguished groups to portray than Ter Borch did. Metsu was a master at conveying light and shade as well as all sorts of different surfaces such as satin, linen, fur, pottery, glass and skin tones. Besides this, he succeeded wonderfully well in intimating the precision of Dou's fine artwork, despite the fact that his brushstrokes were much looser and his areas of colour almost abstract in their approach. It was as if Metsu managed to combine the best of all his contemporaries in his own work.

His contemporary, Johannes Vermeer, probably also knew Metsu personally. Because few of his surviving works were ever dated, it is difficult to determine who reacted to whom, but it seems certain that the two painters were inspired by each other. There is a great affinity between the two oeuvres, both thematically and in terms of technique. Anyone who sees Vermeer's and Metsu's works next to each other can understand more easily why art experts from the 1930s and 1940s mistook forgeries by the master forger Han van Meegeren for authentic work by Vermeer. To contemporary eyes these forgeries seem closer to Metsu's work than Vermeer's, but a few things illustrate how our perception of art changes with time and how we have been able to get a better understanding of the painting techniques of these old masters.

In 1658, Gabriel Metsu married Isabella de Wolff. Her mother, Maria de Grebber, came from Haarlem and was one of the rare woman painters to succeed in gaining renown in the male dominated seventeenth century. Isabella de Wolff has been identified as the model for a considerable number of Metsu's paintings, but it is not implausible that she, just like her mother, was also an accomplished painter.

Lauran Toorians
Translated by Peter Flynn

www.nga.gov

Gabriel Metsu has been published as a supplement to the exhibition and contains a wealth of illustrations. Edited by Adriaan E. Waiboer, the book also includes contributions by Bianca M. du Mortier, Pieter Roelofs and Marijn Schapelhouman (Yale University Press. ISBN 978 0300167245).

A Versatile Precursor

Painter Jan Gossart

While certainly not a household name for the broader public, the Netherlandish artist Jan Gossart (c. 1478-1532) has long been recognized by art historians as a painter of the first rank with a great influence on the development of painting in the Low Countries in the first decades of the sixteenth century. While always represented in surveys of Netherlandish art - such as the canonic *Art before Iconoclasm* exhibition in Amsterdam (1986) - and studied in detail in contributions to scholarly magazines, Jan Gossart has rather surprisingly not been the subject of a monographic exhibition since 1965 (Bruges & Rotterdam). The last *catalogue raisonné* by Sadja Herzog also dates from this period (1968). While fundamental to much of the subsequent research, both these publications are now seriously outdated and the need for a systematic study of Gossart's oeuvre has long been recognized.
Thanks to a noteworthy initiative of Maryan Ainsworth curator at the Metropolitan Museum of Art and an established scholar of Netherlandish painting - both gaps have been filled at the same time. In combination with a splendid exhibition in New York - to be shown in slightly reduced format at the National Gallery in London - a hefty book has been produced that is both an exhibition catalogue and a thorough survey and

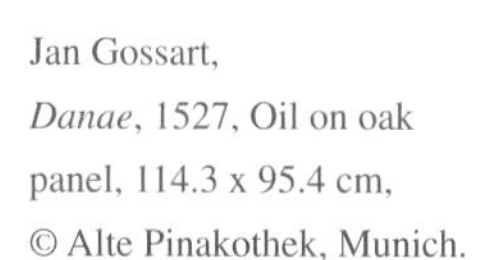

Jan Gossart,
Danae, 1527, Oil on oak panel, 114.3 x 95.4 cm,
© Alte Pinakothek, Munich.

Jan Gossart, *Sheet with a Study after the "Spinario" and Other Sculptures,* c. 1509,
Pen and gray-brown ink, 26.3 x 20.5 cm, © Leiden, University Library, Print Room.

oeuvre catalogue of the life and work of Jan Gossart. The Metropolitan Museum and the Flemish publisher *Mercatorfonds*, which is responsible for the French and Dutch language editions, are to be congratulated for this beautiful publication, which meets the highest scholarly standards and will most certainly be the reference for future studies on Gossart and his environment for many years to come.

Jan Gossart was born around 1478 in Maubeuge, then part of the Burgundian Netherlands but French territory since 1678. Where he was trained is unknown. Both Bruges - specifically the workshop of Gerard David whose influence is strongly visible in his early work - and Antwerp, the city where he was registered as an artist in 1503, have been suggested. Very little is known about Gossart's life and work until the fall of 1508. Why and how it happened remains a mystery, but on October 26 of that year the artist was part of a mission sent out to the papal court in Rome by the regent Margareth of Austria and led by Philip of Burgundy, illegitimate son of Philip the Good, Admiral of Zeeland and Gossart's patron until his death in 1524. This journey, which lasted no more than a year and also took the artist to such cities as Trente, Verona, Mantua and Florence, was not only decisive in the development of his own work, but is above all an important reason why Jan Gossart came to be such an influential and innovative artist. He was surely not the first artist from the Low Countries to travel to Italy, but he was most certainly the first to draw copies of classical statues and architecture such as his often reproduced drawing of the famous *Spinario* amidst fragments of other sculptures and used them to create a new pictorial language after his return. But it was not only the remnants of ancient culture which fascinated Gossart. As new in-depth research proves, he must have seen, admired and copied works of such contemporary Italian masters as Mantegna, Verrocchio and Donatello on his journey to and from Rome.

After his return to the Low Countries, Gossart settled in Middelburg - most probably to be close to one of the main residences of Philip of Burgundy in Suytburg. He quickly became one of the most sought-after artists of his generation, receiving prestigious commissions from patrons at the highest levels in Mechelen, Brussels and Bruges. As Aynsworth and her colleagues demonstrate, Gossart's importance lies not only in the reflection of classical antiquity in his work but also in his technical mastery as a painter, draughtsman and experimental printmaker, his versatility in practicing such different genres as portraits, mythological subjects and religious themes, and the combination of a thorough training in the traditions of the 15th century Flemish masters (above all Van Eyck and Memling) and influences from antiquity and contemporary Italian and German art (most notably Albrecht Dürer and the sculptor Conrad Meit).

Although Gossart seems not to have had a workshop of any size, what is now left of his oeuvre is comparatively large: 63 paintings, 48 drawings and 10 prints are listed. His merits as an artist and his legacy are slightly overrated in the catalogue, which puts him at the same level as Jan van Eyck and claims he was the precursor of the developments of the entire 16th century leading up to Rubens. That is a bridge too far. Gossart was certainly a highly gifted, versatile and innovative artist. He was above all the precursor of a new generation of artists like Jan van Scorel, Jan Vermeyen, Lambert Lombard and, more indirectly, Lucas van Leyden and Dirk Vellert. We are indebted to Maryan Ainsworth and the Metropolitan Museum for spotlighting this fascinating artist with a beautiful exhibition and a comprehensive catalogue.

Manfred Sellink

Maryan Ainsworth et al., *Man Myth, and Sensual Pleasures; Jan Gossart's Renaissance,* New York, 2010 (Dutch language edition by Mercatorfonds, Brussels, 2010).

The exhibition that took place in the Metropolitan Museum of Art, New York (October 5, 2010 - January 17, 2011) is on travel, in slightly reduced form, at the National Gallery, London, February 23 - May 30, 2011 (www.nationalgallery.org.uk). Curiously enough the two institutions do not agree on the spelling of the artist's name. While the Metropolitan uses Gossart as found in autograph signatures and documents, the National Gallery prefers Gossaert, as the name has always been spelled in modern times.

Contributors

Dirk Van Assche
Deputy Editor Ons Erfdeel vzw
dirkvanassche@onserfdeel.be

Jan-Hendrik Bakker
Journalist
jhbakker@kpnmail.nl

Michel Bakker
Archaeologist and Architectural Historian
michel.m.bakker@planet.nl

Marnix Beyen
Professor at the Dept. of History at the Universiteit Antwerpen
marnix.beyen@ua.ac.be

Wim Blockmans
Em. Professor of Medieval History at the Universiteit Leiden / Former Rector of the NIAS
W.Blockmans@nias.knaw.nl

Derek Blyth
Journalist
derekblyth@lycos.com

Viola van Bogaert
Researcher Constitutional Law, University of Aruba and Rijksuniversiteit Groningen
v.v.r.van.bogaert@rug.nl

Nicolas Bouteca
Research Assistant at the Dept. of Political Sciences (GhIPS, Universiteit Gent)
Nicolas.Bouteca@ugent.be

Klaas Coulembier
PhD candidate, Research Unit of Musicology, Katholieke Universiteit Leuven
klaas.coulembier@arts.kuleuven.be

Pieter Coupé
Secretary *Ons Erfdeel. Vlaams-Nederlands cultureel tijdschrift*
onserfdeel@onserfdeel.be

Dirk van Delft
Director Museum Boerhaave, Leiden / Science Journalist
dirkvandelft@museumboerhaave.nl

Luc Devoldere
Chief Editor Ons Erfdeel vzw
luc.devoldere@onserfdeel.be

Carl Devos
Professor at the Dept. of Political Sciences (GhIPS, Universiteit Gent)
carl.devos@ugent.be

Rien Emmery
PhD candidate, Research Unit of Modernity and Society, Katholieke Universiteit Leuven
Rien.Emmery@arts.kuleuven.be

Guido Fonteyn
Journalist
guido.fonteyn@telenet.be

Willem Frijhoff
Em. Professor of Early Modern History at the Vrije Universiteit, Amsterdam
wtm.frijhoff@let.vu.nl

Stefanie van Gemert
PhD candidate Comparative Literature, University College London
svangemert@gmail.com

Piet Gerbrandy
Poet/Critic
psgerb@xs4all.nl

Wim D'haveloose
Critic/Translator
wimdhaveloose@hotmail.com

Hans Ibelings
Architecture Critic
ibelings@cuci.nl

Joost Jonker
Associate Professor, Universiteit Utrecht
Roode.Jonker@inter.nl.net

James Kennedy
Professor of History of the Netherlands at the Universiteit van Amsterdam
J.C.Kennedy1@uva.nl

Joris van de Kerkhof
Journalist
Joris.van.de.Kerkhof@nos.nl

Anton Korteweg
Poet
antonkorteweg@planet.nl

Liv Laveyne
Theatre Critic
livy.laveyne@telenet.be

Nop Maas
Literary Historian/Biographer
nop.maas@planet.nl

Eric Mijts
Dean Faculty of Law, University of Aruba
eric_mijts@hotmail.com

Bertram Mourits
Editor/Critic
bertram.mourits@planet.nl

Cyrille Offermans
Writer/Literary Critic
CyrilleOffermans@home.nl

Frank van der Ploeg
Art Critic
f.vanderploeg@tiscali.nl

Anne-Marie Poels
Art Critic
ampoels@me.com

Reinier Salverda
Director Fryske Akademy
rsalverda@fryske-akademy.nl

Manfred Sellink
Artistic Director Musea Brugge
Manfred.Sellink@brugge.be

Geert Sels
Journalist/Critic
geert.sels@telenet.be

Johanna Spaey
Writer
info@johannaspaey.com

Jan Temmerman
Journalis/ Film Critic
jan.temmerman@demorgen.be

Lauran Toorians
Journalist
laurantoorians@cs.com

Hans Trapman
Professor of Cultural History, Erasmus School of History, Culture and Communication, Erasmus Universiteit Rotterdam
hanstrapman@hotmail.com

Aleid Truijens
Literary Critic/Biographer
aleidtruijens@chello.nl

Hans Vanacker
Secretary *Septentrion.Arts, lettres et culture de Flandre et des Pays-Bas*
septentrion@onserfdeel.be

Ilja Veldman
Art Historian/Em. Professor of Art History at the Vrije Universiteit, Amsterdam
Ilja.veldman@tiscali.nl

Loes Veldpaus
PhD candidate, Technische Universiteit Eindhoven
l.veldpaus@tue.nl

Paul Vincent
Freelance Writer and Translator
p-vincent@btconnect.com

Emile Wennekes
Professor of Musicology/Head of School Media and Culture Studies,
Universiteit Utrecht
e.wennekes@uu.nl

Geert De Weyer
Journalist
geert.deweyer@scarlet.be

Translators

Gregory Ball
Pleuke Boyce
Sheila M. Dale
Lindsay Edwards
Chris Emery
Peter Flynn
Nancy Forest-Flier
Tanis Guest
John Irons
Yvette Mead
Valerie Robillard
Julian Ross
Paul Vincent
Laura Watkinson

ADVISORS ON ENGLISH USAGE

Tanis Guest (UK)
Lindsay Edwards (Belgium)

Colophon

Association

This nineteenth yearbook is published by the Flemish-Netherlands Association 'Ons Erfdeel vzw', with the support of the Dutch Ministry of Education, Culture and Science (The Hague), the Flemish Ministry of Culture (Brussels) and the Provinces of West and East Flanders. The Association 'Ons Erfdeel vzw' also publishes the Dutch-language periodical *Ons Erfdeel* and the French-language periodical *Septentrion. Arts, lettres et culture de Flandre et des Pays-Bas,* the bilingual yearbook *De Franse Nederlanden – Les Pays-Bas Français* and a series of books in several languages covering various aspects of the culture of the Low Countries.

Address of the Editorial Board and the Administration

'Ons Erfdeel vzw', Murissonstraat 260,
8930 Rekkem, Flanders, Belgium
T +32 56 41 12 01, F +32 56 41 47 07
www.onserfdeel.be, www.onserfdeel.nl
thelowcountriesblog.onserfdeel.be
VAT BE 0410.723.635

Kevin Vandenbussche *Head of Administration*
Adinda Houttekier *Administrative Secretary*

Aims

With *The Low Countries,* a yearbook founded by Jozef Deleu (Chief Editor from 1993 until 2002), the editors and publisher aim to present to the world the culture and society of the Dutch-speaking area which embraces both the Netherlands and also Flanders, the northern part of Belgium.

The articles in this yearbook survey the living, contemporary culture of the Low Countries as well as their cultural heritage. In its words and pictures *The Low Countries* provides information about literature and the arts, but also about broad social and historical developments in Flanders and the Netherlands.

The culture of Flanders and the Netherlands is not an isolated phenomenon; its development over the centuries has been one of continuous interaction with the outside world. In consequence the yearbook also pays due attention to the centuries-old continuing cultural interplay between the Low Countries and the world beyond their borders.

By drawing attention to the diversity, vitality and international dimension of the culture of Flanders and the Netherlands, *The Low Countries* hopes to contribute to a lively dialogue between differing cultures.

ISSN 0779-5815
ISBN 978-90-79705-078
Statutory deposit no. D/2011/3006/1
NUR 612

Printed by Die Keure, Bruges, Flanders, Belgium
Design by Luc De Meyer (Die Keure)

Prices for the yearbook 2011, no. 19
Belgium € 37, The Netherlands € 39, Europe € 39

Other Countries: € 45
All prices inclusive of shipping costs

As well as the yearbook The Low Countries, the Flemish Netherlands Association 'Ons Erfdeel vzw' publishes a number of books covering various aspects of the culture of Flanders and the Netherlands.

Wim Daniëls
Talking Dutch.
Illustrated; 80 pp.

J.A. Kossmann-Putto &
E.H. Kossmann
The Low Countries. History of the Northern and Southern Netherlands.
Illustrated; 64 pp.

Isabella Lanz &
Katie Verstockt,
Contemporary Dance in the Low Countries.
Illustrated; 128 pp.

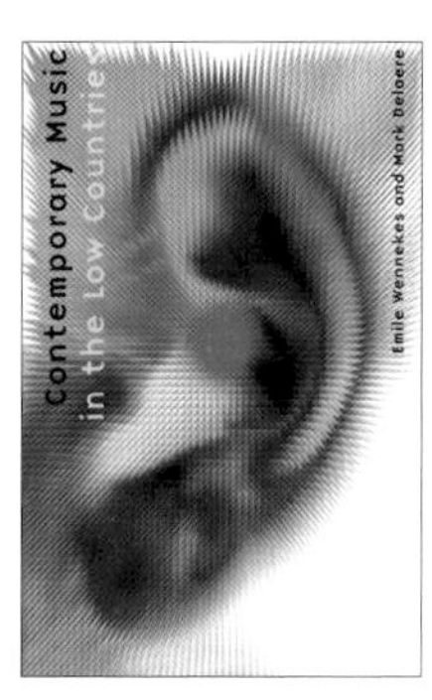

Mark Delaere &
Emile Wennekes,
Contemporary Music in the Low Countries.
Illustrated; 128 pp.

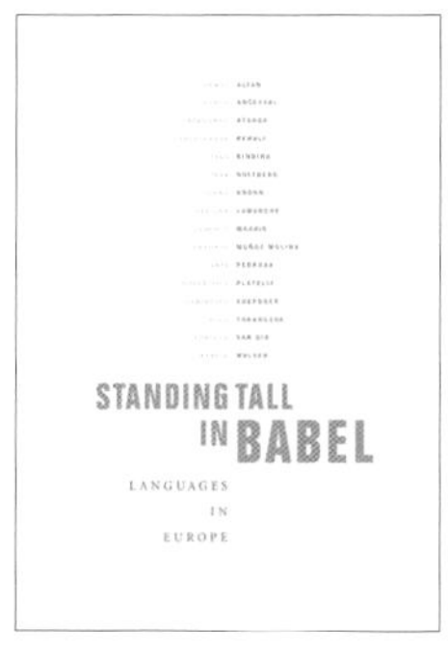

Standing Tall in Babel. Languages in Europe.
Sixteen European writers about their mother tongues.
Hardcover; 144 pp.

Between 1993 and 2010 the first eighteen issues of the yearbook *The Low Countries* were published.

EUROPE
NORTH SEA
GRONINGEN
Groningen
Leeuwarden
FRIESLAND
Assen
DRENTHE
NORTH HOLLAND
FLEVOLAND
Lelystad
Zwolle
OVERIJSSEL
Haarlem
AMSTERDAM
The Hague
Utrecht
UTRECHT
GELDERLAND
Arnhem
SOUTH HOLLAND
ZEELAND
Middelburg
's-Hertogenbosch
NORTH BRABANT
Antwerp
ANTWERP
LIMBURG
Bruges
WEST FLANDERS
EAST FLANDERS
Ghent
FLEMISH BRABANT
Leuven
BRUSSELS
LIMBURG
Hasselt
Maastricht
GERMANY
Wavre
WALLOON BRABANT
HAINAUT
Mons
Namur
Liège
LIÈGE
FRANCE
NAMUR
LUXEMBOURG
LUX.
Arlon
0 km 50
© Carto
Dutch language-area
French language-area in Belgium
Brussels bilingual area : Dutch and French
German language area : in Belgium
Bilingual area : Dutch and Frisian
Capital city
Provincial capital
National frontier
Provincial Boundary